GREEN SHADOWS
THE LIFE OF JOHN CLARE

John Clare in 1820
From the portrait by W. Hilton, R.A.

JUNE WILSON

Green Shadows

THE LIFE OF JOHN CLARE

There I meet common thoughts, that all may read
Who love the quiet fields: I note them well,
Because they give me joy as I proceed,
And joy renewed when I their beauties tell
In simple verse and unambitious songs,
That in some mossy cottage haply may
Be read and win the praise of humble tongues
In the green shadows of some after-day.
For rural fame may likeliest rapture yield
To hearts whose songs are gathered from the field.

Rural Scenes

LONDON
HODDER & STOUGHTON

First printed 1951

MADE AND PRINTED IN GREAT BRITAIN
FOR HODDER AND STOUGHTON LIMITED
BY JARROLD AND SONS LTD., NORWICH

"For what is it to be a poet? It is to see at a glance the glory of the world, to see beauty in all its forms and manifestations, to feel ugliness like a pain, to resent the wrongs of others as bitterly as one's own, to know mankind as others know single men, to know Nature as botanists know a flower, to be thought a fool, to hear at moments the clear voice of God."

LORD DUNSANY

CONTENTS

CHAPTER   PAGE

AUTHOR'S NOTE   11

INTRODUCTION   13

1. CHILDHOOD   18

2. THE BLUE BELL   27

3. MARY JOYCE   36

4. THE MILITIA   44

5. WALKHERD LODGE   50

6. THE SEARCH FOR A PUBLISHER   54

7. A VARIETY OF MINDS   64

8. "POEMS DESCRIPTIVE OF RURAL LIFE AND SCENERY"   71

9. MARRIAGE AND FAME   81

10. DIVIDED LOYALTIES   91

11. THE TEMPTATION OF JOHN BARLEYCORN   101

12. "THE VILLAGE MINSTREL"   109

13. THE LONDONERS   118

14. HELPSTON AGAIN   126

15. TREATMENT BY DR. DARLING   135

16. AUTUMN DAYS   146

17. DELAY CARRIED INTO A SYSTEM   156

18. "THE SHEPHERD'S CALENDAR"   169

19. SORROW AND SICKNESS   178

20. THE STRUGGLE FOR INDEPENDENCE   188

21. THE CLOUDED MIND   198

22. NORTHBOROUGH   206

23. "THE RURAL MUSE"   216

24. HIGH BEECH   225

25. HOMELESS AT HOME   240

26. NORTHAMPTON—THE LAST YEARS   250

A BIBLIOGRAPHICAL OUTLINE   265

INDEX   267

LIST OF ILLUSTRATIONS

JOHN CLARE IN 1820   *Frontispiece*
    (*From the portrait by W. Hilton, R.A., in the National Portrait Gallery*)

FACING PAGE

THE COTTAGE AT HELPSTON WHERE CLARE WAS BORN   64

JOHN TAYLOR   67
    (*From the drawing by W. Hilton, R.A., in the possession of Mrs. Cartwright-Taylor*)

THE BUST OF JOHN CLARE BY HENRY BEHNES, 1828   180
    (*In the Northampton Public Library*)

THE COTTAGE AT NORTHBOROUGH   208

JOHN CLARE IN 1844   240
    (*From the portrait by Thomas Grimshawe in the Northampton Public Library*)

AUTHOR'S NOTE

I THINK THAT MANY PEOPLE share my dislike of unnecessary footnotes, and I have therefore used them only where it was unavoidable, for example, to give the source of a quotation or the explanation of a dialect word. I have, in almost every case, omitted notes as to the source of the extracts from Clare's autobiographical sketches, as these are all taken either from the MS. books at Peterborough or from *Sketches in the Life of John Clare*, which was published with an Introduction by Mr. Edmund Blunden in 1931, and the manuscript of which is at Northampton. The letters written to Clare form six large manuscript volumes which are in the British Museum, and those written by him are most of them at Northampton and the remainder at Peterborough.

Clare's use of punctuation was so sparing that it has been necessary in places to supply this need, but I have done it only where I felt that to print the passage with no more punctuation than he gave would try the reader too sorely. In a few places it is obvious from the sense of the passage that Clare intended a new sentence, and there I have put in the necessary full stop. The spelling is his, and in every other respect the manuscript passages are copied exactly.

My thanks are due to all those who have written about Clare before me. A list of the books that I have used in writing this biography will be found at the end.

I should like to thank Mr. Geoffrey Grigson, who read the MS. and who, though we differ on some aspects of Clare's life and work, has made comments and suggestions which I have found valuable. I am grateful to Mrs. Cartwright-Taylor for permission to reproduce the sketch of John Taylor, and to Major H. C. Brooke Taylor for lending me a block of the drawing.

To the following people, also, my thanks are due: Lord Dunsany for permitting me to quote from his speech to the Poets' Club in 1912; Dr. R. E. Sedgwick and Dr. C. P. Blacker for advice on the medical and psychological aspects of Clare's story; Mr. Reginald Brown, Librarian of the Northampton Public Library, for his kindness in facilitating my work there and in permitting me to publish extracts from the MS. material and photographs of the Grimshawe portrait and the bust by Behnes; Mr. M. Urwick-Smith, Curator of the Peterborough Museum, for kindly allowing me to copy and publish extracts from Clare's notebooks, etc; Mr. Cooper of Northampton and Mr. Protheroe of Peterborough for photographs; Miss Lorna Bailie for help which speeded and lightened the task of preparing this book. To the many other people from whom I have received kindness and courtesy in the course of my work I express my gratitude.

J. W.

INTRODUCTION

JOHN CLARE ONCE DESCRIBED biography as "a parcel of lies". He was apt to make such sweeping statements in moments of irritation, and would probably have qualified it afterwards had he given it any further thought, but it is as well for the biographer to keep that phrase in mind and to tread warily lest his work should, in fact, turn out to be just that. I do not refer to falsification of the facts of a man's life, for, with patience, it is usually possible to ascertain these, and no one who seeks truth will invent them; but the facts are only half of biography, and the other, and equally important half, is the light that is shed upon them.

By that light we are enabled to see a little more, to understand a man's motives, to know what he thought and felt; without such illumination, a biography is nothing more than an enlargement of a column in *Who's Who*, and provides about as much food for thought. And yet how perilous are these rays that we seek to turn upon the thoughts and impulses of men! We must work like detectives, diligently searching for our clues and piecing together the evidence, but having it always in mind that nothing is of use in court unless it can be proved. It is so easy to go a few steps too far, to assume more than one is justified in assuming, to imagine, and be convinced by one's own imagination. It is a knife-edge that the biographer must balance upon, making clear as much as may be, but never taking things for granted or stating as a known truth what is only a supposition.

Our own lives, our innermost thoughts, and the impulses from which our actions spring are so hard to understand, so often wrapped in mystery, that it would appear not only presumptuous but impossible to seek to understand and explain the life of another, and so, indeed, it is unless the limitations are accepted from the beginning. Believing that, and believing that those limitations are quickly reached, I would say in all humility that this book is not offered as a full and comprehensive explanation of Clare's life and character, but only as an attempt to portray him in the light of such knowledge and understanding as is available to me.

Clare's story is an interesting one for a variety of reasons, not least of which is that he provides one of the clearest examples of how inescapable is the destiny of the poet. He had not, when he began to write, any knowledge of the poetry that had gone before, he inherited no tradition, knew no stimulus from the company of intellectuals; all he had encountered as manifestations of the glory of poetry were Thomson's *Seasons*, and the ballads that the villagers of Helpston sang when they gathered round their firesides on winter evenings. His genius needed no spark from outside to kindle the flame; long before he came to manhood, it was burning clearly and brightly, a small pin-point of light that would one day be a blaze.

Clare did not choose to be a poet—he wrote because he had to. He wrote in sickness and poverty, he wrote when he was hungry and weary, when all the world discouraged and mocked at him, when his hopes of the immortality that he so much desired for his poetry were almost dead. Neither joy nor tribulation could lessen that compulsion which he described as "itching after rhyme" —a compulsion so strong that at times he was alarmed to find how utterly it controlled him, how it drove him on to write and write for days on end, scarcely stopping to eat or sleep, until everything was drained from him and he was left like "a beggar by the wayside."

It is very difficult to tell with any certainty when Clare's mental derangement actually began. His mental and physical disorders were closely connected, and it seems fairly certain that his mind had begun to be slightly affected long before he actually suffered his first attack of insanity in 1830. We may conclude that there had always been something in his manner or conversation that suggested abnormality, for the villagers prophesied when he was but a boy that he would lose his reason, and Drury mentioned in 1820 that he had fears for Clare's sanity if he continued to drive himself as he was doing at that time. It is necessary to make allowance in the first instance for the suspicion with which the inhabitants of Helpston regarded a boy addicted to learning, and in the second for Drury's jealousy at Clare coming under the influence of Gilchrist, but there remains the fact that a number of people thought of insanity in connection with him and there must have been something that caused them to do so.

Certainly, until Clare actually became insane and began to suffer from delusions, he showed a more than ordinary amount of balance and common sense in the conduct of his life. In his letters, where he gave his opinions of people and things, of books, of religious and political beliefs, it is always evident how carefully he weighed those opinions and how sound were the conclusions that he reached. In material matters he showed the same good sense; in the face of terrible difficulties he managed to maintain his family by augmenting his slender income with money obtained by field labour. He economised in every way he could, and managed his accounts in a remarkably business-like way, although this was made difficult by the vagaries of his publisher. It was very rarely that his strong emotions got the better of his sense of duty, and on those occasions he suffered agonies of remorse; at other times he mastered completely the temptations to disregard his obligations as a husband and father and as a man of integrity.

Remembering all these things, I think that it becomes evident that it was only in connection with his poetry that Clare appeared to be not as other men. From the very beginning his gift controlled *him*, not he *it*, and under its influence he was swept away beyond the confines of the ordinary everyday world, and became in manner and behaviour sufficiently eccentric to make him suspect in the eyes of his friends and neighbours. It is probable that they erred in their judgment of him because they tried to measure his mind against their own; the proverbially scant recognition accorded to a prophet in his own country meant that Clare's genius was under-estimated and he was regarded first as a Helpston labourer and second as a poet. He was thus measured by the standards of the local peasants, compared with whom he must, indeed, have seemed strange, but even if his neighbours had realised that they could not judge him as one of themselves it is doubtful whether they would have understood the fundamental differences between them.

It is not given to us, any more than it was given to them, to know exactly what it means to a man to be possessed of that tormenting, comforting, bewildering thing that we call genius. We can go so far with him along the road, but whereas the horizon grows no nearer in the longest lifetime of ordinary men and women, the saint and the genius reach it early in life, and, having seen what is beyond, their lives henceforth are not as ours. In time and space they have seen farther than we shall ever see, and everything is intensified tenfold—their joys are more intoxicating, their agonies more terrible, their capacity for all emotion infinitely greater. It is not surprising that sometimes the human mind breaks under the strain, as Clare's broke. No man, we are told, puts new wine into old bottles, yet something very like that has happened now and again in the history of mankind, when a great genius has been born within a human being.

I think it is easy to lay too much emphasis upon the part played by the material circumstances in Clare's life. That they caused him distress, suffering, and a constant, nagging anxiety, is well known, but, had he attained that independence that he so much desired, would he indeed have found tranquillity? I think it went deeper than that. His tragedy was really one of loneliness. The part of him that was peasant, that inherited the peasant's ways, traditions, outlook, held him fast to his native village. The fields and woods that he so passionately loved, the birds and beasts that he watched and wrote about with tenderness and patience, the familiar trees and stones and hedgerows, were, with the poetry which grew out of them, the great loves of his life. To them he turned for solace and companionship, in them he found forgetfulness of material cares. To leave them for the town would have been death to him, yet it was in the town—in the company of Taylor and the circle of contributors to *The London Magazine*—that he found the intellectual companionship that he needed. Between these conflicting joys he must make his choice; he could not have both. It is not, perhaps, strictly accurate to call it a choice, for there was never any question of his deserting Northamptonshire, but the few weeks that he spent in the company of the "Londoners" made it abundantly clear to him how unsatisfying and inadequate was the conversation of his Helpston friends. It was a difficult situation, and it was inevitable that, belonging in part to two spheres so different, he should not belong wholly to either. To the "Londoners", much as they liked him and admired his work, he was always the rustic, while to the peasants of Helpston he was an eccentric, and his learning was regarded with almost as much suspicion as witchcraft.

During the last years of Clare's life, when he was in the asylum, he was forgotten by the public as completely as if that brief spell of fame had never been, and after his death it seemed as though his life and work were doomed to oblivion. There was a slight revival of interest in 1865, when Martin published his life, and again, eight years later, when Cherry's *Life and Remains of John Clare* appeared, but after that he became once more nothing but a shadowy name. The poems, long out of print, languished on the shelves, forgotten, and the great number that had never been published remained locked away in drawers and cupboards while the years passed.

But in this century—particularly in the last thirty years— thanks to the efforts of a few people who know and love his work, Clare has begun to come into his own again. He never desired wealth, and to be famous—in the sense of being flattered and lionised—was a prospect that had no appeal for him. His ambitions were few and simple. He wanted to be independent, and he wanted his poetry to be read by future generations. The first wish was not granted to him, but the second—that of "living a little after life"—has come about, and it is not too much to hope that oblivion will not again overtake his name, and that he will have permanently the place in English literature that he assuredly deserves.

2

I

CHILDHOOD

Between the eastern border of the county of Rutland and the western border of the great fen country that stretches across Lincolnshire and Cambridgeshire to the coast, is a low-lying region called on the map "The Soke of Peterborough". If a triangle is drawn across the area, having for its corners, Peterborough, Stamford, and Market Deeping, it will be found that the small Northamptonshire village of Helpston lies at the heart of the triangle thus formed. It is a long, scattered village, its centre being at the crossing of two roads, and the houses straggling out from there north, south, east, and west into the wide, flat countryside.

Into this village at an uncertain date somewhere near the year 1760, there came a young man, reputed to be a Scotsman by birth, who possessed a fiddle and a glib tongue and went by the name of John Donald Parker. He may have been a schoolmaster by profession, or he may have assumed the role for a time to suit his own convenience, but at any rate he was appointed to the task of teaching the children of Helpston their letters. He used his leisure to court the daughter of John Clare, the parish clerk, and when it was revealed to him that her situation was such as only marriage could render honourable he disappeared from the village and was heard of no more. The girl whom he thus betrayed cannot have felt any great bitterness against him, for she gave to their son at his christening the name that he should have inherited at his birth, and, as her grandson humorously remarked long years afterwards, "her love was not that frenzy which shortens the days of the victim of seduction, for she liv'd to the age of 60".

Such was Parker Clare's entry into the world in the year 1765. He became a day labourer, working for the farmers in the vicinity of Helpston, and when he had grown to manhood he, in his turn, went courting, but with more honourable intentions than his father, for in the autumn of 1792 he married Ann Stimson, whose father was a shepherd and had the care of all the flocks of the village of Castor where he lived.

Parker Clare took his young bride home to Helpston where they lived in a long, low, thatched cottage in the village street which runs south from the cross-roads; the row of cottages, which is still standing, was subsequently made into four, but at that time it was only two, as it is to-day, and both belonged to a retired farmer who occupied one end himself.

Into this home was born, on 13th July, 1793, a son whom they called John. He was one of twins, the other being a girl who was large and bonny while John was so small that his mother said she could have put him into a pint pot. But, contrary to expectation, the little girl died when only a few weeks old while John, the weakling, survived.

It was difficult enough to make ends meet even in those days, but there was to come a time when Parker Clare was disabled, and they looked back to this as a golden age of prosperity. The wages of a day labourer were very small, and the outbreak of war with France in 1793 sent the price of bread on the first stage of the upward journey which was to cause terrible want and misery in many English homes. Even before that, the plight of the peasantry was a pitiful one, and the Acts of Enclosure which were swallowing up the common lands all over England deprived the labourer of the piece of ground on which he might keep his cow or his pig, the proceeds of which often proved the narrow margin by which he managed to live without the humiliation of accepting parish relief. By 1795 the patient endurance of the peasant already showed signs of breaking, for there were riots in several of the southern counties as a protest against the price of bread; but the situation was patched up by the introduction of the Speenhamland system, under which the labourer received a certain weekly sum from the parish, which was in addition to his wages and which fluctuated with the price of bread. The advantage of this scheme was that it was a rough-and-ready insurance against starvation; the disadvantage was that it reduced every labourer, even those in full employment, to the status of a pauper depending on parish money.

Under such conditions it was a hard task to bring up a family, and it was perhaps fortunate that Parker and Ann Clare had only one other child who survived—a girl called Sophy who was born in 1798. There were times when it was difficult to feed even two young mouths, and John, who was never a strong child, needed all the care which his mother lavished on him, and which, with a larger family, she might not have been able to give him. For if the home was poor in money it was rich in kindness and affection, and when John Clare recalled his childhood he was able to say of his parents: "I have every reason to turn to their memories with the warmest feelings of gratitude, and satisfaction; and if doing well to their children be an addition to righteousness, I am certain God cannot forget to bless them with a portion of felicity in the other world."

Parker Clare used to dig his garden in the early morning before he went to work, or at night when he came home, and as it was quite a good size the vegetables that he grew there helped to augment the rather slender meals. There was also an apple tree in the garden which generally bore a good crop of a variety called Golden Ruperts, and the sale of these, except in a bad year, paid the rent of the cottage which was forty shillings. At that time Parker Clare was an unusually strong man and had something of a reputation in the neighbourhood as a wrestler. He could read a little in the Bible and had a liking for old superstitious tales such as the hawkers would sell in the street for a penny. He had a good voice and a long memory for songs and ballads, of which it was his boast that he could sing above a hundred.

Ann Clare doubtless had a store of these old ballads in her memory, too, for singing and reciting and telling stories that had been handed down from antiquity were great pastimes in the evenings when the villagers sat round the fire, but she could not read or write, and "superstition went so far with her that she believed the higher parts of learning was the blackest arts of witchcraft, and that no other means could attain them". Her illiteracy was a source of great regret to her, and she determined, if it were possible, not to let her children suffer the same handicap, but to give them such education as would make good scholars of them.

It was very early in John Clare's life that he first showed that sense of delighted wonder at the shape of the world and everything in it that was later to pervade his poetry, the same sense that stirred in him when he marvelled at the glow-worm or wrote of the

> slender kingcup, burnished with the dew
> Of morning's early hours,
> Like gold yminted new.[1]

[1] "Summer Images."

He was out gathering sticks one summer morning when he was filled with a sudden desire to explore that wonderful and mysterious distance where earth and sky meet. He had often looked at it across the wide expanse of Emmonsales Heath and had imagined that a day's journey would bring him to that brink of the world from which he could look down as into a large pit and see its secret—"the same," he says, "as I believed I could see heaven by looking into the water". So he set out across the heath and wandered on and on until he seemed to be in an alien country, and even the sun and the familiar wild flowers looked different. But he had no fear, for his "wonder-seeking happiness" left no room for that.

> I was finding new wonders every minute and was walking in a new world often wondering to myself that I had not found the edge of the old one—the sky still touched the ground in the distance as usual and my childish wisdom grew puzzled in perplexity.

Night came on before he had realised that the morning was past, and he turned hurriedly to search for the way home. He was quite lost, but some happy chance put him in the right way and at last he recognised the Helpston fields, although they looked different now that he saw them for the first time with the eyes of one who had looked on other scenes. His parents were naturally alarmed at his long absence and half the village had gone out to search for him, fearing that some accident had befallen him.

But except for that one incident Clare gave little sign in these early years that his destiny was to differ in any way from that of the other boys with whom he played. He delighted in all the games of childhood—leap-frog, hop-scotch, hide-and-seek; he fished with thread and a bent pin, fed on nuts and blackberries and peas stolen from the fields, ran races, and joined the other children in singing the songs that they had from their parents. Perhaps most of all he liked the games of make-believe in which the young imagination played the part of Cinderella's godmother and transformed pumpkins into golden coaches. He was already eager to be a man, and in imitation of his father he used to hold a willow-twig which was the plough and drive a team who had names but no substance; at harvest-time when he saw the wagons loaded with sheaves of corn he wanted to lead one of his own, so he cut the lower branches from an old oak tree and used them to carry home his imaginary crop.

he had listened to the ballads of Granny Bains. He more than half believed their stories of ghosts and witches and hobgoblins, and for many years these and other stories like them had such a hold upon his mind that he was fearful of passing certain places on the road when he went home in the evening.

Meanwhile, in the school at Glinton, Clare was making good progress under the tuition of the old schoolmaster, Seaton. No doubt the boy's quick brain made the task of teaching him a pleasure, and Seaton encouraged him not to be content with the rudiments of an education but to go on and hope one day to qualify for the position of usher in a village school. Clare's zest for learning led him to use much of his leisure in reading and writing and struggling with the mysteries of mathematics which he longed to conquer, so that Seaton was always surprised to find him improved every time he came to school instead of having forgotten what he had previously learned. Clean, white paper on which to practise his writing or do his sums was a luxury seldom known to Clare, for he must save three farthings before he could buy a sheet, and farthings were not plentiful, but he used to form his letters or draw squares and triangles on the dusty walls of the barn, and whenever his mother brought back some tea or sugar from the village shop he took the brown or blue paper in which it was wrapped and wrote on that. In the winter evenings he would sit at the kitchen table to do his work—that table which, he said, "old as it was, doubtless was never honoured with higher employment all its days than the convenience of bearing at meal-times the luxury of a barley loaf or dish of potatoes", but which was now covered with pens, ink and paper. His parents watched him with anxious pride, and his mother often stopped her spinning-wheel to look at what he was doing and to say that one day their son would reward them for the trouble they had taken in giving him schooling.

Despite the hours which Clare spent in his searchings after knowledge, he found time to share in such merrymaking as the other villagers enjoyed, and in his autobiographical notes he gave a vivid description of the traditional pastimes of the country folk at the holidays which crowned the year "as thick as the boughs on a harvest-home". At Christmas-time they fetched ivy from the woods and coloured the berries with whitening and the blue-bag; then came St. Valentine's Day, with the excitement of choosing their favourites in the village, and the first of April, with the fun of making fools. There were the sports on May Day, and, a little later, the May Fair when stalls were set up round the Cross at Helpston and there were wonderful toys and sweets for sale; then there was sheep-shearing and harvest-home and Martinmas, when they roasted apples and drank nutmegged ale, played games and told fortunes.

But at other times, when there were not, as on these special days, celebrations in progress to tempt him into company, Clare was beginning to develop a taste for solitude, and on Sundays, instead of joining in the sports and games of the other boys as had been his wont, he went for walks in the woods and fields alone. Solitude was needful to him at that time when perhaps the first vague hints of his destiny began to trouble his soul and bewilder his young brain although he had not, as yet, found expression in verse, and the dawning of genius was not yet clear enough to be a definite thought or to make itself understood. These lonely wanderings developed in him that passion for Nature and all the creatures of the earth that was to be a delight to him through all his long life, and yet was to cause him so much suffering. For, while he walked about the woods or lay in the grass or sat within the shelter of some hollow tree, he watched what went on around him, whether it was a bird building its nest or a spider spinning its web, or "the packman snail" journeying along with his home on his back. The endless patience that enabled him to sit for hours observing the activities of bird and beast, even down to

these tiny loiterers on the barley's beard

was not the least of his gifts, for it made of him a naturalist of the first order, and the blending of his scientific knowledge with his immense love produced some of his most beautiful poetry.

There was also a practical reason that prompted Clare to seek solitude at this time; he had developed an insatiable passion for reading which he was shy of revealing to the neighbours, who regarded such tastes as a sure indication of idleness, so he took his books in his pockets and hid "in woods and dingles of thorns in the fields on Sundays". He devoured any books that he could lay hands on, but mostly, at that particular period, the sixpenny romances which he saved every penny and halfpenny to buy from the hawkers who came to the door. Like this he acquired *Cinderella, Little Red Riding Hood, Jack and the Beanstalk* and several more, and he firmly believed everything that he read in them.

But although he succeeded in concealing the extent of his reading from the villagers they noticed his new habits of wandering off alone into the fields, and they discussed it among themselves, prophesying that no good would come of it.

There were, however, two friends who sometimes shared Clare's leisure hours. One was a boy called Richard Turnill who used to go bird's nesting with him and whose death from typhus while still at school was a great grief to Clare. The other, Mary Joyce, was the daughter of a Glinton farmer and also attended Seaton's school where, although she was four years younger than Clare, they soon became good friends. For Clare, young as he was, the relationship soon grew from a childish friendship into something more, for it was the early and immature stirring, the faint foreshadowing, of a love that was to possess his early manhood and remain with him in a strangely mystical form until he died. Mary's companionship helped to dispel that loneliness which Clare felt in being already set apart from the other boys by reason of his ambitions towards learning, and his unconscious mental and spiritual preparations for the day, not yet envisaged, when the chrysalis would become a butterfly. For, although he was always inarticulate with her and could not share these secret, inner thoughts, there seems to have been a silent understanding between them which made talk on such subjects unnecessary. Clare told the story of that early love in the notes that he made many years later for an autobiography:

I was a lover very early in life, my first attachment being a school-boy affection, but Mary, who cost me more ballads than sighs, was beloved with a romantic or Platonic sort of feeling; if I could but gaze on her face or fancy a smile on her countenance it was sufficient —I went away satisfied. We played with each other but named nothing of love, yet I fancyed her eyes told me her affections; we walked together as school companions in leisure hours, but our talk was of play, and our actions the wanton nonsense of children. Yet young as my heart was it would turn chill when I touched her hand, and tremble, and I fancyed her feelings were the same for as I gazed earnestly in her face, a tear would hang in her smiling eye and she would turn to wipe it away. Her heart was as tender as a bird's.

One day, when they were playing in the churchyard, Clare threw a green walnut which hit Mary in the eye and made her weep. He hid his sorrow and affection, pretending to feel no

regret for what he had done, lest the other children should laugh
at him and accuse him of loving her, but the memory of the incident remained with him and he recalled it long afterwards and
spoke of his shame.

The happy companionship was broken by the termination of
Clare's studies with Seaton. He was now twelve or thirteen, an age
at which most boys, in those hard times, had finished with school
and worked the same long hours as grown men. Parker Clare was
beginning to be badly handicapped by the rheumatism that finally
crippled him, and this meant that he was able to earn less and
there would be dire need in the home unless John could earn
more and so keep up the level of the money coming in. So,
reluctantly, the parents decided that their dreams of making the
boy a great scholar with a job above that of manual labour must
be sacrificed to the necessity of the moment and he must give up
Seaton's school and find regular work. But the master interceded
for him that his education should not be entirely abandoned, and
Parker and Ann Clare were ready enough to listen to him, being
anxious to do their best for the boy; so it was decided that he
should attend a night-school at Glinton, which plan fulfilled both
purposes of adding to his learning and yet leaving his days free for
work.

2

THE BLUE BELL

Clare's parents, considering
that the boy was not strong enough for the heavy work of threshing, made application to have him apprenticed to a shoe-maker,
but he did not relish the idea so it was abandoned, for, he says,
"my mother was determined if I was [bound to] a trade that I
should have my choice". The choice, however, was limited by the
fact that his parents could not afford to pay even a sixpence
towards his apprenticeship and were therefore dependent on
finding someone who would take the boy for nothing. A stone-
mason called Shelton offered to take him, but this calling was no
more to his taste than cobbling and he said, by way of excuse,
that he disliked climbing, although he had often delighted to climb
trees after the nests of kites and magpies. His parents were almost
in despair and began to think that the neighbours' prophecies
would be fulfilled and that their son was an idler who wanted no
harder work than reading books. "But the fact was," Clare wrote,
"I felt timid and fearful of undertaking the first trial in everything." He did not want to leave home nor to work in any trade
that was new to him, and he was filled with dread at the thought
that he must now meet that premature manhood that poverty had
forced upon him; yet, although he was afraid of taking such a big
step as entering into an apprenticeship, he had already a faint
notion that in the end he would come to a calling much more
adventurous than that of a cobbler or a stone-mason.

> I felt a sort of hopeless prospect around me of not being able to
> meet manhood as I could wish, for I had always that feeling of
> ambition about me that wishes to do something to gain notice or to
> rise above its fellows.

Although his parents were disappointed, they would not force
the boy to any work that he did not want to undertake, so he
stayed on at home and worked in the fields, haymaking, harvesting,
weeding in the wheat and doing any odd jobs that fell to his lot.

7

After a while he was offered employment by Mrs. Bellars of Woodcroft Castle, some two or three miles from Helpston, and he began work there as a ploughboy. It was a good job and Mrs. Bellars was very kind to him, but Clare was not happy there and would not make up his mind to settle down. He objected to getting up so early in the morning as he was obliged to do there, and he also complained that in wet weather the moat overflowed the causeway which led to the porch and the boys had to wade through water up to their knees to get in and out, so he left there after one month and went back to his parents who tried in vain to persuade him to return.

Very soon after this another opportunity occurred that filled the anxious parents with hopes of finding Clare some work that would be congenial to him and would offer him good prospects. Ann Clare's brother, Morris Stimson, was footman to a lawyer called Bellamy who lived at Wisbech, and, learning that there was a vacancy in his employer's office for a clerk, he determined to try to get Clare the job. Mr. Bellamy was not unwilling to consider taking the lad, but he wished to see him in order to form an opinion of his character and qualifications, so Clare, who had never been more than eight miles from home, had to make the journey to Peterborough and thence by boat along the River Nen to Wisbech. Ann Clare was anxious for her son to make a good impression, and she dressed him with much care, giving him a pair of gloves to lend refinement to his rough hands and a white neckcloth to distract attention from the fact that his suit was old and his coat-sleeves so short as to be almost nearer his elbows than his wrists.

Clare set out with a great sense of adventure and with high hopes for the approaching interview. In the boat, going down the river, he asked himself questions such as he thought Mr. Bellamy might put to him, and carefully rehearsed his answers; he thought what a fine figure he would cut when he went to see his friends, dressed in the smart clothes of a lawyer's clerk, and he laughed out loud for pleasure and excitement. But then he remembered how shabby he was and how grand was the situation to which he aspired; his spirits fell and success seemed impossible. Diffidence and fear increased in him as he neared Wisbech, and by the time he had found Bellamy's house he was almost too frightened to ring the bell. But he plucked up his courage at last and was relieved when his uncle opened the door and led him to the kitchen. He could eat no tea for thinking of what he was to say to the lawyer and wondering how he should manage to obey his uncle's instructions to "look up boldly and tell him what you can do".

The interview, when it came, was brief, and Clare himself has described it with a nice sense of humour:

> At length the counsellor appeared and I held up my head as well as I could but it was like my hat, almost under my arm. "Aye aye so this is your Nephew, Morris, is he" said the counsellor. "Yes, Sir" said my uncle. "Aye aye so this is your Nephew" repeated the counsellor, rubbing his hands as he left the room. "Well I shall see him agen"—but he never saw me agen to this day.

Mrs. Bellamy gave instructions that Clare was to be made welcome in the servants' quarters until the boat returned to Peterborough two days later, so his uncle looked after him and he spent a whole day exploring Wisbech and amusing himself looking at the shops, in one of which he saw some paintings by an artist called Rippingille who was then doing portraits in the town. Some fourteen years later he was to meet Rippingille, strike up a friendship with him, and spend many evenings carousing with him in London alehouses. But that was still a long way off; at present Clare was a young boy going home with mixed feelings—of relief that he had escaped the ordeal of Counsellor Bellamy's office, and of chagrin that he had met with failure in the enterprise. His own disappointment was soon forgotten in his delight at seeing home again, but to his parents this latest failure of their son was a more serious matter and they may well have wondered whether the boy would ever get steady work.

At this point a piece of good fortune came Clare's way. Francis Gregory, who kept the Blue Bell Inn next door to the cottage where Clare lived, offered him work as a ploughboy for a week or two, and after he had been there for a little while and the arrangement proved satisfactory he hired him for a year. Gregory had six or eight acres of land and a few animals, and as he was very delicate and was often ill, he was glad to have the boy to attend to these. He was unmarried and his mother lived with him and looked after the house; they were both kindly people and seem to have been fond of Clare, for he says "they treated me more like a son than a servant". The work that he gave Clare to do was not heavy, and, as Gregory himself was kept much indoors either by ill-health or by his duties as landlord of the inn, the boy was generally left alone at his tasks. While he was weeding, or tending the horses and cows, he diverted himself by singing over the old ballads and by talking to himself, describing scenes that impressed themselves on his mind, and on occasions this habit served another purpose besides that of entertainment. Mrs. Gregory was a thrifty housekeeper, and as flour was sold more cheaply at Maxey than at Helpston she used to send Clare once or twice a week to fetch a bag of it from this village which was some two miles distant. It was usually late afternoon by the time he started on the errand, so that in winter he had to come back in the dark and was obliged to pass several spots that were said to be haunted by those ghosts and hobgoblins of which the old village women never tired of telling, and Clare found that by talking to himself he could occupy his mind and keep his fears at bay. So he would hurry along with his eyes fixed on the ground, except when a quaking thistle or the murmur of the wind in the trees startled him and made him look round, and as he went he told himself stories of which he was the hero; sometimes he was a soldier, valiant in battle, and sometimes he travelled in foreign lands and found a fair lady with a great fortune, but almost always he told his stories in rhyme. Often he would be so occupied with these imaginings that he would not only forget the ghosts but would also be unaware that he had reached his destination, and would go down the village street at Maxey still muttering to himself until the strange glances that people gave him recalled him to reality and filled him with shame.

Clare was still reading furiously at this time and was turning his attention more and more to poetry although the books that were available to him were very few. He had now two friends who were both of a studious turn of mind and with whom he talked over the things that he read. John Turnill was the son of a farmer and the brother of that Richard Turnill who had been a friend of Clare's schooldays; he was older than Clare and had had the advantage of a boarding-school education so that he was able to give his young friend some help with his studies, but he subsequently obtained a post in the Excise and went away from Helpston. The other boy, Tom Porter, who lived at Ashton Green about a mile from Helpston, was fond of gardening and of wild flowers, and he and Clare used to go out on Sundays to search for rare plants. Clare says "our taste was parallel excepting poetry", and he borrowed and read greedily the few old books that Porter possessed, including Sandys' *Travels*, and Parkinson's *Herbal*. Among the other books and poems that Clare had read by now were *Robinson Crusoe*, *The Scotch Rogue*, Wordsworth's *We are Seven*, and Tannahill's *Jessie, the Flower o' Dunblane*.

He was still spending all his leisure in the woods and fields, watching the birds and insects, listening to "the cuckoo's 'wandering voice' and the restless song of the nightingale"; he stayed away from church on Sundays to go fishing, or to "lie upon a mossy bank where the fir-like fern its under-forest keeps 'in a strange stillness'", and he would sit for hours watching "the little insects climb up and down the tall stems of the wood-grass, or the smooth plantain-leaf". His keen eye and ear made him familiar with the habits and characteristics of all the creatures for whom he felt such an immense tenderness and whom he regarded not as inferiors but as brothers, and he began to experience an intensified delight that was near ecstasy at the beauties of earth. He was growing daily more aware of colour, shape, movement, sound, and the flight of a heron across a grey sky or the clapping of a wood-pigeon's wings among the dark oaks awoke a pleasure and an agony in his soul. This period was, in some ways, one of the happiest in Clare's life, for he was utterly free from those material cares and anxieties that ever afterwards weighed him down, and he was discovering every day and every hour new wonders of the earth that absorbed and fascinated him; but it must also have been a time of great torment, for he was already a poet and bore the poet's burden without the relief of expression. He did not as yet understand why the things that other people thought nothing of should move him to such happiness.

I loved to employ leisure in wandering about the fields watching the habits of birds, to see the woodpecker sweeing away in its ups and downs, the jaybird chattering by the woodside its restless warnings of passing clowns, and the travels of insects, were the black beetle mumbled along, and the opening of field flowers; such amusements gave me the greatest of pleasures but I could not account for the reason why they did so. A lonely nook, a rude bridge or woodland style with ivy growing round the posts delighted me and made lasting impressions on my feelings, but I knew nothing of poetry then, yet I noticed everything as anxious as I do now and everything pleased me as much.

I marked the varied colors in flat, spreading fields checkered with closes of different-tinted grain like the colors in a map—the

copper-tinted colors of clover in blossom, the sun-tanned green of the
ripening hay, the lighter hues of wheat and barley intermixed with
the sunny glare of the yellow carlock and the sunset imitation of the
scarlet headaches[1] with the blue corn-bottles crowding their splendid
colors in large sheets over the land and "troubling the corn-fields"
with destroying beauty; the different greens of the woodland trees,
the dark oak, the paler ash, the yellow lime, the white poplar peeping
above the rest like leafy steeples, the grey willow shining chilly in the
sun as if the morning mist still lingered in its cool green. I felt the
beauty of these with eager delight—the gad flyes noon day hum, the
fainter murmur of the bee fly spinning in the evening ray, the dragon
flye in its spangled coats . . . the wild geese scudding along and
making all the letters of the alphabet as they flew. . . . I observed
all this with the same rapture as I have done since, but I knew
nothing of poetry—it was felt and not uttered. I loved the meadow
lake with its flags and long purples[2] crowding the water's edge. I
listened with delight to hear the wind whisper among the feather-topt
reeds, to see the taper bulrush nodding in gentle curves to the rippling
water, and I watched with delight on haymaking evenings the
setting sun drop behind the Brigs and peep again through the half-
circle of the arches as if he longed to stay.

It was very soon afterwards that the poetic feelings that troubled
him found utterance, but there is some difficulty in placing the
exact date on which Clare wrote his first poem; he was vague
about dates and contradicted himself several times as to the order
in which things happened in those early days. In *Sketches in the
Life of John Clare* he certainly says that it was during the summer
when he worked for Francis Gregory; but Taylor, in the introduction to *Poems Descriptive of Rural Life and Scenery*, for which
Clare supplied facts, says that it was when he was thirteen, which
would have been earlier. At any rate, though the date is uncertain,
the manner in which it occurred is well known. A young man in
the village, a weaver by trade, lent Clare Thomson's *Seasons*, and
the impression it made on him was so great that he determined to
possess a copy himself. He expressed surprise, when he returned
the book to its owner, that it should have been so roughly treated,
for part of "Winter" was missing, but the weaver laughed, and said
he did not think much of it, and thought Wesley's hymns much

[1] Poppies. The name was given to them because of the belief, common among the
country people that their sickly smell caused a headache. They were also called Ear-
aches and Blindybuffs as they were thought to injure the eyes and ears if held close
to them.
[2] The purple loose-strife.

greater, for he was a Methodist; upon which Clare privately decided that "whatever his religion might be, the taste of him and his friends was worth little notice". The young Methodist, however, condescended to inform him that the book could be bought for one-and-sixpence, and, having worried his father to give him that amount, Clare set out for Stamford the next Sunday morning to buy it. He knew so little of town customs that he had no idea that the shop would be shut, and he came home again empty-handed and low in spirits. But the next week, when he was meant to be tending his horses in company with some other boys, he bribed one of them to watch his charges while he went again to Stamford; the amount of the bribe was 2d, of which one penny was for looking after the horses and the other was the price of silence. He got to Stamford so early that he had to loiter about for several hours before the shop opened, but he finally got his book for one shilling.

The sun rose as he was coming back, and the beautiful morning and the pleasure of his new possession filled him with such excitement that he could not wait to read the book, and as he did not like to be seen reading at the roadside on a working day he climbed over the wall into Burghley Park. He was not disappointed at this second perusal, and as he continued his journey homewards the pleasant scenery and the influence of Thomson's verse stimulated him to "descriptive rhyming". The result was "The Morning Walk", and it was soon followed by "The Evening Walk" and by a number of other descriptive poems, some of which Clare kept in his head while others he ventured to commit to paper. To begin with, he was often ashamed of them when they were written, and burned them, but later he "felt a desire to preserve some, and used to correct them over and over until the last copy had lost all kindred to the first, even in the Title". This habit of taking great pains over his poetry was one that Clare cultivated all his life, and his notebooks show how he would write and rewrite a thing, drawing a line through the last version as he completed the new one.

His mind was now filled with new and exciting thoughts about this absorbing business of rhyming, and it was a good thing that Francis Gregory was a lenient master for it is easy to imagine that Clare was somewhat inattentive at his work. All his spare moments were occupied in writing, but he guarded his secret closely and his parents had no idea that their son was a poet, thinking

3

only that his scribblings were done in order to improve his hand-writing. When he was given a penny on Sundays or holidays to buy fruit and sweetmeats he saved it to buy paper, and he used all the shop-paper that came into the house, as well as writing be-tween the lines of old copy-books. His only confidant in this matter was Tom Porter, whose qualifications as a critic were not great and who did not seem impressed with the verses, though he told Clare that he understood them, and he certainly kept the secret.

After a time Clare began to long for the encouragement that a little praise would give him, and determined, without wholly divulging what he was about, to seek the opinion of his parents. So when he heard his father humming over some old ballad or popular song he would say that he could beat it, and after a few days he would produce his own version of it and read it aloud to his family; but they laughed and told him that he need never hope to make songs like them. Clare was discouraged and mortified, fearful that his verses were indeed no better than the doggerel of the ballads, and even more fearful that he might incur further ridicule, so for a time he stopped writing, and when he began again he sought the privacy of the woods where there was no one to inquire what he was doing. There he would sit down to write on the blue or brown scraps of grocer's wrapping-paper, with a pencil that was one of a dozen he had bought for a shilling from a Jew at Stamford Fair.

> I whispered aye and felt a fear
> To speak aloud though none was near,
> I dreaded laughter more than blame,
> I dared not sing aloud for shame,
> So all unheeded lone and free,
> I felt it happiness to be
> Unknown, obscure and like a tree
> In woodland peace and privacy.[1]

After a while Clare thought out a trick by which he might ob-tain the unbiased judgment that he wanted without the risk of being laughed at. He read his poems to his parents and said that they were written by someone else, either holding a book while he read so that they should think the verses were from the printed page, or saying that he had copied them out of a borrowed book. The ruse worked; they praised the poems and said on many

[1] "The Progress of Rhyme."

occasions, "Aye boy, if you could write so, you would do." Clare
was delighted and made use of his parents' criticisms to alter and
correct his work; if they laughed, he knew that there was some
affectation in the verse that he must get rid of, if they could not
understand and desired to have a line repeated, he knew that there
was some obscurity that he must clarify. The poems that they
liked best he stored away, first in an unused cupboard and then,
when that was needed, in a hole in the wall beneath it, but his
mother discovered the hoard, and, thinking that they were only
bits of paper on which he practised writing, she used them for
kettle-holders and fire-lighters whenever she wanted paper. Clare
was afraid to tell her what they really were, lest she should show
them to someone else and ask for an opinion which he felt would
put him to shame, so he said nothing and she continued to destroy
them, but when he wrote anything that he thought better than the
rest, he carried it about in his pocket until the paper was worn
through at the folds.

While Clare was writing as much as he could in all his spare
time, turning his hopes, thoughts, ambitions into verse, he came
upon a remark in the introduction to some book he was reading
that "a person who knew nothing of grammar was not capable of
writing a letter nor even a bill of parcels". This filled him with
consternation, for he had been writing all this time without ever
having learnt any grammar at all, and he hastily bought a spelling-
book as the best means of remedying this grave defect. "But", he
wrote afterwards, "finding a jumble of words classed under this
name and that name and this such-a-figure of speech and that
another-hard-worded-figure, I turned from further notice of it in
instant disgust. For, as I knew I could talk to be understood, I
thought by the same method my writing might be made out as
easy and as proper."

Clare kept this wisdom of simplicity all his life, and it served
him to better purpose than a knowledge of that grammar which
Lowe's *Critical Spelling Book* could not teach but could only make
him hate.

3

MARY JOYCE

THE YEAR AT THE BLUE BELL was a significant one in Clare's life because it saw his feet firmly planted on the path of the poet, and it must be said that without Gregory's kindness and indulgence he could not have made such rapid intellectual development as he did at that time. Gregory died a year or two after he left, but Clare always remembered him with gratitude, and said that he believed "this place to have been the nursery for fostering my rustic song".

But that year was significant for another reason, and here we come to one of the most important points in the story—indeed, to one of the pivots upon which the whole story turns—and find, ironically enough, that it is one of the few pages in Clare's life that was never written. Everything else of importance is told in the MS. material that he left—the fragments of his autobiography, the letters that he wrote and received, his notebooks—but on this one matter he remained, except for a few oblique references, very naturally but provokingly silent. For it was sometime during this year that he met Mary Joyce again, and that his childhood's affection blossomed into a deep and abiding love.

It seems that Clare used to go frequently to Glinton during that winter and early spring, and for a time they were happy in being together, probably without thought of the future; but Clare was acutely sensitive about his poverty, and although he clung to the hope that they might one day marry it must have seemed always a far-off dream to him. In "The Progress of Rhyme" he speaks of the smile of beauty which it was worth making every endeavour to gain:

> Whose smiles I little thought to win
> With ragged coat and downy chin,
> A clownish silent aguish boy,
> Who even felt ashamed of joy.

Later in the same poem, he tells how he wrote verses to her and how everything that was beautiful in the world seemed akin to her:

"   . . . . . nor could I pull
The blossoms that I thought divine
As hurting beauty like to thine.
So where they grew I let them be.

Clare's two early biographers have stated that the reason for their parting, which took place some time later—we do not know exactly when—was that Mary's father objected to the relationship and forbade his daughter to have any more to do with a lad who was not only below her station but was an idler as well. It has since been pointed out that there was no evidence for this idea and that it was Mary herself who realised the hopelessness of such a match.[1] Clare certainly hinted as much in some of the poems which we can presume refer to this love of his, and he said it in one of the only two prose passages in which he mentioned the affair, but he said it in such a way as to lack conviction. He wrote in his autobiographical notes about their friendship in the days at Seaton's school (the passage has already been quoted), and he made no allusion to the fact that they met again when they were older, but he finished his account of the early days with these comments:

When she grew up to womanhood she felt her station above mine, at least I felt that she thought so, for her parents were farmers and farmers had great pretensions to something then; so my passion cooled with my reason and contented itself with another tho I felt a hopeful tenderness that I might one day renew the acquaintance and disclose the smothered passion. . . . I felt the disparagement[2] in situation and fearing to meet a denial I carried it on in my own fancies to every extreme, writing songs in her praise, and making her mine with every indulgence of the fancy.

With such material as is extant, this part of Clare's story must always remain something of a mystery, and any attempt to explain it is entirely a matter of speculation, but it does appear from this passage that Mary never *expressed* feelings of superiority and that they may have existed only in Clare's imagination, having grown out of nothing more than his injured pride. He did not speak to

[1] "*John Clare. A Life.*" J. W. and Anne Tibble.
[2] Clare evidently meant disparity.

Mary of his love before they parted, so that she would have had no opportunity of disavowing the feelings attributed to her by Clare, and after their parting, which perhaps occurred in the heat of a quarrel, Clare may have thought of that and wondered if he had misjudged her. In the poems that he wrote about first love in later years, and particularly in those that he wrote in the asylum, he seems to have been almost obsessed by the idea of a love that is inarticulate.

> I hid my love when young till I
> Couldn't bear the buzzing of a fly;
> I hid my love to my despite
> Till I could not bear to look at light:
> I dare not gaze upon her face
> But left her memory in each place;
> Where'er I saw a wild flower lie
> I kissed and bade my love goodbye.[1]

and

> I loved thee, though I told thee not,
> Right earlily and long.[2]

In a dozen different poems the theme recurs, and there is a ring of regret in the lines as though Clare were always lamenting that youthful silence. It seems as though he wondered whether Mary had really felt herself superior, whether she would, had he spoken, have given him the denial that he so much dreaded. Again, in the prose passage: "She felt her station above mine, *at least I felt that she thought so.*" By then he was no longer sure that he had been right in accusing her of arrogance.

The background of the time must not be forgotten. There was then a greater disparity between the farming and labouring classes than had ever been known before. The price of corn had reached a fantastic level, due to the fact that the import of European corn had been stopped since the Napoleonic Wars began, but the labourers' wages had not risen at all, and consequently, while the poverty of the peasants grew gradually worse the farmers were richer than they had ever been in their lives. Many of them having raised their standard of living to an entirely different level, drove about in carriages, and sent their sons and daughters to expensive schools. There is no reason to suppose that Mary Joyce's father was one of these, but he may have acquired rather

---

[1] "I hid my love."   [2] "The Secret."

exalted notions, and, in any case, the fact that he was a farmer would have been quite enough to fill Clare with suspicion and resentment, for he expressed his dislike of them as a class over and over again in later years.

Clare was always sensitive about his situation in life, and was quick to resent any hint of condescension, as when an article appeared in a newspaper giving an inaccurate account of his financial troubles, and he wrote angrily, "I am no beggar for my income is £36." When he became famous he received letters from many people (who should have known better) to the effect that he must never forget his humble station, must never cease to be grateful to his generous friends and patrons. They are letters that would revolt a man far less sensitive than Clare, and by this hard lesson he learned to swallow his pride. But before all that, in the days when he was courting Mary, his pride and his temper were both less controlled, both liable to be set ablaze by the merest spark, and it does seem very probable that this same pride worked in him until he could no longer bear the situation and fancied Mary's every word and glance a slight. In despair and misery he may then have taken that decision to part that he thought of with regret in after years, and Mary may have been wholly ignorant of the reason for the termination of his visits to Glinton. So much for speculation. Of Clare's part in the story, we only know with certainty that the image of this early love went with him all his days and remained supreme through many other loves, and through all the years of married life; of Mary there is no further trace, except the record of her death, unmarried, in 1838.

During the year when Clare was working at the Blue Bell, there was one event of public interest which made a deep impression on him; this was the Act of Parliament by which lands in the parish of Helpston and various adjoining villages were enclosed. Over a course of years these Acts had been passed, dealing with two or three parishes at a time, until more than half the total acreage of Northamptonshire had come under enclosure. Something has already been said of the hardship that was caused to the peasants by these innovations, but although Clare, in common with the rest, was indignant for material reasons, his strongest objection to enclosure was the grief it caused him to see the familiar landscape so drastically changed. It was always his desire that the loved haunts of his boyhood should remain exactly as they were, and he knew every stone and blade of grass so well that nothing could be altered without his noticing and lamenting it:

> How oft I've sighed at alterations made;
> To see the woodman's cruel axe employed,
> A tree beheaded, or a bush destroyed:
> Nay e'en a post, old standard, or a stone
> Mossed o'er by Age, or branded as her own,
> Would in my mind a strong attachment gain,
> A fond desire that there they might remain.[1]

With such sentiments, it is easy to imagine the horror that Clare felt on witnessing the disappearance of the heaths and common lands where he had wandered as a child, the ploughing up of Helpston Green, the levelling of woods, the fencing of pastures, the destruction of the old hollow trees which had provided shelter for him while he scribbled his poems or devoured the sixpenny romances. Among the victims of "the woodman's cruel axe" was Lee Close Oak, that same tree from which Clare had once broken the lower branches to make himself a harvest wagon, and the carpenter who bought it, learning that it was an old friend of his, had the kind thought of making two rulers from its wood and sending them to him.

Clare's employment with Francis Gregory terminated probably in the spring of 1810, though the dates at this period of his life are somewhat uncertain. He had no idea what he should do next, except for a sudden desire to become a sign-painter which was caused by the bragging talk of a man of that profession from Market Deeping who frequented the Blue Bell. He offered to take Clare as an apprentice, but he wanted a small payment, and there was no money to spare in the cottage at that time, so it was impossible.

It was a serious matter for him to be long out of work, for his father's wages grew less in proportion as his rheumatism grew worse, and the mounting cost of food made existence a struggle. Clare's own health was not good either, for he was suffering at about this time from fits which troubled him in spring and autumn.

> I swooned away without a struggle, and felt nothing more than if I'd been in a dreamless sleep after I came to myself; but I was always warn'd of their coming by a chillness and dithering, that

[1] "Helpstone."

seemed to creep from one's toe ends till it got up to one's head, when I turned senseless and fell. Sparks as of fire often flashed from my eyes, or seemed to do so, when I dropt; which I laid to the fall.

He attributed these attacks to the shock of having seen, when he was younger, a man called Thomas Drake after he had fallen off a load of hay and broken his neck, but the symptoms that he describes are typical of epilepsy. He was cured of these attacks by a certain "Mr. Arnold, M.D., of Stamford" and they only recurred once or twice afterwards, but it was no doubt a consequence of this trouble that spring and autumn were always for him a time of low spirits when he was beset with dark fears that he was wont to refer to as "the blue devils".

While Clare was considering what to do, having reluctantly abandoned his plan of becoming a sign-painter, he heard that an apprentice was required by the Marquis of Exeter's head gardener at Burghley House, and, as he felt that such work would be to his liking besides carrying with it the advantage of good prospects, he went at once, accompanied by his father, to apply for the job. They sought the Master of the Kitchen Garden, and when he appeared with white stockings and neckcloth they thought that such a grand figure could be none other than the Marquis himself, so they took off their hats and bowed low to him before venturing to state their business. The great man agreed to take Clare on and he started work the following week as an apprentice for a term of three years, to which, however, he was not bound.

Clare liked his work which included, among other duties, a journey down to the Hall twice a day with fruit and vegetables, and he saved his money to buy Abercrombie's *Gardening* so that he might learn more about the higher arts of his new calling. But the head gardener despite his neckcloth and stockings, was not a gentleman in temper or in habits and although he liked Clare, calling him a willing boy and treating him better than most, he made life hard for his staff and was very unpopular. He was also addicted to drink which caused Clare to make many nocturnal journeys to Stamford, either to fetch liquor for him or to bring him home from a carousal by his wife's orders. Probably the boy would not have met with a good reception when he came on such an errand, for he said that he was often too frightened to go, and so lay down under a tree in the park and fell asleep. In the autumn mornings he would awake to find the rime covering him like a sheet which was hardly helpful to one of his weak constitution.

But although the head gardener flew into tempers and swore at the lads for no reason—except that his head ached after a night at Stamford—there was not much discipline among the garden staff. They slept in the garden-house and were locked in every night, but they used to get out of the windows, climb over the high garden wall, and made for Stamford. There they visited a public-house called "The Hole in the Wall", where the ale was strong and the merriment lasted until midnight; it was kept by a man who had formerly been a servant at Burghley and who was delighted to welcome the boys and encourage them to drink more than was good for them. It was here that Clare first acquired that liking for strong ale which caused him so much trouble afterwards and which constituted a temptation that he was only able to overcome after a long and difficult struggle. His visits to Stamford were frequent, for when he had not enough money to go drinking, his companions treated him for the sake of his company on the road and to prevent his divulging the secret to their master.

No doubt Clare was ready enough to join in the revels and probably thought it grand to go off to the public-house with the older men, but at heart he did not much care for any of them except the foreman, George Cousins, who read a little and was a simple, honest man. The lack of congenial company and the tantrums of the head gardener caused Clare to grow weary of the place before very long and wish to be gone, so when he had been there nearly a year he decided to run away.

Cousins went with him, and they set off early one morning and travelled the twenty-one miles to Grantham where they slept that night at "The Crown and Anchor"; Clare felt as though they were in another world after this tremendous journey, and the spirit of adventure grew faint in him so that he wished himself at home, but he had now gone too far to turn back. They could not hear of any work at Grantham, so they went on to Newark-on-Trent, where a nurseryman called Withers gave them employment, but the wages they received were very unsatisfactory as he only gave them part, promising the rest if they suited him on further trial; they lodged in the house of a lame man whose son was a carpenter, celebrated for making fiddles. The work was very hard and taxed Clare's strength and he felt lost and unhappy, although Newark was "a very lively town". While they were there he attended a village feast at Baldwick, where he got drunk and offered himself for service in the militia, but when he went to Nottingham to be sworn in he was found to be too short and, much to his relief, was sent back to Newark.

After a while the two wanderers decided that they had had enough of Mr. Withers and his garden and wanted to go home, so for the second time they rose early in the morning and fled, leaving ninepence-halfpenny for the lame man which settled their debts. They reached Stamford that night, but did not dare to show themselves in a public-house, so they slept under a tree and were whitened with rime as Clare had been many times before.

Clare's happiness was great on reaching Helpston again, for the highway of the traveller had no fascination for him and he was always homesick if he was away for very long, but his parents were not so pleased, though whether they imagined that he was still at Burghley or had heard of his disappearance is not recorded. In the latter case perhaps their relief at seeing him safe went some way towards mitigating their disappointment in having him out of work again when they had thought him safely settled for three years.

4

THE MILITIA

AFTER HIS RETURN FROM
Newark, Clare got work again as a day labourer in the fields and
resumed his poetic efforts which had been much neglected during
his absence from home. But his love of rhyming was now known
to the neighbours, who mistrusted anyone with such strange habits
and regarded him as a good-for-nothing, while his abstracted
manner and the practice of talking to himself, to which he had
become addicted when he worked alone in Francis Gregory's field,
led the more uncharitable of the Helpston gossips to say that he
was mad. Clare was hurt by this attitude and felt at times an
intolerable loneliness; it puzzled him that other people could not
see things as he did, and when he walked on Sundays with the
other boys he would try their taste "by pointing out some striking
beauty in a wild flower, or object in the surrounding scenery, to
which they could seldom make an answer; and if they did, 'twas
such as 'they could see nothing worth looking at', and turning
careless to resume their old discourse, and laughing at my 'droll
fancies' as they would call them."

For a time Clare struggled on with his writing because, as he
said in a later poem:

> I felt without a single skill
> That instinct that would not be still,
> To think of song sublime beneath
> That heaved my bosom like my breath,
> That burned and chilled and went and came
> Without or uttering or a name,
> Until the vision waked with time
> And left me itching after rhyme.[1]

But everything seemed against him; those who had seen his
poetry gave him no encouragement, the villagers laughed at him,
and his parents, kind and indulgent though they were, were

[1] "The Progress of Rhyme."

44

convinced that his literary efforts were but waste of time and would, if not checked, keep him from getting an honest living. Faced with such opposition from all quarters, it is small wonder if Clare's faith in himself burned low and he questioned the use of going on; he began to write less and to spend his leisure instead in mixing with the wildest characters of the village.

He was employed in setting down fencing and planting quick lines in accordance with the Act of Enclosure, and his fellow workers were "a motley set of labourers . . . whose whole study was continual contriving to get beer, and the bottle was the general theme from week's end to week's end. Such as had got drunk the oftenest fancied themselves the best fellows and made a boast of it." But Clare said that although he contributed towards the bottle as often as the rest he often missed the tot that was handed round, for his constitution would not have borne it. His head was always a weak one, and it did not take much ale to make him drunk; probably his companions deliberately encouraged him, for when he was "fresh", as he called it, he was noisy and excited, singing and laughing and joining in any wild revels that took place. In such a state he provided a strange contrast to the shy, sensitive, abstracted creature that was his normal self.

But Clare's merry-making with his wild companions was interrupted by the course of events in the outside world. In the spring of 1812, when he was nineteen, the fear of a French invasion, which had considerably alarmed the country, resulted in a great recruiting effort for the militia, and Clare volunteered. What caused him to take this somewhat surprising step he does not say, although he suggests that the only courses open were to pay a fine, to be drawn and go for nothing, or to volunteer and receive a bounty of two guineas, which latter choice was obviously the wisest; on the other hand, he may have been driven to it by the lack of other employment or a sudden longing for adventure, or perhaps the break with Mary had recently occurred and made him wish to leave the neighbourhood. Anyhow he went off to Peterborough with a neighbour's son to be sworn in, and was to go on from there to Dundee to join the regiment. Rumours had spread that the French had already invaded and had reached London, and some even said that they were at Northampton, so the people of Helpston stood at their doors, listening for the sound of cannon and recalling the rebellion of '45 when the rebels reached Derby. When they saw Clare and his companion setting off, they bade them farewell with the cheerful comment that they were not likely to see Helpston again, and Clare began to wish himself well out of the adventure.

This time, in spite of his small stature and poor health, Clare was accepted, but when the "motley multitude" of 1,300 new recruits was assembled at Oundle and sorted out into companies, he, in common with the other less hearty specimens, was placed in that section rudely nicknamed the "bum-tools". The light company were called "light-bobs" and the grenadiers "bacon-bolters" and Clare says that the enmity they felt for each other was as great as that which they all felt for the French. The captain of his company was pleasant enough and exercised great patience in trying to teach his men the rudiments of soldiering, but there was what Clare describes as "a little louse-looking corporal" who had not the same forbearance and who took a delight in finding fault with Clare and making jokes about his awkwardness as a soldier. Certainly the poet was not very martial in his bearing, and he explained in the sketch which he afterwards wrote about this phase of his career, "I was not very apt at learning my exercise, for then I was a rhymer, and my thoughts were often absent when the word of command was given."

But although he recognised his limitations as a soldier, Clare saw no reason why he should be insulted by a corporal or any other man, and when his arch-enemy found fault with him unjustly he answered back, upon which he was threatened with the "awkward squad". Clare grew so desperate at being subjected to this torment that he longed to desert and go home again, but he was afraid that his companions would laugh at him, so he screwed up his courage and determined that the next time he was wrongfully accused he would fall out of the ranks and address the corporal, no matter what the consequence might be. It was not long before the latter fell to his favourite trick of taunting Clare, and this time the poet threw down his gun, seized him by the throat, hurled him down and kicked him. For this he was threatened with the black hole and with whipping, but after the captain had inquired into the matter he was punished with nothing worse than serving an extra guard, and he had the satisfaction of being eyed with considerable respect by the corporal, who never ventured to find fault with him again.

Soon after this, Clare went home and within a short time the Northamptonshire Militia was disbanded. He is said to have

taken back to Helpston a copy of *The Tempest* and a very battered
Paradise Lost, both of which he had bought at a shop in Oundle.

Clare had by this time collected quite a number of books,
which he prized greatly, and he mentions that they included
Abercrombie's *Gardener's Journal*, Thomson's *Seasons*, Fisher's
Young Man's Companion, *Joe Miller's Jests*, and *A Collection of
Hymns*, besides two or three books on mathematics. His mother
had given him, some time before, a small box with a lock and key
in which to keep his clothes and other possessions. The gift was
accompanied by injunctions to think seriously of going into service
of some kind, to leave off writing, and buy no more books.

"I give you this box and you will find it useful when you get
from me to keep your few things together; when you once get
from me, you will think nothing of it and you'll find it far better
than drudging at home year after year, in the barn and the field,
for little or nothing."

But when her son did "get from her" he always came back and
continued "drudging at home", so that the box was not needed
for his clothes but made an excellent hiding-place for his books
and his poetry.

The exact details of Clare's employment in the next two or three
years are not known, but he worked sometimes in the fields and
sometimes in the gardens of the farmers round about Helpston.
He was probably not in great demand among the local em-
ployers, for his thoughts were always occupied with poetry, and
when a verse came into his mind which particularly pleased him
he would sit down at once and commit it to paper, using the crown
of his hat as a writing-desk. For this reason he preferred field work
to gardening, for he could often do his writing undiscovered
behind the shelter of a hedge or bush, whereas the garden provided no very adequate cover and the arrival of his employer
would often startle him and put his thoughts to flight.

The resumption of his poetic labours after he left the militia did
not wean him from his wild companions, and he was often out all
night, sometimes because the drinking and story-telling lasted until
morning, and sometimes because he was too drunk to get home
and so had to sleep in a field. Among his associates were two
brothers, James and John Billings, whose dilapidated old cottage
just outside the village formed a meeting-place for the young men
of Helpston. It was known as "Bachelor's Hall", and its reputation among the more respectable neighbours was not a very good

one, although the frequenters of it seem to have been guilty of nothing worse than rowdy singing, an excess of ale, and occasional poaching.

This latter occupation was one for which Clare's enthusiasm was short-lived, though at that time he used to accompany the Billings brothers on their expeditions to the woods. His eyesight was not good enough for shooting, so James Billings carried the gun, until one Sunday, when he attempted to shoot a hare, the ancient weapon burst, blowing away the barrel and part of the lock. All three were thoroughly frightened, and Clare, taking it to be a warning from Providence, never went poaching again. On another occasion, however, when he had gone into the woods for the harmless purpose of finding a place to write, he narrowly escaped being taken for a poacher. The Marquis of Exeter's keepers passed near to where he was sitting, and he quaked, for to be found trespassing in the woods meant almost certain conviction for poaching. He remained hidden, and they passed by without noticing him, but his fear can be easily understood when it is remembered that, in those days, the minimum punishment for poaching was imprisonment with hard labour.

There were other and less dangerous expeditions that Clare made with the Billings brothers, or, at any rate, with John; they often went fishing together on Sundays, or dug up primroses and bluebells and other wild flowers to plant in the garden of Bachelor's Hall, and perhaps in Clare's garden, too. John Billings was a great believer in ghosts and hobgoblins, and had a cupboard full of penny books such as *The King and the Cobbler* and *The Seven Sleepers*, besides one called *Laugh and be Fat*, which he carried constantly in his pocket. He believed everything that he saw in print and had a great reverence for learning, so no doubt he respected Clare's superior knowledge.

The poet formed some other friendships at this time which did his reputation more harm than the visits to Bachelor's Hall; these were among the gypsies who were often to be found camping on the heath near Helpston. He was fascinated by their dark eyes and strange talk no less than by their manner of living, and, although he knew them to be guilty of poaching and petty pilfering, it angered him to hear the villagers abuse them, for, he said, "I must confess I found them far more honest than their calumniators." He was accepted by the Smiths and the Boswells as a friend who was welcome whenever he chose to come, and he often shared their evening meal with them, which consisted, on occasions, of the flesh of badgers and hedgehogs.

From what Clare says, it is probable that he had a number of light-hearted flirtations at this time, possibly with one or two gypsies as well as the local girls. The only one that we know anything of was quite a serious affair and lasted, on and off, for some time. This was Elizabeth (or Betsy) Newbon, who lived near Ashton Green and who, though not, apparently, blessed with good looks, appeared very attractive to the poet who "fancied she was everything". Her father was a wheelwright and a great student of the Bible, and, when the courtship progressed from the early stage of meeting on Sundays in some prearranged spot to the later stage at which Clare visited her home, the old man used to question him to test his knowledge of the scriptures. "My silence", Clare wrote, "generally spoke my lack of religion, and he shook his head at my ignorance." Finally, after numerous petty quarrels and reconciliations, Elizabeth accused him of "changing affection", and they parted, which does not seem to have distressed Clare unduly.

5

WALKHERD LODGE

In the spring or summer of 1817, Clare was persuaded by an acquaintance, Stephen Gordon, to leave Helpston and get work as a lime-burner at Bridge Casterton in Rutlandshire, where Gordon was employed. It seems that the latter made many fine promises about how profitable Clare would find this work and how many advantages he would derive from undertaking it, but the promises proved empty ones, and Clare afterwards wrote, rather sadly, "the whole addition to my fortunes accumulated here was the acquaintance with a young girl who was destined for my future companion thro' life; and a poor man's meeting a wife is reckoned but little improvement to his condition, and particularly with the embarrassments I laboured under at that time".

The embarrassments were certainly many and grave, for Parker Clare's rheumatism had now finally crippled him so badly that he was forced to give up his labouring work entirely. Clare says that his father's spirit was "strongly knitted with independence" and he had always dreaded the day when he should have to accept the hated parish relief; so, for as long as he was able, he "pottered about the roads putting stones in the ruts for his 5 shillings a week, fancying he was not so much beholden to their forced generosity as if he had taken it for nothing". Five shillings a week did not go very far towards meeting the living expenses of four people, and consequently the whole weight fell on Clare.

The Napoleonic Wars had ended, but the peace had brought, as yet, no relief to the troubles of the poor. The price of corn had fallen from its fantastic war-time level (it had reached 126s. per quarter in 1812); but the Corn Law of 1815 kept it high, forbidding the importation of foreign corn unless the price of wheat rose above 80s. per quarter. The harvest of 1816 was a failure, and the ensuing scarcity sent the price up again to well above that figure, while the labourer not only received no increase in his wages, but was liable to be thrown out of employment by the economies that the farmers were making at the end of the war-time period of false prosperity. The desperation of the people who had endured hunger and want for so long manifested itself in a series of riots in the year 1816 which occurred in the agricultural districts of the eastern counties as well as in the manufacturing towns of the midlands and the north; houses and ricks were set on fire, soldiers were called out, arrests were made and sentences passed on certain of the rioters varying from a year's imprisonment to transportation for life.

Against this background it is not difficult to understand the anxiety that Clare felt at finding three people dependent on him, and knowing that if his health failed or he could not find work they would be faced with the most dire need, if not with actual starvation. The work at the lime-kiln, even if it did not come up to the expectations that Stephen Gordon had planted in Clare's mind, provided a better wage than day-labouring in the fields at home.

To begin with, they worked "from light to dark (and in some emergencies all night)" so that they could get some extra money with which to remedy the shabby appearance that they both presented. In about six weeks Clare had saved some fifty shillings, and he intended to purchase "a new olive-green coat, a colour which I had long aimed at, and for which I was measured already ere I left home". But some unforeseen expense prevented him from paying for it just then, and whether he ever realised this ambition, he did not say.

Clare liked the town of Bridge Casterton and the surrounding countryside, but had not the same feeling towards the house where he lodged. It was a professional lodging-house where they took in men of all descriptions, without discrimination, and "when they all assembled round the evening fire, the motley countenances of many characters looked like an assemblage of robbers in the rude hut dimly and mysteriously lighted by the domestic savings of a farthing taper". In addition to the uncongenial company, Clare had another complaint to make of the establishment: "We were troubled at night with treble fares in each bed, an inconvenience which I had never been used to."

When he had been at the lime-kiln for a short time, Clare's employer, a man called Wilders, learned that he had been a gardener at Burghley and put him to work in the garden of the New Inn at Casterton, which he owned.

On Sundays Clare used to go for walks which most frequently took him in the direction of Tickencote, a little farther along the River Gwash, for it was here that the labourers from the lime-kiln went to drink their ale at a small public-house called "The Flower Pot". Probably Clare did not stay long with them, for he was writing hard at that time and no doubt wished for his favourite solitude, to sit under a hedge, to write or think or

> . . . musing lie,
> Mark the wind-shaken trees,
> And cloud-betravelled sky.[1]

It was in the fields near Tickencote that he first saw Patty, and he was so eager to discover who she was and where she came from that he climbed on to the top of a pollard tree so that he might see which way she went, for, he said afterwards, "I was in love at first sight." But she disappeared from view, and it was only by chance that they met again some weeks later when Clare was on his way to Stamford. He then learned that her name was Martha Turner, though she was called Patty, and that she was the daughter of William Turner, a cottage farmer, of Walkherd Lodge.

Clare was to have played the fiddle for some dancing in Stamford that evening, but after this encounter he either forgot about it or decided that the dancers could do without his music, for he left the Stamford road and went with Patty to her home, some four miles away, which "became the introduction to some of the happiest and unhappiest days my life has met with".

He started home in a state of blissful abstraction, full of dreams of the future, and when twilight overtook him his uncertainty as to the path that would lead him home changed to a positive knowledge that he was lost. Thinking it useless to go on in the darkness, he climbed over a hedge and sat down on a baulk, or grass strip between two pieces of arable land, and while he sat there he composed a ballad and the song "Of All the Days", both of which were later included in *The Village Minstrel*. The ballad was probably the one in which he tells the story of the meeting that had taken place that day:

> When nature's beauty shone complete,
> With summer's lovely weather,
> And even, shadowing day's retreat,
> Brought swains and maids together;

[1] "Summer Images."

Then I did meet a charming face,
But who—I'll be discreet:
Though lords themselves without disgrace
Might love whom I did meet.

He intended, when the moon rose, to cross the same hedge again and get on to the right track, but on the far side of the hedge, where he expected to find himself on the Common, he saw something shining in the moonlight which he took to be a piece of ground that had been eaten bare by sheep and cows in the hot weather; fortunately, he bent down to feel it and discovered, to his horror, that he was standing on the bank of the river where one step would have ended his life. He sat down again under the hedge and waited for daylight before he ventured farther.

After that Clare went often to Walkherd Lodge in the evenings, and always on Sundays, chiefly because he liked to be with Patty but also partly because he wanted to get out of the lodging-house where the "assemblage of robbers" was not much to his taste. On his way to or from the Lodge his thoughts were often occupied with poetry, and he would sometimes stop to write down a verse as it came into his mind. He was, he said, "the companion of the evening and very often the morning star", and he came to know the surrounding countryside almost as well as his native fields. With the seventeen-year-old Patty he wandered about the woods and heaths on summer evenings "in more than happiness". In a neighbouring wood there were wild lilies of the valley which she liked to pick, and Clare used to go with her and take back handfuls of them to Walkherd Lodge.

Patty seems to have welcomed Clare's courtship from the beginning, but there was considerable opposition from her parents who thought a penniless young lime-burner was not a good enough marriage. A shoe-maker from Stamford was courting her at the same time, and as he had his own shop and every prospect of getting on in the world, while Clare had none, they considered him a much more desirable husband for their daughter and tried their hardest to persuade her to agree with them. But Patty knew her own mind and would have none of her parents' advice, so the shoe-maker disappeared from the scene, leaving Clare in undisputed sway to walk in the woods with Patty while "happy time went on".

6

THE SEARCH FOR A PUBLISHER

WHILE CLARE WAS OCCUPIED in courting Patty Turner, he was also occupied in quite another direction, that of endeavouring to find a publisher for his poems. His father's disablement and the consequent difficulties of his family made him wonder if he could turn his literary work to good account, and the idea seemed at least to provide him with an excuse for paying some attention to those restless stirrings of ambition which in his less exalted moods he had felt compelled to dismiss as sheer nonsense. It might have taken him a very long time to turn thought into action, for he had met with so much ridicule from those who knew about his poetry that he was ashamed to speak of it and always fearful lest strangers should learn his secret, but in this instance that "John Barleycorn" that was his enemy for so many years proved his good friend.

Clare had determined to have a manuscript book in which to write his best poems, and when he went to Deeping Fair he tried to buy one from a bookseller named Henson. There was nothing in the shop that met Clare's needs, so Henson promised to bind one up for him and send it, but he was evidently filled with curiosity to know what a young labourer was going to do with a manuscript book. Clare says that "being at that time released from my timid embarrassment of reserve from a free application of ale in the fair, I bluntly told him my intentions and as he was a printer of that extent of business in having types sufficient to enable him to print a pamphlet or small book now and then, when he could happen of employment, he doubtless fancy'd I was a bargain; so he wished to see some of my poems".

Clare took him a selection soon afterwards which included the sonnets "The Setting Sun" and "To a Primrose", both of which subsequently appeared in his first published volume. The former is a comparison between the departure of the sun at evening and the departure of the Christian's soul at the close of his life, while the other sonnet is a purely descriptive poem:

Welcome, pale Primrose! Starting up between
Dead matted leaves of ash and oak, that strew
The every lawn, the wood, and spinney through,
Mid creeping moss and ivy's darker green;
How much thy presence beautifies the ground:
How sweet thy modest, unaffected pride
Glows on the sunny bank, and wood's warm side.
And where thy fairy flowers in groups are found
The school-boy roams enchantedly along,
Plucking the fairest with a rude delight:
While the meek shepherd stops his simple song,
To gaze a moment on the pleasing sight;
O'erjoyed to see the flowers that truly bring
The welcome news of sweet returning spring.

Henson liked the poems that Clare took him, and expressed himself willing to print them, showing the poet, as a proof of his ability to do so, a *Life of Joseph* which was then in the press—"which," Clare says, "tho' I little understood the elegance of printing, I thought it deserved small praise as to that matter".

But the only thing that Clare really minded about was that the poems *should* be printed, so he entered into negotiations with Henson, who told him that the best course would be to publish by subscription. The idea was not at all to Clare's liking, for he felt that it would be "little better than begging money from people that knew nothing of their purchase", and the thought of the jeers that he would meet with when he issued his prospectus was more than enough to check his ambition for a time; but, realising that there was no other way in which he could hope to get his poems published, he finally decided to brave the ridicule and began to save up his money until he should be able to pay Henson the £1 necessary for the printing of 300 prospectuses.

Clare's omission of dates from his autobiographical notes makes it impossible to say with certainty when these dealings with Henson actually began, but it was probably in the spring of 1817, just before he went to Bridge Casterton. Towards the end of the year, he went to work in another lime-kiln at Pickworth, and it was while he was there that he made his decision to have the prospectus printed—a decision to which he was urged, no doubt, by his ambitions in love as well as his ambitions in literature.

Pickworth, some three miles distant from Casterton, Clare described as "a hamlet which seems by its large stretch of old foundations and ruins to have been a town of some magnitude in past times, tho' it is now nothing more than a half solitude of huts and odd farm houses scatter'd about some furlongs asunder". He and Gordon lodged at a public-house which was a lonely spot, for "as the road had forgotten the few fragments of the town that remained it seemed to stand out of the world's eye".

At the Pickworth kiln Clare worked long hours, and he was also writing a great deal, so that, between these activities and his visits to Walkherd Lodge he can have got little rest. The £1 at length was saved, "and getting a many more poems written, as excited by change of Scenery, and from being over head and ears in love, above all the most urgent propensity to scribbling, I fancy'd myself more qualified for the undertaking, considering the latter materials much better than what I had done, which no doubt was the case".

He therefore wrote to Henson, asking him to go forward with the printing of the prospectuses, and to write the necessary address to the public which Clare felt sure the bookseller was better qualified to do than he was. But Henson replied that Clare must compose the address himself. The task presented great difficulties to the poet who, although he was happy enough in writing verses, was ill at ease when he tried his hand at prose, and the subject was anyhow a delicate one which he did not know how to approach. He made several attempts which did not satisfy him, and his efforts were hampered by his having little time and no privacy in which to work, so he kept on putting off the task and it seems that months went by without anything being accomplished, until at last Clare decided that, for good or ill, he must produce *something*. Circumstances favoured his resolution, for he was sent to work, about that time, at another lime-kiln, owned by his employer, at Ryhall, two or three miles from Pickworth, and the journey to and from work gave him the necessary opportunity to think over his composition undisturbed. He would sometimes sit down five or six times in the course of his walk to wrestle with the troublesome sentences and write down his ideas. One morning, on his way to work, he made one of these pauses, and, as he sat under a hedge, he turned over in his mind the difficulties that beset him—the indigence of his parents, his own vain efforts to get out of debt, and the added anxieties of his "ill-timed love". He felt suddenly the futility of his struggles, and exclaimed aloud "What is Life?" A poem immediately began

to take shape in his mind, and he hastily wrote down the first
two verses:

> And what is Life?—An hour-glass on the run,
> A mist retreating from the morning sun,
> A busy, bustling, still repeated dream.—
> Its length?—A minute's pause, a moment's thought.
> And happiness?—A bubble on the stream,
> That in the act of seizing shrinks to nought.
>
> What is vain Hope?—The puffing gale of morn,
> That robs each flow'ret of its gem,—and dies;
> A cobweb hiding disappointment's thorn,
> Which stings more keenly through the thin disguise.[1]

Clare then continued his journey to work, but the address to the
public occupied his thoughts to the exclusion of all else—even
lime-burning—so he sat down on a lime-scuttle, took out his
pencil, and wrote the address as best he could, determined that,
good or bad, it should be dispatched that day. In the evening,
when he left the lime-kiln, he set out for Stamford, but on the way
there he was still in an agony of indecision, wondering whether
he should give up the whole idea or wait until he could get the
advice of a friend. But there was no friend whose advice was
likely to be of much use to him, and when he had turned the matter
over in his mind he came to the conclusion that the attempt might
do him some good and, at the worst, could do him no harm.

> If my hopes of the Poems failed, I should be not a pin worse than
> usual,—I could but work then, as I did already,—nay, I considered
> I should reap benefit from disappointment. Their downfall would
> free my mind from all foolish hopes, and let me know that I had
> nothing to trust to but work.

With this thought in his mind, Clare dropped down on a stone-
heap before he reached the town and read his composition
through a second time, carefully correcting what he thought
wrong, for he had no faith in Henson's ability to do so, and knew
that he must rely on his own intelligence to produce something
that would not be laughed at.

> When I got to the Post Office they wanted a penny, as I was past
> the hour, but as I had none, and hating to look so little as to make the

[1] This poem, with three more verses, was published in *Poems Descriptive of Rural
Life and Scenery*.

confession, I said with a little pettishness, that it was not mine, and that I should not pay for other people's letters. The man looked a little surprised at the unusual garb of the letter, which I was half ashamed of—directed with a pencil, written on a sheet of paper that was crumpled and grizzled with lying in one's pocket so long, and to add to its novelty sealed with shoe-maker's wax. I saw his smile and retreated as fast as I could from the town.

Henson's letter, dated 24th November, 1818, promised that the prospectuses should be printed at once, and that he would bring them on 1st December to the Dolphin Inn at Stamford where Clare was to meet him. His purpose in arranging a meeting, as Clare discovered when he arrived at the appointed place, was to present his bill which was for £1 5s. instead of the £1 agreed upon. "This," Clare says, "led me into his principles of over-reaching and encroaching, and from that time I considered him in his true light as being no friend of mine further than interest directed him, which turned out exactly the case."

The title of the prospectus was *Proposals for publishing by Subscription, a Collection of Original Trifles, on miscellaneous Subjects, religious and moral, in Verse, by John Clare, of Helpston.*

The book was advertised to be published as soon as three hundred subscribers had been obtained; it would cost three shillings and sixpence, and would be printed "on a superfine yellow wove foolscap paper, in octavo size". The sonnet "The Setting Sun" was printed as a specimen, and the Address to the Public which had caused Clare so much trouble read as follows:

The Public are requested to observe, that the Trifles humbly offered for their candid perusal can lay no claim to eloquence of poetical composition; whoever thinks so will be deceived, the greater part of them being Juvenile productions, and those of later date offsprings of those leisure intervals which the short remittance from hard and manual labour sparingly afforded to compose them. It is hoped that the humble situation which distinguishes their author will be some excuse in their favour, and serve to make an atonement for the many inaccuracies and imperfections that will be found in them. The least touch from the iron hand of Criticism is able to crush them to nothing, and sink them at once to utter oblivion. May they be allowed to live their little day and give satisfaction to those who may choose to honour them with a perusal, they will gain the end for which they were designed and their author's wishes will be gratified. Meeting with this encouragement it will induce him to publish a similar collection of which this is offered as a specimen.

While Clare and Henson were talking together in The Dolphin, a man came in to whom Henson offered one of the prospectuses, but the stranger, after glancing at it, walked out of the room without troubling to say a word. Clare's spirits were sadly dashed, but soon afterwards a clergyman came in who read the prospectus with interest, and told Henson to put his name down as a subscriber; this was the Revd. Thomas Mounsey, master of Stamford Grammar School.

Henson promised to begin printing the book as soon as they had got a hundred subscribers, and Clare went back to Pickworth with high hopes, taking the encouragement of Mr. Mounsey to be a sign of the reception that his prospectuses would meet with everywhere. He quite quickly procured seven names for his subscription list, one of them being that of a baronet, and he wrote to Henson, "Good God, how great are my Expectations, what hopes do I cherish! as great as the unfortunate Chatterton's were, on his first entrance into London, which is now pictured in my Mind; and undoubtedly, like him, I may be building 'Castles in the Air'; but Time will prove it."

But Clare's eager hopes were soon shattered, for the list of subscribers did not grow and the number remained at seven. Henson, after a time, wrote or said something which led Clare to believe that the list had reached the required number, and the poet took a week off from Pickworth in order to go home and arrange matters for the publication. Clare implied afterwards that this was a deliberate deception on the part of the bookseller, but there would seem to be little point in such a manœuvre and it is more likely to have been a genuine misunderstanding. When Clare arrived at Stamford he learned the true facts, and received from Henson the crushing news that he must advance £15 before the printing could begin. Such a sum was, of course, utterly impossible, for he had not "15 pence nor 15 farthings", and there was therefore no alternative but to give up the idea of publishing the poems.

Besides the bitter disappointment of seeing what appeared to be the end of all his hopes, Clare had to suffer the chagrin of feeling himself ridiculous in the eyes of all his acquaintances, for by the circulation of the prospectuses his ambitions had become widely known and now that they had come to nought there was ample opportunity for the uncharitable to jeer at his presumption. To add to his troubles, he was now without employment, for the frost had set in and the lime-kilns could not be worked.

> I knew not what course to take. I had got no work to go to and I hardly dare show my face to seek for any—everybody seemed to jeer at my foolish pretensions and . . . fallen hopes—enquiry stood on tiptoe with questions, go where I would, and I hated to hear them. I evaded them as well as I could. I felt uncommonly uneasy and knew not what to do. I sometimes thought of running away and leaving home were I might be at peace among strangers (for my disappointment was fast growing into a byword) and I went to Stamford twice to enlist in the artillery which was recruiting there but my variety of minds prevented me; besides my love matters etc. was a strong tether that I could not easily break—I went so far at one time as to take the money [for] a recruit but the sergeant was a better man than such usually are and said he took no advantage of a man in liquor (for I was fresh at the time) and let me off with paying the expenses of the drink. But I was wanting in height, which might be a better plea than the sergeant's honesty.

In the straitened circumstances to which Clare was now reduced, he was much distressed to receive a bill for fifteen shillings from a bookseller called Thompson who kept the "New Public Library" in the High Street at Stamford, and from whom he had been taking the *Enquirer*, a quarterly magazine; he said ruefully that he was still playing the fool and could not help running unnecessary expenses even then. As it was quite impossible to comply with Thompson's demand for immediate payment, Clare felt that he must demonstrate that he was not without prospects, hoping thus to induce the bookseller to wait for his money with a good grace; so he wrote a note, enclosing three or four prospectuses and the names of a few subscribers, which Tom Porter took for him to Stamford. Thompson was not interested in the prospectuses and told Porter that he wanted his money and would take care that he got it, but to Clare's good fortune it chanced that the conversation was overheard by Edward Drury who was about to succeed (or perhaps had already succeeded) Thompson as owner of the shop.

Drury, who had only lately come to Stamford, was first cousin to John Taylor, the London publisher and bookseller, and being an acute business man with a not unsound judgment in literary matters, he saw that this chance encounter with the work of the young peasant poet might well be turned to his advantage. He therefore entered into conversation with Tom Porter, and, after asking various questions, he paid Clare's debt and expressed his intention of knowing more of him.

Drury's own account of the incident differs somewhat from Clare's, for, in a letter to Taylor he said that while the argument was in progress between Thompson and Porter he "observed a piece of dirty paper, that had enveloped the letter brought by the man, had writing like verse on it; and picking it up found the "Sonnet of the Setting Sun" signed J. C.—Learning that it was most probably written by Clare, as his love of '*song-writing*' was common talk and fun to the village, I paid 18*s*. in dispute and sent home the books."

This inaccuracy annoyed Clare, who wrote some years afterwards that "his account of first meeting with the 'Sonnet to the Setting Sun' in MS. is all a hoax, and of no other foundation than his own fancy; but whether a mistake or intended falsity, I can't justly assert".

Drury kept to his intention of learning more about Clare, and a few days later he took Robert Newcomb, the proprietor of the *Stamford Mercury*, and sought him out at Helpston. It was a Sunday, and Clare was at Bachelor's Hall with the Billings brothers, whither his sister Sophy ran to fetch him home with the news that two gentlemen were waiting to see him.

Clare was shy and awkward with the visitors, but he showed them what manuscripts he had and told them that the rest were with Henson at Market Deeping, who had undertaken to print them. Newcomb said that if Clare had pledged himself to an agreement with Henson they did not want him to break it, but that if he was free to do what he liked with his poems they would pay him instead of demanding payment to print them.

As Henson had broken his word and apparently set very little store by honour in the matter, Clare felt that he was no longer bound, and he therefore promised to get the MSS. from Henson and take them over to Stamford, when Drury would arrange with him about printing them. As they were leaving, Newcomb invited Clare to dine with him the following week, but his second thoughts apparently led him to fear that Clare might take advantage of this, for he opened the door again and said, "If you get the MSS. from Deeping, Mr. Clare, we shall be glad to see you; if not, we can say nothing further about the matter."

Clare's pride was so much hurt by this that he wished he had stayed at Bachelor's Hall instead of coming home to be insulted, and he took good care to avoid Newcomb's house when he went to Stamford later in the week. His mother had fetched the MSS. from Henson, and he was therefore able to deliver them to Drury, receiving a guinea as "earnest to the bargain", and also being shown Byron's poems for the first time.

Drury, before making any further move in the matter, decided that it would be prudent to get a reliable opinion on Clare's poems, so he sent them to the Revd. Mr. Twopenny, of Little Casterton, who returned them with the comment that "he had no objection to assist in raising the poor man a small subscription, though the poems appeared to him to possess no merit".

Clare was both mortified and angered to learn of this reply, and there is a letter from him to the Revd. Isaac Knowles Holland which must have been written about this time when Drury had grown dubious because of the adverse criticism and Clare's hopes once more hung in the balance.

All that hurts me is the Necessity of taking to hard Labour again—after all my hopes to the Contrary. A Clergyman of the Church of English propos'd raising a subsn. for me but as he spoke very coldly of pieces I sent him my proud spirit declin'd the offer and despis'd such unintentional humanity when at the same time, like the Poet Marvell, I had not sixpence to bless me.

When I know the fate of my book you shall have a Lampoon on that Learn'd and humane Gent: who while he offer'd to foster the branch with promises was actually crushing the blossom of genius in o'erwhelming Ruin.

Holland was a Nonconformist Minister—or, as Octavius Gilchrist called him, a "Calvinistic preacher"—with whom Clare had become acquainted during the time that he was endeavouring to get his poems published. He showed Clare great kindness which had in it no hint of condescension, and he is reported to have said of "The Village Funeral," "If this kind of poetry does not succeed, the world deserves a worse opinion than I am inclined to give it." Clare corresponded with him until he went to live at St. Ives some time after 1820, and he lent the poet a number of books, including the poems of Burns, Pope, and Shenstone.

Clare's spirits, so cruelly dashed by Mr. Twopenny, were soon to rise again, for Drury luckily did not abandon his idea of printing the poems on the advice of one man, but sought the opinion of Sir

John English Dolben, who was more encouraging. Drury was sufficiently satisfied by this to send the poems to his cousin, John Taylor in London, and he told Clare that his poems "were crowned with the utmost success I could wish for, as they were in the hands and met the favourable opinion of a gentleman who could and would do them justice; but he would not tell me his name. And a painter of profiles was in the town whom he engaged to take my likeness. These things were trifles to remember but they were great at their beginnings; they made me all life and spirits."

7

A VARIETY OF MINDS

IN THE SPRING OF 1819 CLARE returned to work in the garden of the New Inn at Casterton, remaining there throughout the summer. He was busy with his poetry and he usually went to Stamford on Sundays to take to Drury whatever he had written during the week. He was apparently given the freedom of the shop to read what books he liked, besides being supplied with new tunes for his fiddle, and he was so eager to begin these pleasures that his Sunday journey was often made in the early morning so that he arrived to breakfast with Drury, sometimes even rousing the poor man from his bed. A wet day, which meant that no work could be done in the garden, was welcomed as another opportunity for a walk to Stamford, and Clare needed no prompting to take advantage of all that Drury's shop could offer towards improving his knowledge of literature and widening his intellectual horizons.

During the latter part of the winter, when he had been at Helpston, he had not seen much of Patty, but with his return to Casterton the courtship was resumed. Although he was now once more full of hope that his poverty would eventually be relieved by the proceeds of his poems, he was still struggling to keep his parents and sister, as well as himself, on his wages of nine shillings a week with the addition of five shillings from the parish, and it was therefore impossible for him to contemplate marriage until his situation had improved. Under these difficult circumstances it is perhaps not surprising that, as Clare's early biographer euphemistically expressed it, they loved "not wisely but too well", and although the summer was a happy one it was followed by an autumn that brought both cares and quarrels. Patty's parents and friends, impressed by Clare's association with Drury and the prospect of his poems being published, began to revise their opinions of the match and to encourage him with frequent invitations to Walkherd Lodge, but he, with characteristic pride, was nettled by their sycophancy and showed his independence by staying away, or

The cottage at Helpston where John Clare was born

coming only at rare intervals. It seems that Patty then accused him of coldness, which annoyed him still further, and their anxiety about her condition, which was not yet known to her parents, aggravated the situation between them.

Towards the end of the year, Clare's employer decreased his wages to seven shillings a week, so he left Casterton and went home. He said that the place was, on the whole, "one of the best I ever met with. I left it with regret and rather wish'd to return, as I liked the town, and the fields and solitudes were wild and far better than the fenny flats that I had been used to."

During the winter Clare sought refuge from the troubles of his "amorous intrigues and connections with Patty" in a flirtation with a girl called Betty Sell, who lived at Southorpe and whom he met at Stamford Fair; but it only added to his troubles, for the flirtation "grew up into an affection that made my heart ache to think it must be broken, for Patty was then in a situation that marriage only could remedy".

Clare, in great agitation of mind, was torn between his duty to one girl and his affection for the other, and had no particular wish to marry either of them, or indeed anyone, as yet, for responsibilities already lay heavily enough upon his shoulders.

I felt awkwardly situated and knew not which way to proceed. I had a variety of minds about me and all of them unsettled; my long-smothered affections for Mary revived with my hopes, and as I expected to be on a level with her bye and bye I thought then I might have a chance of success in renewing my former affections; amid these delays Patty's emergency became urgent. She had revealed her situation to her parents when she was unable to conseal it any longer, who upbraided her with not heeding their advice and told her as she had made her bed hard she should lye on it; for on my first arrival at Casterton a young shoe-maker paid his addresses to her, whose visits were approved of more by her parents than her self, and when I had disinherited him of her affections they encouraged him to come on and tried and urged to win her mind over to his and their wishes. When I reflected on these things I felt stubbornly disposed to leave them the risk of her misfortunes, but when she complained of their [harshness] I could stand out no longer and promised that my prosperity should make me her friend and to prove that I was in earnest I gave her money to [maintain her] independence till we should be married. This behaviour pacified them and left her at peace.

5

Martin, in his *Life of Clare*, says that it was some blunt speaking on the part of Drury that persuaded Clare to his decision, but whether Drury did or did not express his opinion there is every reason to suppose that Clare would have acted as he did without it. His standards of honour and loyalty were as high as any man's, and the occasions when he failed to live up to them were always followed by fits of agonising remorse. If his sense of what was right had not led him to decide on marriage with Patty, his sense of pity would no doubt have done it instead, for he said that "the wide mouth of the world was open against her, swallowing everything that started to discredit her", and he had always been moved to defend those whom the world attacked, whether it was the gypsies or the Billings brothers.

Clare wrote afterwards:

I was little fit or inclined for marrying, but [for] my thoughtless and ram-headed proceedings (as I was never all my life anything else but a fool, committing rashly and repenting too late), having injured her character as well as my own,—as for mine, I cared not a farthing about it, 'twas bad enough I knew, and made ten times worse by meddling lyars, but the ruination of one whom I almost adored was a wickedness my heart, however callous it might be to its own deceptions, could not act.

But, although Clare's mind was occupied with such disturbing problems, he found time, during the winter, to write some more poems and to continue his visits to Drury, though these were now less frequent, as the walk to Stamford was considerably longer than it had been when he went from Casterton. It was on one of these visits—probably in November, 1819—that he met John Taylor, and discovered him to be the editor of his poems, and the "gentleman who could and would do them justice" of whom Drury had spoken so mysteriously.

Taylor was then a man of thirty-eight, dark, and, if we are to believe his portrait, uncommonly handsome. He was the son of James Taylor, a Retford bookseller, and went to London in 1802, where he worked first in Messrs. Lockington and Allen's bookshop, "The Temple of the Muses", and afterwards in the publishing firm of Messrs. Vernor and Hood, of whom the latter was the father of Thomas Hood, the poet. In 1806 Taylor entered into partnership with James Augustus Hessey and they started a publishing and bookselling business at 93, Fleet Street. Thirteen

years later, when Clare met him for the first time, the firm of
Taylor and Hessey had come to be widely known as publishers of a
high class of literature, having on their list such names as Keats,
Hazlitt, Cary, and Reynolds. Taylor's sound judgment led him at
once to perceive the merit of Clare's poems, and he undertook to
edit them himself, being confident of the poet's genius and of the

John Taylor, from the drawing by Hilton, R.A.

reception that his work would get from the public, both for its
intrinsic worth and for the interest attaching to it as being the
production of a labourer.

Taylor was staying with Octavius Gilchrist, who had a grocery
business in Stamford and who was to show Clare much kindness
during the next few years. Hearing that Clare was with Drury,
and feeling both a desire to see him and a wish to foster further
acquaintance between poet and publisher, Gilchrist sent a servant

round to the bookshop to invite him to dinner. Clare, overcome
with shyness, was unwilling to go but was finally persuaded to do
so, and seems, despite his embarrassment at entering into such fine
company, to have enjoyed his evening, for, in describing it afterwards, he said, "I read an account of Woodcroft Castle from
Wood's *History*, and Taylor talked over some sayings and doings
of the living authors."

Gilchrist, in an article on Clare in *The London Magazine* of
January, 1820, described this visit:

Clare announced his arrival by a hesitating knock at the door—
"between a single and a double rap",—and immediately upon his
introduction he dropped into a chair. Nothing could exceed the
meekness and simplicity and diffidence with which he answered the
various enquiries concerning his life and habits, which we mingled
with subjects calculated to put him much at his ease. Nothing, certainly, could less resemble splendour than the room into which Clare
was shown; but there was a carpet, upon which it is likely he had
never previously set foot; and wine, of which assuredly he had never
tasted before.

Clare's description of the evening was written in verse, entitled
"The Invitation", and he sent it to Gilchrist soon afterwards—
perhaps as a sort of apology for what he had felt to be his social
shortcomings. The poem begins with the servant's arrival at
Drury's, and "Johnny's" embarrassment at being bidden to
dinner, describes his entry—ushered in by a lady—and goes on
to speak of what he found within:

> The finery dazzled a'e his sight,
> Rooms far too fine for clown's to bide in,
> He blinkt, like owls at candle-light,
> And vainly wished a hole to hide in.
>
> He sat him down most prim the night—
> His head might itch, he dare not scratch it;
> Each flea had liberty to bite,
> He could not wave a finger at it.
>
> But soon he proved his notions wrong,
> For each good friend, tho' finely 'pearing,
> Did put clown's language on his tongue,
> As suited well the Rustic's hearing.

When he met with kindness and courtesy, as in this case, no one was more ready than Clare to laugh at his awkwardness in the unaccustomed company in which, from now on, he was, on occasions, to find himself; but his speed in making a joke of himself was matched by the speed with which his anger was roused when others showed contempt or presumed to mock at his manners.

Clare was encouraged by his meeting with Taylor and by the knowledge that his literary affairs were in good hands, but hope does not fill an empty stomach and, although Drury gave him small sums of money from time to time—under no agreement, but an erratic system of good will—things were still so difficult that Clare wrote to the Revd. Knowles Holland, "If Poets in General had no better Encouragement to write than I have at present—I think they must be mad to pursue it."

Parker Clare's rheumatism was no better, and there was now no hope that it ever would be; Lord Milton had sent him, some time before this, to the sea-bathing infirmary at Scarborough which had done him some good, but he had tried to walk part of the way home in order to save money, and had thereby made himself worse than before. Ann Clare had been for some years past afflicted with dropsy, and the sickness of both parents and the fact that they could be given so little in the way of comforts added to Clare's anxieties.

It was probably in the winter of 1819 that the idea of making Clare a school-teacher was first mooted, though by whom is not certain. Clare mentioned it in a letter of about that time which was addressed to Holland, and in which he asked him to tell Lord Milton that the poems were going to be published.

> Please to hint the Dedication—if he will not agree to it I am undone but I am in no fear as to that when you come to Inform him that I am the son of the *Lame Man* at Helpstone.[1] Please to hint Likewise the Intention of Sending me to the National School to enable me to act in the Capacity of School master which has dropped from the Want of Friends.
>
> P.S. the sooner done the better as I am afraid Drury will interest himself in the matter.

Whether the postscript refers to the National School suggestion or merely the approach to Lord Milton, it is difficult to determine,

---

[1] Clare always spelt the name of the village with the final "e" as did many people at that time.

but evidently nothing came of the former on that occasion, and Drury *did* interest himself. For Clare was soon afterwards scribbling a note for him at the foot of a page in his manuscript book: "You will hear from me no more while[1] the book is out—unless anything particular required—I hope you have not forgot your promise of sending me to some School—I shall certainly reap great benefit from such an advantage."

Taylor was then approached, and wrote to Clare:

> If you and Mr. Drury can see any good likely to result from your coming to London for the Purpose of being educated as a Teacher in the National School I would pay your Expenses.—The time required for your Instruction would be about 2 months, after which you might, if you were well qualified, succeed in getting Employment as a Master in some School in the Country.

He added a warning that "the strictest moral Conduct" was necessary if he were to enter such a profession and hinted that Clare's liking for ale might prevent him from leading quite such a sober life as would be expected of him. Perhaps Clare was alarmed by this, or perhaps the thought of spending two months in London deterred him, but we hear no more of the scheme.

[1] Dialect for till.

8

"POEMS DESCRIPTIVE OF RURAL LIFE AND SCENERY"

Even before Clare's first volumes of poems was published, we see the beginnings of those jealousies between his friends and patrons that later reached such a pitch as to make considerable difficulties for him. On 2nd January, 1820, Drury wrote to Taylor, expressing genuine concern for the poet's welfare, but the perspicacity with which he viewed the problems of Clare's life and work was mixed with a jealously monopolistic attitude towards him. Gilchrist, in befriending Clare and giving encouragement to his work, had poached on what Drury considered to be his preserves, and the latter hinted broadly to Taylor that the kindly grocer was mishandling his protégé.

It is to be greatly feared that this man will be afflicted with insanity if his talent continues to be forced as it has been these 4 months past, he has no other mode of easing the fever that oppresses him after a tremendous fit of rhyming except by getting tipsy. A simple pint of ale very often does this, and next morning a stupor with headache and pains across the chest afflicts him very severely. Then he is melancholy and completely hypochondriac—you will easily suppose how true is my account when I assure you he has rhymed and written for 3 days and 3 nights without hardly eating or sleeping. I therefore watch with a degree of fear Mr. Gilchrist's proceedings.

Clare was already busy collecting the results of this furious activity for a second book of poems, although he hardly dared to speculate upon the fate of the first, being sometimes filled with tremendous hopes and sometimes with despair at the seeming futility of imagining that he could ever rise to fame. But his fears were soon set at rest and his wildest hopes fulfilled. *Poems Descriptive of Rural Life and Scenery* was published on 16th January, 1820, with an Introduction by Taylor in which he gave an outline of Clare's life and circumstances and said of the poems that they were "the genuine productions of a young Peasant, a

71

day-labourer in husbandry, who has had no advantages of education beyond others of his class; and though Poets in this country have seldom been fortunate men, yet he is, perhaps, the least favoured by circumstances, and the most destitute of friends, of any that ever existed".

One thousand copies of this first edition were printed and quickly sold, a second and third edition of equal size followed, and by the end of the year the fourth edition was in print. It was well reviewed in a number of periodicals, including *The Eclectic Review*, *The Gentleman's Magazine*, *The New Monthly*, and *The Analectic Magazine*.

The Antijacobin Review said of the poems:

> If they do not possess the polish of Bloomfield, or the wild energy of Burns, they are free from those impurities (and even impieties) which disgrace the latter; and equal the former in unaffected piety; and in giving a true picture of rustic life, and those scenes with which the author was best acquainted.

This, though not a brilliantly perceptive piece of criticism, was kindly meant; so, too, was the article in *The New Monthly* which pointed out Clare's imitations of Burns and his inability to equal him, but said:

> If associations are only wanting to convey an image correctly to the mind, Theocritus or Virgil could bring forward none but what this untaught Northamptonshire hind enumerates. Their works are to him, as they were to the Ayrshire peasant, "a fountain shut up, and a book sealed" but Clare is acquainted with a language less understood than Greek or Latin—the language of the human heart, and he reads it in a book which requires no commentary—the book of nature.

In May, the *Quarterly Review*, which had heaped abuse on the poems of Keats, printed a nine-page article on Clare's poems, written by Gilchrist and polished by the hand of the editor himself. Upon this, a writer in *The Monthly Magazine* commented, "for once the disadvantages of education are treated with indulgence by the high-bred Mr. Gifford. We had supposed that the extraordinary academical pampering which his own genius received in his youth, had rendered him incapable of appreciating the merits of talent struggling with indigence." But, long before

Mr. Gifford had graciously signified his approval of the book, it had become a favourite topic of conversation in London drawing-rooms, where people wondered that an uneducated peasant could write poetry, and where not to have read it was to be out of fashion.

Clare received the first news of the book's success from Holland, who rode over one wet day and opened the door of the cottage to shake Clare by the hand and say, "Am I not a good prophet?" He had that morning received a letter from a friend in London, telling him of the stir that the poems had made, and he had lost no time in coming to tell the poet. There is a story that Clare wanted to offer him food and drink but had none, and Holland, understanding the situation at once, said, "I had intended having some dinner at the inn round the corner; but if you will allow me, I will have it sent here, and take it in your company". He then had several trays of food brought from the Blue Bell, and the whole Clare family had a good dinner.[1]

The immediate result of Clare's literary success was that he was summoned to visit the various great houses in the neighbour-hood, the first being Milton, the residence of Lord Fitzwilliam who owned much property in the county, and whose heir, Lord Milton, had been responsible for sending Parker Clare to Scar-borough some years before. While his book was being prepared for publication, Clare had written to Lord Milton, asking permission to dedicate it to him, but his Lordship was just setting off for Italy and forgot to answer the letter. When the book was out, Clare's mother took one to Milton, and the poet then received a note from Lord Milton telling him to come himself and bring ten more copies.

Clare's agitation at receiving such a summons can be imagined, but it was impossible to refuse, and there was therefore no alter-native but to summon up his courage. He had been to Milton once before, when he was about nineteen or twenty; on that occa-sion the parish clerk had taken him there to introduce him to Lord Milton and ask if something could be done to help him—a request which, although Milton promised to remember, had never been granted. The recollection of this previous visit was no encouragement to Clare, and he suffered agonies of apprehension that he would do or say something wrong and make himself appear ill-mannered or ridiculous.

[1] Martin's *Life of John Clare*.

Drury wrote to him with some good advice on the subject of his clothes:

> Let me recommend you not to wait on his Lordship in your "Sunday clothes" which are more suitable to a "Squire of high degree" than humble John Clare. The dress you wear at Stamford with clear clean shirt, clean stockings and shoes will occasion the Lord Milton to judge more favourably of you.
>
> I send you one of my Shirts which you will perhaps be disposed to make use of—tucking in the frippery of the frill under your clean waistcoat. A nice silk handkerchief will also be useful.

It would be worth while, Drury suggested, to tell Lord Milton of the kind attention which Clare had received from General Birch-Reynardson a few days previously in Drury's parlour; he was also to mention that one of his poems, "The Meeting", had been set to music by Haydn Corrie and was to be sung at Covent Garden by Madame Vestris.

On arrival, Clare was ushered into the servants' hall, where he was offered food and drink, which he could not take because his agitation was too great, but, when he was finally received by Lord Milton, the "quiet, unaffected manner" of the latter put him more at his ease. He told Clare that he had heard of the poems from Mr. Mossop, the vicar of Helpston. Lady Milton also talked to Clare, asking him questions and expressing a desire to give him a book if he would name one that he liked. He wanted Shakespeare, and the request was at his "tongue's end", but he did not like to make it for fear that he should appear presumptuous, so his chance was lost. Lord Fitzwilliam was present, with his wife, at the interview, and told Clare to beware of booksellers, and "not to be fed with promises". On his departure they gave him a handful of money which was more than he had ever possessed in his life. It was seventeen pounds.

Soon after this, Clare was invited to visit Burghley by Mr. Pierrepoint, brother-in-law of the Marquis of Exeter, but on the Sunday when he was to go it was snowing, and he postponed his visit, not because he minded bad weather, but because he feared that he would arrive with his clothes too wet and his shoes too muddy to enter the house. So he went the next day, and when he got there the porter asked him sharply why he had not come before; on being told the reason, he said, "They expected you, and you should stand for no weathers, though it rained knives and forks with the tynes downward. We have been suspected of sending you away."

He was sent for by Lord Exeter, and was conducted by a footman upstairs and through winding passages where, he says, he was "almost fit to quarrel with my hard-nailed shoes at the noise they made on the marble and boarded floors, and cursing them to myself as I set my feet down in the lightest steps I was able to utter". Lord Exeter received him kindly, and asked to see some of his MSS. which he had been instructed to bring with him. He expressed regret that his sister, Lady Sophia, could not be present as she was ill and had sat-up too long the day before, expecting Clare's arrival. After about half an hour of conversation, in the course of which Clare was presented with the *Pleasures of Hope*, Lord Exeter noticed his embarrassment, for the poet looked frequently from the door to his dirty shoes, wishing himself "out of danger of soiling such grandeur". He therefore told him that he had better go or he would miss his dinner in the servants' hall, but Clare was quite unable to find his way back through the many passages, and had to admit to Lord Exeter that he was lost. His host then opened the door and led the way, but before they reached the servants' quarters he made a halt to tell Clare that he could offer him no work in the gardens at present but would grant him an allowance of fifteen guineas a year for life.

From the interest that these two families took in Clare he derived some benefit, both now and afterwards, but there were many people whose interest sprang, not from a regard for the poet or his work, but merely from idle curiosity at the phenomenon of a literary ploughman. Within a short time of the publication of his book, Clare began to be bothered by these people, who came to the cottage and had him fetched from his work in the fields so that they might see him, and who wasted an hour of his time before they went away, leaving him no better off for the doubtful pleasure of their acquaintance. Of some of these visitors Clare said with a rather bitter humour, "I got invitations to correspond and was showered with promises of books till my mother was troubled and fancied that the house would not hold them, but her trouble was soon set aside, for the books never came."

There is no doubt that this curiosity was one of the factors that contributed to the great success of the first volume, but it proved, in the long run, a disadvantage to Clare, for it equally contributed to the comparative failure of the later volumes and was harmful to his reputation. The way in which the fashionable world seized upon this novelty and made of it a nine days' wonder was not calculated to make the more serious readers of poetry think well of Clare, and when the later volumes appeared, containing poems in which he had progressed immeasurably from the early days, the novelty had worn off so that the curious no longer cared to read him, while the others remembered the foolish way in which he had been lauded before, and ignored him too.

There were, however, some acquaintances that publicity brought him who proved true friends and who showed Clare much kindness. Chief among these were Mrs. Emmerson and Lord Radstock. The former, wife of a London picture-dealer, lived in Berners Street. She had a sincere admiration for Clare's work, and, although her literary judgment was not always sound, she had a fairly wide knowledge of English poetry and a slight acquaintance with a few people in the world of art which enabled her to be a help to Clare. Her heart was of the proverbial gold, and although, in the early days of the friendship, she sometimes wrote rather foolishly and tried to establish a sort of "literary flirtation", she gained in common sense with the passing of time, and showed herself to be a staunch friend to Clare when he sorely needed one. The first of the hundreds of latters that she wrote to him is dated 21st February, 1820, and she enclosed in it a copy of Young's *Night Thoughts*, and expressed her appreciation of Clare's poems.

Lord Radstock's first letter was not written until considerably later, but Mrs. Emmerson had drawn his attention to Clare's poems and he showed his admiration of them by sending the poet a copy of Blair's *Sermons* enclosed in a letter from Taylor during February. The second son of the third Earl Waldegrave, he had been raised to the peerage of Ireland in 1800 for distinguished naval services and had taken the title of Baron Radstock. He was vice-admiral of the Blue in the victory over the Spanish fleet off Cape Lagos in February, 1797; his kindness and generosity were quite as sincere as those of Mrs. Emmerson, but his pious platitudes and his doubtless unintentional condescension sometimes tried Clare sorely. The Admiral determined to do all he could to help Clare in financial matters and to see that the business side of his literary work was properly managed, and he certainly did give considerable assistance in this way, but it was unfortunate that he quarrelled with Taylor in the process, thus creating an embarrassing situation for Clare who did not want to side with either of them.

The introductions thus begun by correspondence were soon to be renewed in person, for early in March Clare accompanied Gilchrist on a visit to London. They went by the Stamford coach, and Clare wondered if he had not changed his identity as well as his occupation, as he looked from his luxurious conveyance at the men ploughing and ditching in the fields as he had done for so long himself.

He spent a week in London, during which time he stayed with Gilchrist's brother-in-law, a German called Burkhardt, who kept a jeweller's and watchmaker's shop in the Strand. On the night of their arrival Madame Vestris was singing one of Clare's songs at Covent Garden—"The Meeting", set to music by Haydn Corri—and they were to have gone, but by the time they had alighted from the coach at the George and Blue Boar, Holborn, and made their way to Burkhardt's house, it was too late. Instead they took a walk in the moonlight to Westminster Bridge so that Clare might see the Thames, of which he afterwards wrote: "I heard large wonders about its width of water, but when I saw it I was disappointed, thinking I should have seen a freshwater sea, and when I saw it [it] was less in my eye than Whittlesey Mere." On this walk he expressed astonishment that they should see so many ladies walking about the streets, and was told that they were girls of the town, as a modest woman rarely ventured out by herself at nightfall. During the next few days, he was taken to see Westminster Abbey and Vauxhall, went to the Playhouses to see Kean and Macready, Knight, Munden and Emery, visited some of the shops, and found London, its sights and customs, so bewildering that he said "everything hung round my confused imagination like riddles unsolved".

Clare dined several times with Taylor, and there met various other writers, with some of whom he was to become better acquainted on his next visit; certain others seem to have caused him some disillusionment, for he says: "I had had a romantic sort of notion about authors and had an anxious desire to see them, fancying they were beings different to other men; but the spell was soon broken when I became acquainted with them." Among the new acquaintances that Clare made at these dinners were

J. H. Reynolds, close friend of Keats, and himself a poet published by Taylor and Hessey, and H. F. Cary, who translated Dante and later (in 1825) became assistant keeper of printed books at the British Museum. Cary took an immediate liking to Clare, whose poetry he already admired, and the kindness which he showed him through long years of friendship was put to practical use very soon after their first meeting, for on 8th March, 1820, he wrote to his brother-in-law, the Revd. Thomas Price, asking him to review Clare's poems and to make his comments as "favourable as your conscience will allow". Price was probably quite willing to comply with this request, for he had already told Cary that he found the poems "*surprising and beautiful*". Cary gives a brief description of Clare in the letter: "He has the appearance rather of a big boy who has never been used to company than of a clown, though his dialect is clownish enough; and, like all true geniuses he was longing to be at home again and is now there. He is modest and unpresuming."

Clare also met for the first time James Augustus Hessey, Taylor's partner, with whom he afterwards corresponded a good deal, and he, of course, improved his acquaintance with Taylor, who wrote to his brother that Clare had "pleased us all by his simple, manly, and sensible conduct and conversation". At Taylor's wish Clare visited the painter William Hilton, R.A., and sat for his portrait which is now in the National Portrait Gallery; for him, Clare says that he felt such a sincere liking as he might have felt for "a neighbour of the Country".

No doubt, in meeting all these people, Clare was shy and embarrassed, being very conscious of his unpolished manners, his dialect and his rough clothes, and there is a story that, in order to hide the latter defect, he borrowed an overcoat from Taylor, and wore it all the time until he left London; but most of the acquaintances that he made during his visit seem to have had enough tact and kindness to put him at his ease, and whatever he may have suffered in the way of embarrassment it did not prevent him from observing everyone with a keen eye and afterwards making some very perceptive remarks.

Of Lord Radstock, to whom he sat next at dinner with Taylor, he said:

> Lord Radstock at first sight appears to be of a stern and haughty character, but the moment he speaks his countenance kindles up into a free, blunt, good-hearted manner—one whom you expect to hear

speak exactly as he thinks. He has no notion of either offending or pleasing by his talk and cares as little for the consequences of either. There is a good deal of bluntness and open-heartedness about him, and there is nothing of pride or fashion. He is as plain in manner as the old country squire. A stranger would never guess that he was speaking to a Lord, though his is one of the oldest families in England.

It was Radstock who introduced Clare to Mrs. Emmerson, and Martin's account of their first meeting tells how she lamented the poet's "desolate appearance" and wept, with what Clare considered a theatrical air, that "so much genius and so much poverty" should go together. This stung his pride, and he answered her with "a few cold and sarcastic words", for which Lord Radstock reproached him when they left the house. But, if this was so, Clare understood Mrs. Emmerson better at subsequent meetings. *How* well he understood her is clearly shown by what he wrote some time afterwards:

> She has been, and is, a warm, kind friend, of tastes, feelings and manners almost romantic. She has been a very pretty woman and is not amiss still, and a woman's pretty face is often very dangerous to her common sense; for the notice she received in her young days threw affectations about her feelings which she has not got shut of yet; for she fancies that her friends are admirers of her person as a matter of course and acts accordingly, which appears in the eyes of a stranger ridiculous enough. But the grotesque wears off on becoming acquainted with better qualities, and better qualities she certainly has to counterbalance them. She, at one word, is the best friend I found, and my expectations are looking no further. Her correspondence with me began early in my public life and grew pretty thick as it went on. I fancied it a fine thing to correspond with a lady, and by degrees grew up into an admirer, sometimes writing as I felt, sometimes as I fancied, and sometimes foolishly, when I could not account for why I did it.

Lord Radstock, having formed a very favourable opinion of Clare, decided that he was worthy of help, and from then onwards made every effort to improve his financial position and to aid the sales of his poems, in which activities he was assisted by Mrs. Emmerson, whose zeal excelled his own. The immediate result of the Admiral's adoption of Clare's cause was that a private subscription was started for the benefit of the poet and his family, to which the firm of Taylor and Hessey contributed £100 and Lord Fitzwilliam a similar sum.

Cary had noticed that Clare, despite the excitements of London, was "longing to be at home again", and he felt no great regret when at the end of the first week in March, he and Gilchrist took the coach from Holborn back to Stamford, whence he returned to Helpston.

9

MARRIAGE AND FAME

A FEW DAYS AFTER HIS RETURN from London—on 16th March, 1820—Clare married Patty Turner at Great Casterton. Her uncle, John Turner, gave her away, and he and Clare's sister, Sophy, signed as witnesses, while Patty's own signature was but a cross, for she could not write. Clare gave two contradictory accounts of the feelings with which he entered into matrimony. In the notes for his autobiography, he implied that he did what he knew to be his duty with a heavy heart: "I held out as long as I could and then married her at Casterton Church." But in *Sketches in the Life of John Clare* he gave no hint of unwillingness: "I had that opportunity of easing my present trouble by making her amends. I therefore made use of it, and married her March 16th, 1820, and my only repentance was that I had not become acquainted with her sooner than I did."

He could not take his wife home at once, for there was no room in the part of the cottage in which Parker and Ann Clare lived, and his hope of getting another house had not materialised. Lord Radstock had written to Lord Milton, asking him to provide a cottage, rent free, for Clare's lifetime, and in April Milton summoned Clare to discuss the matter, but the poet was away from home with Gilchrist. The latter wrote afterwards about Clare's untimely absence, and comforted him with the assurance that Lord Milton was "not one of impulses and caprices and what he designed there is no fear of his abandoning because you chanced to be out of the way with a friend". But, in spite of this, the meeting was never achieved, and although Clare wrote himself to Lord Milton, he heard no more of the project. It then happened that the other part of the Clares' cottage became vacant, so he took it and brought Patty there; although he had written a poem on "Proposals for Building a Cottage" in which he had exactly described the house of his dreams, he probably did not much regret it, for his affection for the Helpston cottage was such that it would have hurt him to leave it. The neighbours and visitors often advised him to get a bigger and better-looking house, but Clare took no notice of them, and remained where he was, "following my old occupations and keeping my old neighbours as friends, without being troubled or disappointed with clinging ambitions, that, shine as fine as they may, only tempt the restless mind to climb so that he may be made dizzy with a mocking splendour and topple down headlong into a lower degradation than he left behind him."

It was difficult for Clare to resume the ordinary routine of his life and to go back to his writing and his work in the fields, for he was constantly interrupted by visitors and by the necessity of answering the many letters that he received. The *Northamptonshire County Magazine*, the *Stamford Mercury*, and various other local papers had now spread his fame far and wide through the surrounding countryside, and the news had naturally caused much interest. Early in April he was invited by General Birch-Reynardson to visit Holywell Hall, which lies a mile or two north of Pickworth where he had worked for a time at the lime-kiln. The visit was marked by a rather amusing incident of which Clare has given an account:

> After looking about the gardens and the library, I was sent to dinner in the Servants' Hall, and when it was over the housekeeper invited me into her room where the governess came and chatted in a free manner, and, asking me to correspond with her, gave me her address. The housekeeper wished me to write an address to her son, in imitation of Cowper's lines on his mother's picture. The governess was a pretty, impertinent girl and mischievously familiar to a mind less romantic than my own. I felt startled into sudden surprises at her manner, and in the evening on my return home I was more surprised still when, on getting out of the park into the fields, I found her lingering in my path, and, on coming up to her, she smiled and told me plainly she was waiting to go a little way home with me. I felt evil apprehensions as to her meaning, but I was clownish and slow in smiles and advantages to interpret it. She chatted about my poems and resumed the discourse of wishing me to correspond with her which I promised I would. When we came to the break of the heath that stands in view of Patty's cottage I made a stop to get rid of her, but she lingered and chattered on till it grew very late, when a man on horseback suddenly came up and asked the road we had come from, when she, thinking it was the General, hastily retreated. But, on finding her mistake, she returned and resumed her discourse till it grew between the late and early, when I wished her good night and abruptly started without using the courage of shaking her by the

hand. I felt excessively awkward all the way home, and my mind was filled with guesses and imaginings at her strange manner and meanings. I wrote one letter to her and intended to be very warm and very gallant in it, but, fancying that she only wanted me to write love letters to have the pleasure to talk about them and laugh at them, my second mind wrote a very cold one in which I inserted the second address to a Rosebud in humble life, in which I requested no answer nor hinted a second adventure, so there the matter or mystery ended, for I never unriddled its meaning, tho' it was one of the oddest adventures my poetical life met with. It made me rather conceited as I fancied the young lady had fallen in love with me. She came from Birmingham; I shall not mention her name here.

Among the visitors who found their way to the cottage at Helpston at this time, was Chauncy Hare Townsend, who was then a student at Cambridge, and with whom Clare corresponded for a time. He gave Clare, on leaving, a folded paper which proved to be a sonnet and a pound bill, and he afterwards sent him Beattie's *Minstrel*. Clare was evidently worried about the impression that he had made on Townsend, for during their interview he was apparently seized by that "natural depression of spirits in the presence of strangers that took from me all power of freedom or familiarity and made me dull or silent". He wrote to apologise for his behaviour:

> Your first visit found me in a gloomy, desponding condition that often gets the sway, but when I have been inspired with a pint of "John Barleycorn" and in one of my sunshiny moments, you would not know me. I am a new man and have too many tongues. Though your visit did not find it, still I can be cheery; but in my sullen fits I am defiled with the old silence of rusticity that always characterized me among my neighbours before I was known to the world.

To this Townsend replied some months later:

> I am sorry that you should owe any exultation of spirits to what our favourite Burns calls John Barleycorn. . . . I would have you shun the very first circle of the vortex which finally engulfed him.

Unfortunately, all Clare's visitors did not give him such good advice, and some of them took him to the Blue Bell and treated him to drinks, thinking it the best way to overcome his shyness and reserve—which, no doubt, it was, but his temptation to drink was already strong enough without that sort of encouragement. His bouts of drinking occasioned his friends some anxiety, and in March Gilchrist wrote to him concerning a headache of which Clare had complained: "Is not the headache the denunciation threatened in scripture,—'Woe unto them that drink strong drink.' When will you leave off these sad doings, John Clare, John Clare!"

If Clare's headache on that occasion was caused by too much ale, he was afflicted soon afterwards with an illness which was not attributable to such a simple cause, and which seems rather to have been brought on—or, at least, aggravated—by complete mental and physical exhaustion. The degree of his illness was much exaggerated in the reports of the neighbours, and Drury, who was in London, heard that he had had "a fit . . . of a dangerous kind"; he communicated the news to Hessey, who was much alarmed and wrote to Gilchrist for more precise information, which the latter gave in a letter dated 23rd April. Clare, he wrote, had gone some ten days previously to visit a certain Dr. Willy who lived somewhere near Stamford, and on the way home, being somewhat exhausted with his long walk, had rested under Uffington Bridge and had fallen into a kind of stupor, from which he awoke much alarmed. The incident had increased the fear, which was always in the back of his mind, that he might suffer a recurrence of the violent fits that had so troubled him when he was younger. "He has, he admits," Gilchrist wrote, "a violent fit of rhyming upon him just now, and cannot pass five minutes without jingling his poetic bells, till he says he is quite frightened."

Clare himself said that he was "worse in health than you can conjecture or than myself am aware of", and Taylor wrote on 27th April in considerable anxiety to inquire if the "momentary ague" was a symptom of inflammation of the chest, and to recommend blistering.

There is unconscious irony in another letter which Clare received just then; it was from a certain Captain Sherwill who was a friend of Sir Walter Scott's and who had started a correspondence with Clare some time before by expressing his admiration of his poetry. Learning of his illness, he wrote begging Clare to be regular in all his habits—". . . and as to your meals, we all eat too much—two thirds of what is usually taken would be sufficient, while the other is eaten for pleasure". Sound advice, indeed, to one whose hunger was rarely satisfied, and then not with such food as would give proper nourishment, so that he resorted to the strong ale which he loved as the only means of substituting a comforting warmth for an aching void!

But the illness, with its attendant fears and depression, passed off, leaving Clare to work throughout the summer in tolerable health and spirits. It seems probable that he was doing some work in the fields at this time, although there is no actual record of this until August, when he was helping with the harvest, but he was certainly writing hard, and the furious bouts of "rhyming" put a great strain upon him, both mentally and physically. He wrote to Taylor on 20th May:

> When I am in the fit I write as much in one week as would knock ye up a fair size Vol.—and when I lay down the pen I lay it down for a good long while—recollect the subjects are roughly sketched in the fields at all seasons with a pencil. I catch nature in every dress she puts on so when I begin to rhyme and polish up I have little to do in studying description. I am like the boy that gets his horn book alphabet by heart and then can say his lesson with his eyes as well shut as open.

Clare was preparing his poems for the second volume, and the "polishing up" was a process on which he expended much time and trouble, writing and rewriting a poem perhaps half a dozen times; as he finished a new version, he would draw a line through the old one, and write in the margin beside it a comment such as "d—d stuff" or "cursed silly—J. C." He was writing very frequently to Taylor at this time, and, having no one at home with home he could discuss his poetry, he was glad to tell the publisher about his plans for work, about what he was reading and what was occupying his thoughts.

Taylor wrote long letters back, full of good advice and encouragement, commenting on Clare's ideas and setting forth his own opinions on literature, religion, and many other subjects. Soon after Clare's return from London, Taylor wrote that Keats had been to dine with him: "He was very sorry he did not see you—when I read Solitude to him he observed that the Description too much prevailed over the Sentiment.—But never mind that—it is a good Fault."

Keat's succinct and perceptive comment drew from Clare a criticism of "Endymion" which is interesting as it emphasises the different attitude of the two poets towards Nature.

Keats keeps up a constant allusion (or illusion) to the Grecian mythology, and there I cannot follow; yet when he speaks of woods, Dryads and Fauns and Satyrs are sure to follow, and the brook looks alone without her Naiads to his mind. Yet the frequency of such classical accompaniments make it wearisome to the reader, where behind every rose bush he looks for a Venus and under every laurel a thrumming Apollo. In spite of all this his descriptions of scenery are often very fine. But, as it is the case with other inhabitants of great cities, he often described Nature as she appeared to his fancies, and not as he would have described her had he witnessed the things he described. Thus it is that he has often undergone the stigma of Cockneyism, and what appears as beauties in the eyes of a pent-up citizen are looked upon as conceits by those who live in the country. These are merely errors, but even here they are the errors of poetry. He is often mystical, but such poetical licences have been looked on as beauties in Wordsworth and Shelley, and in Keats they may be forgiven.

Yet, despite their wholly different approach, the gulf between Keats and Clare is not so enormous. As Mr. Middleton Murry has said in comparing them, "the association of the great name and the small one has a curious congruity", and it is tempting, if futile, to speculate on the friendship that might have sprung up between them had they met. They so nearly *did* meet on Clare's first visit to London, but Keats was not sufficiently recovered from his illness to go out until after Clare had left; and, before the latter's second visit, Keats had gone on the journey to Italy from which he never returned. They sent each other messages through Taylor, and there is said to be a letter still extant which bears the handwriting of both poets; the apparent explanation of this being that Keats, when in the publisher's office one day, wished to note down an amendment to two lines of "Lamia" and picked up a letter from Clare off Taylor's desk to write his note on the back of it.[1] Thus near together did their ways lie for a time, and yet never touched.

Unfortunately, Taylor's letters in the spring of 1820 contained comments on some less pleasant matters than literary criticism, for his quarrel with Drury, which had begun before the publication of the first volume, ended in April or May in a spirit of considerable bitterness, and there were already signs of

---

[1] Mr. Samuel Loveman of Cleveland, Ohio, wrote to *The Dial* in July, 1917, to say that this letter was in his possession, among the bundle of unpublished letters from Clare to Taylor.

friction between the publisher and Lord Radstock, which flared
into a violent quarrel later in the year. It was both difficult
and unpleasant for Clare to be asked to take sides in these
disagreements, which, in each case, were between two people
who had both been kind to him, and he was bewildered and
distressed.

It was, of course, not unnatural that the so-called partnership
between Drury and Taylor should lead to trouble, for each
considered that he had discovered Clare and was solely responsible
for his fame. The rights and wrongs of it are difficult to sort out;
Taylor was probably guilty of trying to ignore his cousin's share in
the business, which was no small one, for it was Drury who had
first seen the possibilities of the peasant poet and had undertaken
to print his work, but Drury was by no means blameless and
seems to have indulged in some rather sharp practice. In one of
Clare's notebooks is the statement: "Drury has persuaded me to
write down in his account book, and under my accounts with him,
that I have sold him my first Vol. for £20, which is to be deducted
from my account, as he only wishes to have a check against Taylor
and Hessey, who he strongly thinks will cheat him." The receipt
was wanted simply for Drury's convenience, for he did not pay £20
nor deduct it from Clare's account; neither was the sum paid by
Taylor and Hessey, although Taylor stated in the Introduction to
The Village Minstrel that "the present Publishers gave Clare
twenty pounds for his Poems".

Not content with his first move, Drury wished to secure the
future. He used every opportunity to poison Clare's mind against
Taylor, and he took advantage of the poet being the worse for
liquor to make him sign an agreement which allowed Clare a
quarter profit. The news of this got out and caused Taylor some
anxiety, but he was eventually able to achieve a settlement with
Drury, and wrote to tell Clare of it:

> We have settled to give E. D., on condition that he sends up the
> agreement for us to destroy it, one half of whatever profit we may
> derive from the present or future Poems, retaining in our own Hands
> the sole management, and perfectly uncontrolled in what we think
> proper to give the Author—E. D. has been repaid the Copyright and
> all other Expenses, and I have charged nothing for my Trouble as
> Editor so far. . . . I should have proceeded with the next Volume
> just as if no Agreement existed, had he remained fixed in his Deter-
> mination to abide by it—We meant to act the same by him, had he

taken no such steps to protect his own Interests, and therefore it is no
Sacrifice to do it now—You shall have at least half of all the profits,
and he shall sustain no loss by our advancing any sums we may deem
right to you. These things I state for your Information, for I have no
Disguise.

Clare, while this quarrel raged over his head, continued with his
work and, in his leisure, did his best to answer the letters of his
other correspondents, the chief among them being Mrs. Emmerson,
whose flowing handwriting covered a double sheet of notepaper
almost every week and generally conveyed a reproof to Clare for
the tardiness of his replies. Captain Sherwill, too, continued to
write, and in April he approached Scott, who was in London for
the purpose of receiving his baronetcy, and and asked him to do
something for Clare. Scott gave him a copy of *The Lady of the Lake*,
and £2 to be spent on books; he refused to inscribe his gift, which
hurt Clare who had thought him "a different person", but the
money purchased Currie's *Life of Burns*, Southey's *Life of Nelson*,
and Chatterton's *Life and Works*, all of which gave him great
pleasure. His voyages of discovery in the realm of literature continued apace and were much helped by the gifts that he received
from certain of his patrons and those who admired his work;
among the poets that he mentions reading at this time are Pope,
Dryden, Wordsworth, and Byron. He also got a great deal of
pleasure from playing his fiddle—a better one than in the days at
Casterton, for Hessey had sent him his own in March, and Clare
had laid the old one on the shelf because he was too fond of it to
sell it.

Lord Radstock, meanwhile, persevered in his efforts on Clare's
behalf with his customary zeal. On 25th April, Mrs. Emmerson
wrote that "our noble and dear friend" had used his influence
with the Bishop of Peterborough to solicit his friendship for Clare,
and she advised the poet to cultivate that friendship by every
means in his power.

Lord R., to convince the Bishop of the purity of your political
principals [*sic*], read some extracts from a letter which you wrote to
me on the subject of the Q . . . s conducts, and your sentiments of
loyalty and attachment to your King and constitution with which the
Bishop expressed himself much pleased.[1]

[1] George IV had succeeded to the throne in January, 1820, and had promptly
announced his decision to divorce his wife which had caused considerable uproar both
in Parliament and in the country.

The Subscription List, which Lord Radstock had opened soon after Clare's visit to London, met with considerable success, and on 28th April £250 was invested in Navy 5 per cents; Taylor was appointed trustee, and a few months later was joined in this office by Richard Woodhouse, a lawyer who was a close friend of both Taylor and Hessey. In June, a further sum of £125 was added, thus making a total of £375, which was made up of the sums contributed by Lord Fitzwilliam and the publishers, and by some twenty smaller donations, including those of Prince Leopold, the Duke of Bedford, the Duke of Devonshire, and Lord John Russell. In addition, Clare was to have an annuity of £10 which Earl Spencer had settled on him in response to a plea from Dr. Bell of Stamford, whose acquaintance Clare had made at one of his Sunday breakfasts with Drury when he was lime-burning at Pickworth. These sums, together with the £15 from the Marquis of Exeter, gave Clare an annual income of £43 15s. This seemed to him a promise of security at last, and with his first book still selling well and his second in preparation he had every reason for high hopes and confidence in the future.

He was sensible of how much he owed to Lord Radstock's efforts in this matter of the Subscription List as well as in the sale of his poetry, and that knowledge made it all the more difficult for him when a disagreement occurred between them. As long ago as February, Radstock had complained to Taylor about two poems in Clare's first volume which he considered improper—"Dolly's Mistake" and "My Mary"—but the publisher had evidently handled the situation with tact and no more had been said. The subject, however, was to be raised again, for on 11th May Mrs. Emmerson wrote urging Clare to submit to his Lordship's wishes and to agree to the omission from the next edition, not only of the improper poems, but also of certain lines which Radstock found even more objectionable because they showed "radical and ungrateful sentiments".

In these lines, which occurred in "Helpston" and "The "Dawnings of Genius", Clare had called a ploughman

> That necessary tool of wealth and pride

and had written of

> Accursed Wealth! o'erbounding human laws,
> Of every evil thou remainst the cause.

Mrs. Emmerson pointed out that Lord Radstock was "at once an ornament and blessing to mankind" and quoted him as saying: "Tell Clare if he has still a recollection of what I have done, and am still doing for him, he must give me unquestionable *proofs* of being that Man I would have him to be—he must *expunge— expunge!*"

Clare was, not unnaturally, incensed at this, and wrote to Taylor: "d—n that canting way of being forced to please, I say—I can't abide it and one day or other I will show my Independance more strongly than ever".

Taylor then announced that the third edition was already printed and it was therefore too late to remove the offending lines. He wrote to his brother: "We have published the 3rd edition of Clare which seems likely to go off with as much spirit as its predecessors. I am much annoyed by Lord R's Puffing in the *Post* and *New Times* and am determined to put an end to it, for I cannot but think it is disgraceful to me and injurious to Clare's fame as well as his feelings." As the fourth edition was not likely to be printed for a few months, there was a temporary lull in the battle, which was later renewed with increased vigour on both sides.

IO

DIVIDED LOYALTIES

Patty moved to the cottage
at Helpston either at the end of April or during May, and on
2nd June their first child was born—a daughter who was christened
Anna Maria. Clare wrote a poem "To an Infant Daughter", in
which he expressed his fear of what life might bring to the child,
and hoped that she would be free from his own failings and would
not "itch at rhymes".

> Lord knows my heart, it loves thee much;
> And may my feelings, aches, and such,
> The pains I meet in folly's clutch
> Be never thine:
> Child, it's a tender string to touch,
> That sounds "thou'rt mine".

Clare sent the poem to his publishers, and Hessey acknowledged
it with a favourable comment, but he was wise enough to consider
the possible effect that the news might have on some of the poet's
patrons, who would remember that he had only been married
three months, and he advised Clare not to make it public. "None
of your friends here but Taylor and myself are acquainted with the
addition to your family—keep your own Counsel and we shall not
betray you." The poem was published the following year in *The
Village Minstrel*, but with certain omissions, for the original
version contained a rather unkind allusion to Patty of which Clare
later thought better.

The poet makes no comment on his relations with Patty in the
existing letters of that time, but the implications of a remark that
he made later are that things did not go too smoothly to begin with.
Indeed, the circumstances attending their marriage were not such
as would engender harmony—the local gossip about Patty's
condition, the anger of her parents, Clare's indecision, and the
necessity of starting their married life in separate establishments.
Because of this situation at home Clare probably gave more

encouragement than he would otherwise have done to Mrs. Emmerson's foolish, though harmless, advances, and it was only natural for Patty's jealousy and suspicion to be roused by the frequent letters from the lady in London. At the time of his marriage, Mrs. Emmerson had told Clare:

> Your "dear Patty" must not be jealous that I write thus to you; I do it for her sake in part, for in comforting and cheering your drooping spirits with the warm language of true friendship, I am at the same time, securing her future happiness in you!

In July, she sent him a portrait of herself which she wished him to put in a private drawer: "Eliza . . . begs not to be exposed to public view, she would live with you in your happy Cottage *unknown* to the *curious* or *ill-natured!*" And, on 23rd August, she told him:

> I've ever addressed you in your own very affectionate language— for we may unblushingly acknowledge ourselves lovers in poesy. . . . I read all your kind letters to my husband and our noble friend Lord R., and my replies to them . . . how far you are so candid in reading mine to your "dear Patty" I cannot judge.

Meanwhile Lord Radstock continued to press for the alterations to the fourth edition of *Poems Descriptive of Rural Life and Scenery*, and Taylor, whose irritation with the old Admiral was growing daily, counselled Clare to hold out for what he thought right.

> I like your Independence, Clare, and am sorry that any persons should be so ill-judging as to try to scream you up to the Squeak of Flattery. Take your own Course; write what you like; if you feel obliged, say so if it suits you; if not, scorn to utter Falsehood even in Rhyme.

He was inclined to let the offending lines remain, and expressed himself willing to abide the consequences, but by September he was obliged to change his opinion, as Lord Radstock had signified his intention of having no more to do with Clare if his wishes in the matter were ignored. "When the Follies of the Day are past," Taylor wrote, "with all the fears they have engendered we can restore the Poems according to the earlier Editions."

Clare received frequent letters from the protagonists in the dispute, each making indignant complaints about the behaviour of the other, and in this atmosphere of jealousy and suspicion it was difficult for him to know whom he was to trust. Radstock made uncomplimentary allusions to Taylor in most of his letters, and Mrs. Emmerson sometimes did the same, although, for the most part, she spoke well of the publisher; she had, however, something to say about another friend of Clare's, whom she considered should add a D to his initials, as "grunting and snarling appear to be his trade", but she added that it might be unjust to the DOG. Presumably this refers to Octavius Gilchrist, though what he had done to call forth this remark is not recorded.

It is not surprising if Clare's confidence in Taylor was a little shaken by the frequent insinuations of Lord Radstock and of Drury, who continued to abuse his cousin either openly or by innuendo; he was also vexed by what he considered the publisher's *volte-face* when Taylor declared that he was now of the opinion that it would be expedient to consent to the amendments to the fourth edition. Evidently Clare wrote about this and expressed his doubts as to Taylor's handling of the new volume, now in preparation, for Hessey dispatched a tactful letter to Helpston in order to reassure him. "You may rely on finding in Taylor a sincere friend and a discreet adviser, and one who is well able to appreciate the merit of your Poetry and well qualified to stand, as you phrase it, 'between you and the Public'. "

During July, Clare's mother was taken ill, and the doctor in Stamford had to perform an operation on a badly poisoned finger. Drury wrote to Hessey that they were very anxious about her and that her condition was complicated by the dropsy from which she suffered; she was installed in lodgings in Stamford, and Clare visited her every other day, while Patty and his sister, Sophy, went on the intermediate days. By August she was recovering, and was well enough to go home.

Clare was then working in the harvest, but was constantly bothered by importunate visitors, of whom he complained in a letter to Taylor:

> It's no use making resolutions to work, you see, now—they will not let me keep quiet as I us'd to be. They send for me twice or three times a day out of the fields and I am still the strangers' puppet show. What can their fancys create to be so anxious and so obstinate of being satisfied? I am but a man (and a little one, too) like others. Still, as they will come, I will still sit in my corner in readiness for them and rhyme and jingle away in the teeth of trouble and scrat away on my "Cremona" string to make the best use of the world while I am in it.

Of one of these visitors, Clare gave an amusing account:

Among the many that came to see me there was a dandified gentleman of unconscious oddity of character, that not only bordered on
the ridiculous but was absurdly smothered in it. He made pretensions to great learning and knew nothing. On his first coming he
began in a very dignified manner to examine the fruits of experience
in books, and said he hoped I had a fondness for reading as he wished
to have the pleasure to make me a present of some. He then begged
my walking stick, and after he had got it he wanted me to write my
name on the crook. I really thought the fellow was mad. He then
asked me insulting liberties respecting my first acquaintance with
Patty, and said he understood that in this country the lower orders
made their courtship in barns and pigsties, and asked whether I did.
I felt very vext and said that it might be the custom of high orders
for aught I knew, as experience made fools wise in most matters, but
I assured him he was very wrong respecting that custom among the
lower orders. Here his wife said he was fond of a joke, and hoped I
should not be offended, but I saw naught of a joke in it and found
afterwards that he was but a scant remove from the low order himself,
as his wife was a grocer's daughter. After he had gossiped an hour,
he said, "Well, I promised to give you a book, but after examining
your library I don't see that you want anything, as you have a great
many more than I expected to find. Still, I should make you an offer
of something. Have you got a Bible?"

I said nothing, but it was exactly what my father had long wanted,
and he instantly spoke for me and said, "We have a Bible, Sir, but I
cannot read it, the print is so small. So I should thank you for one."
The man looked very confused and explained by his manner that he
had mentioned the very book which he thought we had, to escape
giving it.

In spite of the prosperity that Clare had lately felt was coming
his way, he found the need for money to pay his day-to-day
expenses during the summer, and the payment for his work in the
fields was erratic and inadequate. He had received no payment
as yet for his book, except occasional sums which Taylor sent
without any proper account, and the sum of £7 10s. advanced by
Hessey (in Taylor's absence) as a half-yearly payment of dividends
did not go very far. Clare thought to ease the situation by selling
some poems to a music publisher, but this scheme met with disap-
proval in London, and drew forth a protest from Mrs. Emmerson.

At the beginning of October, Clare wrote to tell Taylor of an
unfortunate incident that had worried him considerably.

I made a cursed blunder last week at Drury's shop . . . the Marquis of Exeter came in and very condescendingly asked me how I did—I, not knowing him, said very bluntly, "Middling, thank ye, Sir." He next asked me when my poems would come out, as that, he said, caus'd him to call. "Sometime ere the spring, sir, I dare say", was my answer. He looked hard in my face and went out—and when I was informed who it was I was most confoundedly vex'd, and all the way home, at every stile I got to, sat and repeated it over to myself how I acted, which every repetition made more ridiculous.

Clare must have been too shy, on his visit to Burghley, to look the Marquis in the face, and had, therefore, carried away no recollection of his features.

Taylor proposed visiting Clare at Helpston that autumn when on his way from London to Retford, but the plan was never carried out. The publisher was very busy with more work than he had time to do, and was making slow progress with editing Clare's new poems. Drury remarked sourly, with his usual hit at Taylor, ". . . you may think yourself well off if you get a sight of your Book *complete*, on this side Xtmas. If once he gets down in the country 'tis goodbye to you and I for what with dinnering and visiting, rusticating and water-placing, he never gets on with anything during the summer."

But Taylor's mind was much occupied just then with his anxieties about Keats, and he or Hessey sent frequent reports of his health in their letters to Clare. At the end of June, Hessey had mentioned that he had "been spitting blood for several days", and on 14th August Taylor wrote:

Keats you know broke a Blood vessel and has been very ill. He is now recovering and it is necessary for his getting through the winter that he should go to Italy. Rome is the place recommended. You are now a richer Man than poor K., and how much more fortunate. We have some Trouble to get through 500 Copies of his Work.

As it was impossible for Keats to raise enough money to pay for the journey to Italy, Taylor and Hessey with difficulty managed to advance him a loan of £150—a gesture which was as generous as it was timely, for the likelihood of seeing their money again was not great—and on 27th September Taylor was able to tell Clare:

Keats is on the Water going to Naples, and has been for nearly a Fortnight, but I fear that contrary and strong Winds have still kept him tossing about in the cold English Channel. If he recovers his

Strength he will write to you. I think he wishes to say to you that
your Images from Nature are too much introduced without being
called for by a particular Sentiment.—To meddle with this Subject
is bad Policy when I am in Haste, but perhaps you conceive what
it is he means; his Remark is only applicable now and then when he
feels as if the Description overlaid and stifled that which ought to be
the prevailing Idea.—He likes your first pastoral which E. D. copied
and sent very much indeed; but I am afraid it is not poetical or select
enough in certain Parts of the Soliloquy.

Towards the end of November, Clare's health was troubling
him again, and he complained of nervous disorders and acute
depression, while his mind was constantly occupied with thoughts
of death. Hessey wrote to sympathise with him, and Mrs.
Emmerson tried to encourage him, saying that she knew by
experience what it was to labour under such depresssions.

When such fantasies of the brain take hold of the imagination it is
absolutely necessary for us to rouse our best energies to combat with
such demons as you have named: Call forth all your philosophy—
your Reason—the giant Resolution, and these combined, my dear
Clare, will soon conquer such fiends of the imagination. Is it for such
as you, and me, to fear death? Oh no; rather let us view it as a thing
to be desired—let us by avoiding evil be ever ready to meet death
whenever it may please God to call upon us.

Clare's indisposition was not helped by the fact that the tension
between Taylor and Lord Radstock now broke out into open
warfare, and the cottage at Helpston was bombarded with wordy
epistles from each side, full of invective against the other. Lord
Radstock complained of Taylor's disrespect and his secrecy about
Clare's affairs, and Mrs. Emmerson wrote to the poet: "I regret
to learn that Mr. T—— does not act so respectfully to Lord R——
as he deserves from him, and equally regret his keeping you in
such total ignorance of your affairs. It is most unpardonable of
him." Taylor had refused to dine with Radstock, despite the
inducement of a haunch of venison, and had "pleaded Business
and retired Habits as an Excuse" which had offended the old
Admiral more deeply than ever.

Lord Radstock then wrote to the publisher, urging that there
should be a written agreement between him and Clare to which
Taylor replied on 11th December.

The concluding sentence in your Lordship's letter, reminds me of a
conversation in which you proposed certain terms for the publishing

of Clare's future works—and I then replied, that without any such obligation, we were at the time benefitting the author more than your proposal would have bound us to do—whence it was likely that our conduct to him in subsequent instances would be equally liberal. But, my Lord, if you think your arbitration will be advantageous to Clare—I as a *Publisher* can have no objection to it: in the meantime I shall suspend those labours which are not within the province of a publisher—for I have many other subjects on which I ought to bestow my time.

To this Lord Radstock replied the next day, saying that he recollected having a conversation with Taylor on the subject of his dealings with Clare, but could not remember the whole substance of it. Taylor had apparently mentioned, at that time, the agreement that Southey made with his publishers—i.e. that the publishers defrayed the whole of the expense of publication and that the profits arising from the sale should be equally divided—and had expressed himself willing to adopt this or any other plan that Radstock might suggest.

That your subsequent conduct (as publishers) towards Clare [the Admiral went on] would be as liberal as in the outset I never doubted —but still I apprehend in matters of real business no man's word (however well established his integrity) would be sufficiently binding, unless accompanied by some written document.

As the case now stands between you and Clare—I understand that no terms whatever have been offered. He would therefore I think be to blame, to resign his Manuscripts to any publisher whatever, without a specified security for his labours.

You talk of suspending your "present labours, as not coming within the province of a publisher"—In this I shall only observe that had Clare's poems appeared without an "Introduction" and no Lord Radstock had stepped forth in support of the work, my own opinion is, that a second edition of the poems would not yet have showed itself—That your labours were great respecting the little vol. in question, I most willingly allow—but that you were amply remunerated I am equally convinced.

The sting in the tail of his Lordship's letter was more than Taylor could tolerate, and the icy note which he sent in reply gives some idea of his outraged feelings:

My Lord,
The observations contained in your Lordship's last letter, have materially altered the complexion of our correspondence—I will

7

write to Clare to know whether we are to treat with him, or your Lordship, for the copyright of his next volume; and upon his answer will depend whether I shall again have the honour of addressing your Lordship.

He then wrote Clare a detailed account of the correspondence and quoted passages from it. "Unless you commission Lord Radstock to interfere in this Matter I know of no Right that he has to write to me on the Subject, and if he possessed ever so good a Right the observations he has allowed himself to make on my Conduct would disincline me to have any further Communication with him." Taylor proposed an agreement on the terms of half-profits, as Lord Radstock had suggested, for he thought it would serve "to keep off Meddlers like him"; he allowed that Radstock possibly meant well, and advised Clare not to quarrel with him, lest he should be called ungrateful. "Verily", Taylor ended bitterly, "they have their Reward who bestow Kindness for the sake of Return."

Mrs. Emmerson wrote to Clare on 17th December, and said that the break between Taylor and Lord Radstock had done him great harm; she advised him to press for the agreement but not to remove his manuscripts from Taylor and Hessey, as that would mean a long delay in the publication of the new book. Clare, trying his hardest to steer the difficult middle course, had no desire to seek a new editor for his work, thus indefinitely postponing publication, or, worse still, incurring the risk of not getting it published at all, and he was confident of Taylor's integrity as well as his ability; but he recognised Lord Radstock's kind heart and good intentions, and was wholly in agreement with him as to the dilatory and unbusinesslike fashion in which the publishers handled his affairs.

Taylor sent Clare's half-yearly dividend on 24th December, with some more acid remarks about Lord Radstock, and with the news that he was busy with the editing of the poems, and on the 30th Mrs. Emmerson wrote again to the effect that she would do her best to pour oil on the troubled waters; she believed Taylor's intentions were honourable but he had been too reticent about the whole business.

Clare wrote to his publisher expressing his confidence in him and offering to bind himself for future books as well as the one at present under discussion, and Taylor replied on 1st January, 1821, that he could not accept his suggestion. As matters stood at the moment, he felt sure of Clare's goodwill without any such bond, and should a difference arise between them it would be unjust to tie him down. "That foolish Lord R. has no Conception of such Sentiments as these; what a wretched world he moves in, to have learnt no better at his time of life than thus to estimate his Friends as he pretends to call them."

Clare's sense of fairness was evidently roused by this remark, for he pencilled a note above it, "very unjust". The poet's own comment on the quarrel, written about this time, emphasises his appreciation of the fact that the Admiral had been actuated in all he had done by a sincere desire to help him, and that the proposals that he had made to Taylor had been perfectly reasonable.

> Lord Radstock was my best friend. It was owing to him that the first Poems succeeded. He introduced them into all places where he had connections, got them noticed in newspapers and other [periodicals], and if it did nothing more it made them known. He kindly undertook to settle my affairs with my publishers, which they kindly enough on their parts deferred, and it's not settled yet. He wrote Taylor a letter wishing him to draw up an agreement in "black and white", as his Lordship expressed it, as faiths in men were not to be trusted. Taylor pretended to be insulted at this and wrote his Lordship a genteel saucy one that settled the affair in the present confusion of no settling at all. Nay, they will neither publish my poems nor give them up.

So no agreement was signed, and things went on as before, except that Taylor and Lord Radstock avoided each other and only on rare occasions communicated, when it was done through a third party—Clare or Mrs. Emmerson.

The storm which thus died down, together with the events of later years, raises the question of what really *was* Taylor's attitude to the business side of Clare's literary career. After reading his letters and studying his relations with the poet through the long years of their association, it is impossible to doubt that he was a sincere friend to Clare and never intended otherwise than to do his best for him; yet the facts of their business dealings are disconcerting—are, indeed, such as would prompt one to say, if the publisher were not John Taylor, that he had deliberately cheated Clare. In fact, the answer to the problem seems to be that Taylor was unbusinesslike to an incredible degree, that he resented anyone challenging his methods, and that he regarded the profits from his various authors, not as sums which must be properly accounted for and paid to the people concerned, but as a sort of central fund out of which he could take money for whichever one needed it most. Thus, part of the money which was advanced to Keats in 1820 was probably what was owing to Clare, and although Taylor may have felt that he was justified in this "rob Peter" system, it was not business. Clare himself was kept in complete ignorance of how his affairs stood for *nine years* after the publication of his first book, and when, after repeated requests, an account was finally sent to him in 1829, it contained some very surprising things, of which more will be said later. And yet, with Clare as with Keats, Taylor did not hesitate to do the generous thing when he considered that the moment of crisis had come, and we know that he contributed to the cost of keeping Clare at the private asylum in Essex for four years.

In the course of his career, Taylor quarrelled with several of his authors, and caused others to express their dissatisfaction with him—Lamb, Hazlitt, de Quincey, Hood, Landor, Charles Brown. His arbitrary business methods, the swiftness with which he took offence, and his autocratic dislike of criticism made him difficult to get on with, but, even so, it is a formidable list. And yet— there is always that "and yet" with this man whose life and actions present so many contradictions—he had vision, he had faith in the genius of two unknown poets, and he had the courage to publish what he believed worth publishing even if, as in the case of Keats, he had "Trouble to get through 500 Copies".

11

THE TEMPTATION OF JOHN BARLEYCORN

C̶LARE MARKED THE ARRIVAL OF
1821 by sending Taylor a New Year's message for Keats: "Give
my respects to *Keats* and tell him I am a half mad melancholy dog
in this moozy misty country he has lately cast behind him, but I
feel something better." His depression of spirits and melancholy
thoughts of death persisted throughout January, and he asked for
a will form from Woodhouse so that he might put his affairs in
order; he was being attended, at that time, by Dr. Skrimshire, of
Peterborough, who, it seems, had been sent to him by Lord Milton.

By February, however, he was more cheerful, and on the 13th
he wrote to Taylor: "In respect of travelling into the unknown
hereafter, I hope that mine may be a long way off and yours
longer, to stay and write my life and edit a collected book of
the poetry, so that I shall have no dread on my mind of being
scandalised with a bad character."

The editing of the new volume continued slowly, and Taylor
sent the first proofs on 23rd January; the title was under discussion,
and, after dismissing the original choice of "Ways of a Village",
they decided on *The Village Minstrel*. Taylor consulted Clare
about any textual alterations that he considered necessary, and
generally accepted the poet's judgment when they disagreed.
"Whatever Remarks suggest themselves let me have them," he
wrote, "for I always weigh the alterations again and very often
restore them nearly as at first. So whatever you have to say, say
freely." His frequent letters to Clare were full of advice and encouragement, and he did not withhold the word of praise when he
thought it due. In December, he had commented on the "Sonnet
to the Ivy", in which the lines occur:

> Where thou in weak Defiance strivest with Time,
> And holdest his Weapons in a dread Suspense.

This figure [Taylor wrote] is I think of the highest Order of
Poetry; and I would also observe the happy Epithet of "thy green

Darkness overshadowing me". But go on whenever you feel disposed, and only then, for at such Times your Mind will urge you to compose Verses for its own Relief, and depend upon it I shall be pleased with what you do.

His criticisms were rarely of poetic faults but usually of grammatical ones, and Clare, who still retained his hatred of grammar from the days when he had studied Lowe's *Critical Spelling Book*, often found much difficulty in putting them right. In a fit of exasperation, after struggling to alter a verse in which Taylor had found a mistake, he wrote to the publisher, "grammar in learning is like Tyranny in government—confound the bitch, I'll never be her slave".

In February, Taylor sent news of an event which had caused a stir in the literary world; John Scott, the editor of *The London Magazine*, was challenged to a duel as the result of a quarrel with Lockhart, son-in-law and, later, biographer of Sir Walter Scott. The duel was averted, but Lockhart's second, Jonathan Christie, felt that he had been insulted and himself called out John Scott, who was killed in the ensuing combat.

Taylor had also to report that he had received a letter from Keats' friend, Joseph Severn, dated from Rome three weeks earlier, in which he said that the doctor believed Keats could not live more than a fortnight.

Clare, meanwhile, in improving health, sent an account of an illustrious visitor:

The Marquis of Exeter called on me yesterday and enquired very condescendingly and kindly after the new vols and told me to be sure to let him know when they come out. This is something good in the wind, I hope—but I could not master my d—d stupidity to beg pardon for the blunder I committed at Stamford in not knowing his Lordship. My senses always leave me when I get before these great men, but 'twas uncommon kind of his Lordship to come over to Helpstone.

A few days later he was commenting that he had not heard from Radstock or Mrs. Emmerson for some time, and he added, with some asperity, "God send they may find out a new 'Child of Nature' to foster and flatter, whose name is rather fresher than mine."

At the beginning of March, Clare was deeply distressed at the threat to two dearly loved elm trees which stood behind his cottage, and he wrote to Taylor about it:

> My two favourite elm trees at the back of the hut are condemned to die—it shocks me to relate it, but 'tis true. The savage who owns them thinks they have done their best, and now he wants to make use of the benefits he can get from selling them. O, was this country Egypt, and was I but a caliph, the owner should lose his ears for his arrogant presumption, and the first wretch that buried his axe in their roots should hang on their branches as a terror to the rest. I have been several mornings to bid them farewell. Had I one hundred pounds to spare I would buy them reprieves—but they must die. Yet this mourning over trees is all foolishness—they feel no pains— they are but wood, cut up or not. A second thought tells me I am a fool; were people all to feel as I do, the world could not be carried on—a green would not be ploughed—a tree or bush would not be cut for firing or furniture, and every thing they found when boys would remain in that state till they died. This is my indisposition and you will laugh at it.[1]

To one who felt as he did, a destiny of suffering was inevitable, no matter what the outward circumstances. Many years later he was to express, in one of his most moving poems, the protective love which he felt for all created things, and especially for those which other men thought worthy only of contempt.

> E'en here my simple feelings nurse
> A love for every simple weed,
> And e'en this little shepherd's purse
> Grieves me to cut it up; indeed
> I feel at times a love and joy
> For every weed and every thing,
> A feeling kindred from a boy,
> A feeling brought with every spring.[2]

Taylor, with kindly understanding, saw at once how much Clare would be hurt by the destruction of the trees, and on 9th March he wrote: "You are perhaps not the best Person to bargain

---

[1] It is interesting and perhaps not entirely irrelevant to compare Clare's lament for the elms with the sorrow expressed by a later poet. Gerard Manley Hopkins wrote in his Journal on 17th April, 1873, "The ash tree growing in the corner of the garden was felled. It was lopped first: I heard the sound, and looking out and seeing it maimed, there came at that moment a great pang, and I wished to die and not to see the inscapes of the world destroyed any more."

[2] "The Flitting."

for them, as you have so high an Opinion of their Value; but if they are not likely to be cut down for a Week longer or if you can put off the evil Day till then, Gilchrist who is in Town, will return in a day or two, and we will get him to *buy the Trees*, or at least their *Life for the present*, from the Owner." A few days later he wrote again to say that he had not seen Gilchrist before the latter left London, and that Clare had better approach the owner himself and find out what he wanted for the trees.

But the poet was by that time resigned to the fate of the elms, comforting himself with a poem to "Old elm, that murmured in our chimney top", and although he thanked Taylor for his offer he said "let them dye like the rest of us".

In the same letter he said that he had seen Gilchrist,

and according to custom staid two days in the Town and made myself confoundedly drunk the last night. I roll'd to Drury's who can certainly say plenty to degrade me if he pleases. . . . I hate Stamford but am dragged into it like a Bear and Fiddler to a wake. People that advise me to keep at employment soberly at home are the first that tempt me to break from it.

Clare was engaged in a bad bout of drinking in the early spring which caused his friends some anxiety. In February, Drury had written that he hoped Clare was keeping to his resolution to avoid "Swig" for it would be a pity if he did not live to see the success of his labours:

. . . for I do not despair of seeing you with a good substantial house of your own containing 2 Acres of garden, a good Library room looking into the garden, a dog at your feet, sofa under your bum, pier glass over your chimney piece, and the rest of the walls occupied with elegant paintings among which your own phiz by Hilton in a frame thick as a bedpost.

Taylor's warning was couched in soberer terms, and was contained in a letter that brought sad news.

The Life of poor Keats is ended at last: he died at the age of 25— He used to say he should effect nothing [upon] which he would rest his Fame till he was 30, and all his Hopes are over at 25. . . . Poor Fellow! Perhaps your Feeling will produce some lines to his Memory. One of the very few Poets of the Day is gone—let another beware of Stamford. I wish you may keep your Resolution of shunning that

Place for it will do you immense Injury if you do not—you know what I would say.

On 7th April, the publisher wrote to thank Clare for sending some poems and also the sketches from his life in prose, which he thought very good; he took the opportunity of administering a longer and more severe reproof. "But I am all on the other hand full of Concern at your late unfortunate Fit of Drinking." Those who were not so much distinguished and esteemed, Taylor said, delighted in encouraging the poet's defects and dragging him down to their own level.

> I would have you do yourself Justice—What a pity it is that [you] should love these Knaves or Fools better than yourself—better than Friends, Family Life, Fame,—nay even better than that very gift of Poesy which you so highly value—I would not be thought intrusive, and I know you can think over all the Arguments better than I can state them,—or I would just hint at last whether your Talents be not conferred on you by a wise Providence, and if so whether it be not a sin or profanation to trample upon the ruined wreck of God's Image in you, and forfeit his good opinion for such Men and such Allurements as they offer. . . . [Bear] up a little longer against the attacks of John Barleycorn and your age will fortify your Body as well as your Mind to withstand his levelling Weapons.

During March, Clare suffered another fit of depression, and he wrote to Taylor:

> Life's not much to be regretted when we loose her. She is such a lump of trouble and deception that I myself care not how soon I am done with her, and if there was not such a fence of pains and heartaches between this world and death I should at this moment certainly be trying to break the bounds for a breakneck leap into that unriddled blank of fancys, terrors and confusions.

But his mood of despair yielded to the delight of spring, when,

> The dew is on the thorn,
> And the primrose underneath
> Just agen the mossy root
> Is smiling to the morn.
>
> With its little brimming eye
> And its yellow rims so pale
> And its crimp and curdled leaf—— [1]

[1] "The Primrose Bank."

Soon he was writing cheerfully again, and was also hard at work, not only with his poems, but with several efforts in prose, including a novel, which he had been encouraged to attempt by Taylor's praise of his autobiographical sketches.

His domestic affairs were running more smoothly now than in the early days of his marriage, and in a letter to Taylor he expressed the happiness that he was finding with Patty:

> Patty keeps the address to an Infant Daughter by her as I first wrote it, and she wished to hear of the objectional verse and thought it a compliment, so little does she know of poetry—I am very glad you left the verse out—for I have found out by experience, which is a good adviser, that I possess a more valuable article in her than I at first expected, and believe her from my soul an honest woman. Her calumniators were all of that sort of lyars that wish to make others as disgraceful as the world knows themselves to be. This sort is very plentiful here. Patt and myself now begin to know each other and live happily, and I deem it a fortunate [day] in my life that I met with her. She thanks you kindly for blotting out the injury on her character in the above poem, and is proud she has got such friends, I assure you. The cut of her face always delighted me more than any other, and had I never seen her my attempts at poetry would never have been resumed after my removal at Casterton.

At the end of April, Taylor and Hessey bought *The London Magazine* from Baldwin, Cradock and Joy for £500; Taylor was to edit it, and most of the former contributors promised to continue writing for it, among them Lamb, Hazlitt, and Wainewright. Taylor wrote to Clare to tell him of the new venture, and suggested that they should publish some of his poems in the magazine, and that he should try writing some articles for it.

This addition to Taylor's already numerous duties further delayed the publication of Clare's poems. It had now been decided that *The Village Minstrel* should appear in two volumes, and the 1st May was the date originally planned, but on the 9th there were still three more proof sheets that had not been seen by Clare, and it was evident that the publication day was a long way off.

Drury advised Clare to write to Taylor "in terms rather harsh and yet coolly so, not in a passion", and Mrs. Emmerson was concerned that the long delay would mean bringing out the poems at an inauspicious moment. In spite of his quarrel with her "noble and dear friend", she believed that Taylor would treat Clare with the strictest justice, and she had expressed herself "decidedly of your opinion that no man is better qualified to do honour to your productions", but she wrote to Clare on 5th June:

> . . . the procrastination is most shameful—every family of consequence who patronized your 1st volume will in another month be out of Town—What can be the motive of your Publishers they alone can say—but the interest of the Author is most certainly neglected.

To Clare, waiting eagerly for the first copies of his book, the delay seemed endless and unnecessary, and the disappointment came at a bad time, for he was saddened by the loss of a second daughter who was born on 2nd June and died a few days later. Hessey wrote on 23rd that the book was now ready except for the Introduction, which Taylor had had to put aside while his father and another gentleman were visiting Fleet Street. Early in July, he sent Clare some copies of the book, without the Introduction, which were for the Marquis of Exeter, and a week or so later Taylor wrote that if Clare understood his harassing life as book-seller, publisher, editor, author and printer's devil to *The London Magazine*, he would pity him.

At the end of the month Mrs. Emmerson reported that her husband had been to the shop in Fleet Street to inquire about the book, but could get no more precise information than that it would be "out in a few days". On 7th August, Taylor wrote that he was at work on the Introduction again, and that "as the work could not be brought out when the Town was in full Season it is of less Consequence now whether it be this Day published or this Day month."

Shortly after this, Gilchrist went to London and told Taylor that Clare, bitterly disappointed, was seeking consolation in ale, and that if he allowed any further postponement he would be killing the poet with intemperance. So, on 29th August, Taylor sent the proofs of the Introduction at long last; it was just over 4,000 words, occupying some twenty pages of the book, and he had been writing it since the middle of June.

The accompanying letter to Clare was written in an injured tone, and showed that he considered it very unjust of him to be so impatient; he said that having passed Midsummer he would have preferred to wait until November or December, when their book season began, to publish the poems, but Gilchrist's news had left him no alternative but to bring out the volume at once.

> I thought you felt more Regard for me than to plunge into old Excesses and lay the Sin at my Door. Be assured that had it been possible the work should have been published long ago,—and if I could have found anyone who would have taken the Editing off my Hands, so as to have done it to my Mind, I would gladly have given them £100. I am overworked and have much more Reason than you to think of dying; and if I were not temperate and forbearing it would be too much for me.

Meanwhile, Clare, in spite of his disappointment and consequent intemperance, was writing to Taylor, "Still I am yours sincerely and affectionately and ever shall be". He was working in the harvest fields as usual, and was less troubled by the interruptions of visitors than he had been last year.

On 11th August, he made a strange reference to that early love of his which lay hidden away and still troubled his heart:

> I have not had dossity[1] enough about me to answer your last till now—but you'll excuse me. I have had the horrors agen upon me by once agen seeing devoted Mary. I have written the last doggerel that shall ever sully her name and her remembrance any more; 'tis reflections of the past and not of the present that torment me.

[1] Energy.

12

"THE VILLAGE MINSTREL"

"THE VILLAGE MINSTREL" WAS published towards the end of September; two thousand copies were printed, and each of the two volumes contained an engraving as frontispiece, one being of Hilton's portrait of Clare, and the other of a sketch of the cottage at Helpston. In the Introduction, Taylor gave an account of the events which had led up to the publication of the first book, mentioned Clare's marriage and the birth of his daughter, and printed part of the letter which the poet had written about his favourite elm trees. He skilfully paid a tactful tribute to Clare's patrons, and gave a list of the principal contributors to the Fund, with the amounts that they had given; but, although this was undoubtedly a clever piece of psychology, it was unfortunate that his zeal in enumerating the generosities of the great houses of the county, tended to give an impression that all was now well with the poet. Certainly, he said that his finances were "somewhat too much straitened to support his family with comfort", and expressed the hope that his means of living would be increased by the publication of the new work and the continued sale of the other, but his talk of Clare's "possession of a little fortune" and the establishment of his future income on a firm basis was enough to convince many people that sufficient help had now been given and that his prosperity was assured. In fairness to Taylor, however, the difficulty of his task must not be minimised, for he had to keep constantly in mind the necessity of flattering Clare's patrons if any help was to be expected from them in the future. He concluded the Introduction with an appeal to readers and critics to bring the necessary generosity and high-mindedness to their study of the work, so that they might perceive and appreciate its beauties. No doubt the thought of Keats was in his mind when he said:

> Poets of all ages have been cherished and rewarded, and this, not as of mere favour, but from a feeling that they have a claim to be considered. If of late years a less generous treatment has been experienced by any, it is not chargeable on the nature of man in general,

but on an illiberal spirit of criticism, which, catching its character from the bad temper of the age, has "let slip the dogs of war" in the flowery fields of poesy. We may hope that kinder feelings are returning, that "olives of endless age" will grace the future Belles Lettres of our country, and that especially the old and natural relation of poet and patron may be again acknowledged, as it has been in the present instance.

The title-poem was a long one which Clare had begun in 1819 and in which he attempted "to describe my own feelings and love of rural objects", but he was not satisfied with it and wished afterwards that he had withheld it for more revision, as he felt that it did not "describe the feelings of a rhyming peasant strongly or locally enough". The other poems were, for the most part, descriptive, but they showed clearly enough the progress that Clare had made; some of them had been written several years before and were therefore contemporary with the first book, but in the more recent ones Clare had begun to shed that cloying quality that pervaded much of his earlier work, the tendency to put down everything, without selection, and thus sometimes to lose the poetic image in a welter of detail of a rather pedestrian kind. The detail now was, if anything, even more minute, but it was uplifted by the awakening power of his pure imagination, by the deepening of his love and compassion for all the creatures of the earth, and by a sure instinct for the right word. The patient observation of the naturalist and the creative vision of the poet were blending to produce images of great beauty, although Clare was to travel much farther yet along the road to perfection.

In "To the Butterfly", he tells the insect:

> Oft I've seen thy little leg
> Soft as glass o'er velvet glides
> Smoothen down thy silken sides;
> Then thy wings would ope and shut;
> Then thou seemingly wouldst strut:
> Was it nature, was it pride?

And in a sonnet, "The Arbour", he speaks of his native vale

> Where tiny blossoms with a purple bell
> Shiver their beauties to the autumn-gale.

He found a sort of glorious intoxication in the very names of all
the flowers that he loved, and he delighted to reel off lists of them,
as in "The Wild-Flower Nosegay", but the list in his hands is
transformed into the re-created scene of Spring:

> Crimp-frilled daisy, bright bronze buttercup,
> Freckt cowslip-peeps, gilt whins of morning's dew,
> And hooded arum early sprouting up
> Ere the white-thorn bud half unfolds to view.

There were several poems to Mary, written before that "last
doggerel" that he had mentioned to Taylor, and he looked back,
in each of them, to the days when they had been happy together,
and contrasted them with the sadness of the present.

> Where the dark ivy the thorn-tree is mounting,
> Sweet shielding in summer the nest of the dove,
> There lies the sweet spot, by the side of the fountain,
> That's dear to all sweetness that dwells upon love:
> For there setting sunbeams, ere even's clouds close 'em,
> Once stretched a long shadow of one I adore;
> And there did I meet the sweet sighs of the bosom
> Of one ever dear, though I meet her no more.

There was a poem "To the Right Honourable Admiral Lord
Radstock", and a sonnet "To the Memory of John Keats", as well
as one called "Sorrows for a Friend", in which Clare mourned the
death of Richard Turnill, the friend of his childhood.

He was already, at the age of twenty-eight, looking back to that
childhood with nostalgia,

> As one, awakened from a vision sweet,
> Wishes to sleep and dream it o'er again.

And many of the poems in *The Village Minstrel* reflected this longing
for days that were gone. He was to utter it again and again, in
later poems, in letters, in his notebooks.

> There is nothing [he wrote once] but poetry about the existence
> of childhood, real, simple, soul-moving poetry, laughter and joy of
> poetry, and not its philosophy; and there is nothing of poetry about
> manhood but the reflection and the remembrance of what has been—
> nothing more.

And, again:

> Surely our play-prolonging moon on spring evenings shed a richer lustre than the mid-day sun that surrounds us now in manhood, for its poetical sunshine hath left us, and we have learned to know that. For, when boys, every new day brought a new sun. We knew no better, and we were happy in our ignorance. There is nothing of that new and refreshing sunshine upon the picture now. It shines from the heavens upon real matter-of-fact existences and weary occupations.

Reviews of the new book appeared in a number of periodicals, including *The Eclectic Review*, *The New Monthly*, *The Gentleman's Magazine*, and *The Literary Gazette*. The critics spoke well of it, although some of them complained about his use of provincialisms and others suggested that he had imitated Beattie's *Minstrel*, an accusation which he had predicted in April, 1820, when he read Beattie for the first time, having received it as a present from Townsend.

He had met with this sort of criticism over the first volume, when certain of the reviewers remarked that he had imitated Burns or Bloomfield, but, although it annoyed him, he accepted it as the way of a critic, and it was only when someone added Crabbe's name to the list of those whom he was said to have aped that he gave vent to his wrath. For Crabbe was not only a poet for whose work Clare had not much admiration, but he was also a parson, and, as a race, Clare disliked parsons as much as farmers.

> What's he know of the distresses of the poor [he wrote angrily to Taylor], musing over a snug coal fire in his parsonage box? If I had an enemy I could wish to torture, I would not wish him hung nor yet at the devil—my worst wish should be a week's confinement in some vicarage, to hear an old parson and his wife lecture on the wants and wickedness of the poor and consult a remedy, or a company of marketing farmers thumbing over politics in an ale-house, or a visionary Methodist arguing on points of religion. Either is bad enough—I know not which is the best.

These feelings were probably caused, or at least aggravated, by the numerous letters which Clare received from unknown clergymen after his rise to fame, bidding him not to forget his humble station, but to be grateful to his generous patrons and never aspire to higher walks of life than that in which he was born. Clare's material ambitions did not, at any time, extend beyond the desire for such security as would safeguard his family from hunger and himself from financial worries, leaving him free to write, but all this unsolicited advice, couched in terms of the greatest condescension and mixed with expressions of piety, revolted him as well as wounding his pride. He was a very tolerant man, believing that everyone had a right to their opinions, but the only things which he could never tolerate at any price were what he called "cant and humbug".

His own faith was an essentially simple one. He was always faintly suspicious of the outward manifestations of religion, and felt nearer to God in the fields than he did in church, but the simplicity of his creed was part of his very nature and did not arise from lack of thought; in fact, he read widely on religious and philosophical subjects, and at times he was troubled by doubts which he strove to overcome by discussion with Taylor and Mrs. Emmerson, and by earnest study and meditation. In one of his notebooks he wrote:

> The way to Heaven is a direct road and we have little to do with the turnings, for, like the bye-roads from a turn-pike, they lead to private possessions and private interests and have little to do with our objectives and nothing with our interests for Eternity.

Early in September, Clare wrote to Taylor about the visitors who came to Helpston to see him, and said that had he known four years ago that he would ever have so much flattery he would surely had died of vanity, "but let me wait another year or two and this peep-show will be over—and my vanity, if I have any, will end in its proper mortification and [learn] that John Clare the thresher, in the onset, and neglected rhymer, in the end, are the only two comfortable periods of his life". There was no reason, at that time, to suppose that Clare would become a "neglected rhymer", but within a few months he was to see his prophecy beginning to come true, for by December only eight hundred copies of the book had sold and it was evident that it would not achieve a sale comparable with that of the first volume.

In October, Taylor visited Clare at Helpston on his way back to London from the north, and wrote an account of the day that he spent there for the November number of *The London Magazine*. In it he described meeting Clare about half a mile from the village as he was going with Patty and her sister to receive his quarter's salary from the Steward of the Marquis of Exeter. Clare turned

8

back and went with Taylor to Lolham Brigs, and thence to the
village; the former place was the scene of a poem, "The Last of
March", which was published in *The Village Minstrel*, and Taylor
marvelled at Clare's skill in finding poetic material in what he
considered to be a dull, flat countryside.

In the cottage Taylor saw the water-colour of Hilton's portrait
of Clare, which the artist had copied and sent to the poet's father
who was now sadly crippled and hobbling about on two sticks;
Clare's little daughter, Anna, he described as "a fine lively pretty
creature, with a forehead like her father's, of ample promise".
They had a meal of bread and cheese, with beer from The Blue
Bell, and afterwards Taylor looked at the poet's library which
included the works of Burns, Cowper, Wordsworth, Coleridge,
Keats, Crabbe, and about twenty volumes of Cooke's poets, as
well as *Nithsdale and Galloway Song* by Allan Cunningham,
to whom Clare wished to be introduced. Clare then walked with
Taylor as far as Barnack, where they parted, Taylor going on to
Wansford to take the London coach, and Clare to Casterton
where Patty's family were celebrating Michaelmas.

Taylor remarked, in this article, upon Clare's sound judgment
in literary matters, and his power of argument:

> His language, it is true, is provincial, and his choice of words in
> ordinary conversation is indifferent, because Clare is an unpretend-
> ing man, and he speaks in the idiom of his neighbours, who would
> ridicule and despise him for using more or better terms than they are
> familiar with. But the philosophic mind will strive to read his
> thoughts, rather than catch at the manner of their utterance; and will
> delight to trace the native nobleness, strength and beauty of his
> conceptions, under the tattered garb of what may, perhaps, be
> deemed uncouth and scanty expressions.

In November, Mrs. Emmerson was reproving Clare for the
silence that he had maintained for some time, both to her and to
Lord Radstock; the latter, she said, was hurt and offended by
what he called Clare's "unbecoming conduct". Soon afterwards
the silence from Helpston was apparently broken by a letter which
confessed to another carousal at Stamford, for on 21st December
Mrs. Emmerson wrote again:

> You tell me, by an act of inebriety you have made yourself "ridi-
> culous and have been suffering for it this week past". . . . But why
> suffer the goodness of your heart to mislead your understanding by

taking you into society no longer suited to your situation **and** pursuits in life?

The good lady, who was always anxious to keep the **peace**, added a postscript to her letter: "If you should write to Lord R. don't mention the Stamford matter."

Clare was in need of money early in December, and Taylor sent his dividend money rather before it was due, in response to an urgent request. At the same time, he promised Clare payment of six guineas for the poems that had been published in *The London Magazine*, and said that he would send it with the £5 which was owing from Lord Spencer's annuity, but he delayed sending the latter until 1st February and never sent the six guineas at all.

But, in spite of difficulties, the New Year found Clare hard at work and expressing his resolution "in the teeth of vexation to surmount disappointment by unwearied struggles". His fits of violent creative energy left him exhausted and depressed, and the bouts of drinking in which he sought relief from his troubles were invariably followed by terrible remorse which only lowered his spirits still further. He was now writing a novel of village life, in addition to the various poetical projects that he had on hand, and he was constantly busy with his observation in the fields and woods, the results of which he carefully entered in his notebooks. His comments on birds, flowers, and insects, which were liberally scattered through the notebooks among poems, essays, and occasional copies of letters, were fragmentary but always written with an accuracy of detail and a descriptive power that makes them a delight to read.

> Hawks are beautiful objects when on the wing. I have often stood to view a hawk in the sky, trembling its wings and then hanging quite still for a moment as if it was as light as a shadow and could find, like the clouds, a resting place upon the blue air.

On his walks and at his work Clare only wanted solitude, but at other times he felt an acute loneliness, for, although he seems to have enjoyed peace and happiness at home, there was no one there with whom he could discuss his poetry, the books he read, and the thoughts that filled his busy brain. During his visit to London, and in his correspondence with Taylor, he had tasted the delight of such discussion, and the contrast between the literary society of Fleet Street and the illiterate society of Helpston makes it evident that, if Clare was to know peace of mind, he needed to be remarkably adaptable. There was never, in his attitude towards his family and neighbours, any trace of scorn or shame. If he called them ignorant it was certainly not meant as a term of abuse, for he did not regard his learning as a cause for conceit. He *wanted* the company of the villagers, for it was his natural background and he was happy in it, but he wanted intellectual companionship as well, and it was one of his sorrows that, except for a few brief weeks, it was denied to him.

He had, however, two good friends with whom he spent some very happy days, wandering in the fields or talking over their common interests; both these men were servants at Milton. Artis was an archaeologist in his spare time, and was always busy with Roman coins or bits of pottery that he had unearthed, while Henderson was a naturalist who was "never wearied with hunting after the Emperor butterfly and the hornet sphinx in the Hanglands Wood, and the orchises on the Heath". Clare spent three days at Milton in January, studying Roman remains with Artis, which gave him some respite from his work, but he was soon busy with it again and was writing to Taylor of a new scheme that he had in mind.

His old friends the Billings brothers had got into financial difficulties and had been obliged to mortgage their house—that same dilapidated "Bachelor's Hall" where Clare used to meet the young men of the village in days gone by. There was also some land—about seven acres—and the mortgage had been acquired by a Jew to whom the brothers now found they were unable to pay the interest. Clare wanted to take over the mortgage, which he felt would help his old friends as well as himself, and, as the Fund money was tied up and he could not use that, he suggested that Taylor should buy the copyright of his poems for the next five years for £200. But Taylor disapproved of the whole scheme and declined to buy the future interest in his poems as he said that it was impossible to estimate their value, and such a transaction would prove injurious to one party or the other. Lord Milton, however, lent £20 to pay off the interest, and "Bachelor's Hall" was saved.

In February Clare was writing to Taylor:

The Muse is a fickle Hussy with me. She sometimes stilts me up to madness and then leaves me as a beggar by the wayside, with no more life than what's mortal, and that nearly extinguished by melancholy forbodings. I wish I lived nearer you, at least I wish London would creep within 20 miles of Helpstone—I don't wish H. to shift its station. I live here among the ignorant like a lost man, in fact like one whom the rest seems careless of having anything to do with. They hardly dare talk in my company for fear I should mention them in my writings, and I find more pleasure in wandering the fields than in musing among my silent neighbours who are insensible to everything but toiling and that to no purpose.

From a note written, a few weeks later, on the MS. of "April", we learn how the "fickle Hussy" kept him from his rest:

This was written yesterday and this morning in the Season of Memory. Pray tell me how you like it and that quickly, and if its too late for the Mag I shall feel sorry but I could not help it; I've done all I could and sat up most part of last night to do it, when the headache was very mortifying and the bed very enticing. I am much better.

In March, Taylor wrote about *The Village Minstrel*:

It is certain that the last work does not [sell] like the first, but you must remember that the first was a Surprise to everybody, that it excited the strongest Sympathy, and that numbers bought it from a regard for the Author's Circumstances and from the general Talk there was about it—Now, the real Admirers of Poetry are left alone in the List of Purchasers, and their Numbers are very few.

Taylor's cogent reasons for the remarkable success of the first book accounted only in part for the comparative failure of the second. The higher price may have had something to do with it— 12s. as compared with 5s. 6d. for the first—but there is also no doubt that Clare was unlucky in coming before the public at a time when there was already such a galaxy of poets to command the attention of the reader. Wordsworth, Coleridge and Southey were still writing, while, of the younger generation, Byron and Shelley, to name only two, were already famous. Among all these literary celebrities it is perhaps not surprising that one known only as a peasant poet who had created a stir with his first book should be elbowed out and forgotten.

13

THE LONDONERS

THE ADVENT OF SPRING DID LITTLE, this year, to banish Clare's melancholy—in fact, he believed that his spirits were always at their lowest ebb in spring and autumn, and he wrote to Hessey on 2nd April:

> The blue devils are my constant companions and I feel very ill, so much so as almost to feel alarmed at times; flutterings run from my head to my knees as if something was alive in my veins. What it is I can't tell, but I must be better after a bit.

Mrs. Emmerson, who had lately moved from Berners Street to Stratford Place, thought that a holiday in London might do him good, and suggested that he should come and stay. Clare wanted to go, but, thinking of the expense, was dubious until Hessey wrote to add his persuasions to those of Mrs. Emmerson, and sent £5 for his journey.

Shortly before his departure, Clare received a friendly note from the poet Bloomfield:

> Neighbour John,
> If we were still nearer neighbours I would see you and thank you personally for the two volumes of your poems sent me so long ago, I write with such labour and difficulty that I cannot venture to praise or discriminate like a critic, but must only say that you have given us great pleasure.
> I beg your acceptance of my just published little volume; and, sick and ill as I continually feel, I can join you heartily in your exclamation: "What is life?"

Clare determined that he would stop at Biggleswade on his way home from London and visit Bloomfield, but it turned out that family affairs caused him to make the return journey in haste, and, as he wrote afterwards, "my purse got too near the bottom for a stoppage on the road, and as it was too great a distance to walk home this, with other matters, prevented me from seeing him".

Clare had no companion this time to accompany him on the journey by coach from Stamford to Holborn, for Gilchrist had been ill for some time and was not well enough to start for London until several days later. He was smarting under some very hard blows that he had received in a violent and lengthy literary warfare in which the chief combatants were himself and the Revd. W. Lisle Bowles, but which, before it ended, involved Byron and Campbell. It started as a discussion on the poetry of Pope, but developed into a series of thinly disguised personal attacks in pamphlets and in articles which were published in *The Quarterly Review* and *The London Magazine*.

On arrival in London, Clare went to Fleet Street, where he stayed for a few days with Taylor before moving to Mrs. Emmerson's house in Stratford Place. He liked to sit in Taylor's window and watch the crowds passing up and down Fleet Street, which was to him a most remarkable sight.

When Gilchrist reached town he took Clare to visit the great Mr. Gifford, editor of *The Quarterly Review*, who gave the poet "a hearty shake of the hand", congratulated him on his last book, and warned him several times to beware of booksellers (which was no doubt aimed at Taylor, for whom he had no liking). The next day they called on John Murray, Byron's publisher, in Albemarle Street; he was also very friendly to Clare, and presented him with a copy of *Translations of Perseus*.

The poet was still bewildered by the London streets and did not venture far afield by himself. He learned the way to the Royal Academy and used to go there very often because he knew nowhere else, but Thomas Bennion, the head porter at Taylor and Hessey's, sometimes acted as his guide, and the two struck up a friendship which, it seems, they often toasted in a convenient alehouse.

Another and rather different friendship which began during this visit was with Edward Rippingille, an artist whom Clare met at Mrs. Emmerson's house. It was his work that Clare had seen and admired in a shop window at Wisbech many years earlier, when he had gone there to be interviewed by Counsellor Bellamy. Rippingille had come up from Bristol, where he was then living, and was enjoying the gaieties of London, to some of which he introduced his rustic friend. Clare said of him:

He is a rattling sort of odd fellow, with a desire to be thought one, and often affects to be so for the sake of singularity, and likes to treat his nearest friends with neglect and carelessness, on purpose, as it were, to have an opportunity of complaining about it. He is a man of great genius as a painter and, what is better, he has not been puffed into notice like the thousands of farthing rush-lights (like myself, perhaps), in all professions, that have glimmered their day and are dead. I spent many pleasant hours with him while in London. His greatest relish is punning over the bottle, for he is a strong dealer in puns. We acted a many of life's farces and cracked a many jokes together, many of them bad ones, perhaps, and without kernels. We once spent a whole night at Offley's, the Burton alehouse, and sat till morning. . . . He affected to be little ta'en with worldly applause, and was always fishing for it—he was very careless of money and squandered it away as a thing of no other use than to spend.

Clare went on some shopping expeditions and wrote home with the news that he had purchased presents for his wife and sister— probably lengths of material, but he does not say what they were.

I have at last performed my promise. They are both of the same price and both my choice, but that's no reason why they should please Patty and Sophy—two very difficult creatures on that point, as I have before experienced. But if they don't suit I make no more attempts to please—let them remember that.

He was anxious about the tame birds that he cared for at home, and bade his father, "Remember to take care of the Doves."

Taylor now held a dinner-party each month for the con- tributors of *The London Magazine*, among whom there were, as already mentioned, some of the foremost writers of the day; during his stay in London Clare attended at least one of these dinners and met some of his fellow-authors on several other occasions at Taylor's house. He said that, next to the delight of looking in booksellers' windows, his greatest amusement while in town was

the curiosity of seeing literary men. . . . Some of them I went purposely to see, others I met in literary parties, that is, the confused contributor's dinners at Taylor's and Hessey's. I had no means of meeting the constellations of genius in one mass—they were mingled parties. Some few were fixed stars in the world's hemisphere, others glimmered every month in the "Magazine". Some were little vapours that were content to shine by the light of others—I mean dabbling critics who cut monthly morsels from genius, whose works are on the waters, free for all to catch at that choose. These, bye the bye, I could observe had a self-satisfaction about them that magnified molehills to mountains. I mean that little self was, in its own eye, a giant, and that every other object was mere nothing. I shall not mention names here, but it is evident I do not allude to friends.

Clare wrote detailed descriptions of several of the "Londoners" —notably, Reynolds, Lamb, Hazlitt, Cary, and Wainewright— which show how remarkably keen was his observation and how swiftly and accurately he sized up their characters. Most of them, in turn, described and commented on Clare, and it is amusing to read the opinions that each formed of the other across the table of these literary dinner-parties.

Lamb, who, as "Elia", was contributing regularly to *The London Magazine*, took a great liking to Clare and used to tease him mightily, which Clare took in good part, often giving back as good as he got. Wainewright described their wordy warfare some time later when he looked back on these gatherings as things of the past.

> Alas! good Clare, never again shalt thou and he engage in those high combats, those wit-fights! Never shall his companionable draught cause thee an after-look of anxiety into the tankard!—no more shall he, pleasantly-malicious, make thy ears tingle and thy cheeks glow with the sound of that perplexing constrainment, that conventional gagging-bill, that grammar, till in the bitterness of thy heart thou cursedst Lindley Murray by all the stars! Not once again shall thy sweetly simple Doric phrases and accent beget the odious pun. Thou mayest imbibe thy ale in peace, and defy Priscian unchecked,—Elia is gone!

Lamb called him "Princely Clare" and "Clarissimus", and Hood says that when the two of them walked down the Strand arm-in-arm after they had dined, people would call out, "Look at Tom and Jerry", because they resembled Hawthorn and Logic in the plates to *Life and London*.

Clare's picture of "Elia", written after he had visited his home, brings him at once before us:

> He is very fond of snuff, which seems to sharpen up his wit every time he dips his plentiful finger into his large bronze-coloured box, and then he sharpens up his head, throws himself backward in his chair, and stammers at a joke or pun with an inward sort of utterance

ere he can give it speech, till his tongue becomes a sort of packman's strop, turning it over and over till at last it comes out whetted as keen as a razor; and expectation, when she knows him, wakens into a sort of danger as bad as cutting your throat. But he is a good sort of fellow, and if he offends it is innocently done. Who is not acquainted with Elia, and who would believe him otherwise? As soon as the cloth is drawn, the wine and he become comfortable; his talk now doubles and trebles into a combination, a repetition, urging the same thing over and over again, till at last he leaves off with scarcely a "good-night" in his mouth, and disappears, leaving his memory like a pleasant ghost hanging about his vacant chair. And there is his sister Bridget, a good sort of woman, though her kind cautions and tender admonitions are nearly lost upon Charles, who, like an undermined river bank leans carelessly over his jollity, and receives the gentle lappings of the waves of women's tongues unheedingly till it ebbs, and then, in the same careless posture, sits and receives it again.

Of another jovial wit, J. H. Reynolds, Clare says:

He was the most good-natured fellow I ever met with. His face was the three-in-one of fun, wit and punning personified. He would punch you with his puns very keenly without ever hurting your feelings, for if you looked in his face you could not be offended, and you might retort as you pleased—nothing could put him out of humour, either with himself or others. . . . He sits as a careless listener at table, looking on with quick knapping sort of eye, that turns towards you as quick as lightning when he has a pun, joke or story to give you. They are never made up or studied; they are the flashes of the moment, and mostly happy. He is a slim sort of make, something, as you may conceive, of an unpretending sort of fashionable fellow without the desire of being one. He has a plump, round face, a nose something puggish, and a forehead that betrays more of fun than poetry. His teeth are always looking through a laugh that sits as easy on his unpuckered lips as if he were born laughing. He is a man of genius, and if his talents was properly applied I believe he would do something. . . . He carries none of the Author about him. An hearty laugh, which there is no resisting, at his jokes and puns, seems to be more recompense than he expected, and he seems startled into wonder at it, and muses a moment as if he turned the joke over agen in his mind to find the "merry thought" which made the laughter. They drop, as it were, spontaneously from his mouth, and turn agen upon him before he has had time to consider whether they are good or bad. He sits in a sort of surprise till another joke drops and makes him himself again.

Reynolds' impression of Clare, though less colourful, shows as much perception as Clare's of him. He was, he says, "a quiet and worthy, yet enthusiastic man", guileless yet suspicious, a true observer of nature, "but a man alive to more . . . than town apprehensions."

Hazlitt was very different from the cheerful Lamb and Reynolds.

> He sits a silent picture of severity. If you was to watch his face for a month you would not catch a smile there. . . . When he enters a room, he comes stooping, with his eyes in his hand, as it were, throwing under-gazes round at every corner as if he smelt a dun or a thief ready to seize him by the collar and demand his money or his life. He is a middle-sized, dark-looking man, and his face is deeply lined with satirical character. . . . For the blood of me I could not find him out—that is, I should have had no guess at him, of his ever being a scribbler, much more a genius.

It is to be doubted whether the subjects of these thumb-nail sketches realised how keenly they were being studied, nor what sure estimates Clare was forming. As a poet, they all recognised his genius, but as a man, they were inclined to under-estimate his wit and shrewdness—a tendency which is shown by Hood's remarks upon him in his *Literary Reminiscences*:

> In his bright, grass-coloured coat and yellow waistcoat (there are greenish stalks too, under the table) he looks a very Cowslip, and blooms amongst us as Goldsmith must have done in his peach-blossom. . . . It must have been at such a time when Hilton *conceived* his clever portrait of C——, when he was "C in alt". He was hardy, rough, and clumsy enough to look truly rustic—like an Ingram's rustic chair. There was a slightness about his frame, with a delicacy of features and complexion, that associated him more with the garden than the Field, and made him look the Peasant of a Ferme Ornee. . . . There was much about Clare for a Quaker to like; he was tender-hearted and averse to violence. How he recoiled once, bodily taking his chair with him—from a young surgeon, or surgeon's friend, who let drop, somewhat abruptly, that he was just come "from seeing a child skinned!"—Clare, from his look of horror, evidently thought that the poor infant, like Marsyas, had been flayed *alive*! He was both gentle and simple.

Hood says that the doorkeeper of the Soho bazaar was so suspicious of Clare's rustic dress that he hesitated to admit him, and that one night, when they dined at Wainewright's, Clare was last in ascending the stairs and the "gentleman's gentleman" tried to shut him out as an interloper.

The one of all the party who was perhaps Clare's best friend, and with whom he afterwards stayed at Chiswick, was H. F. Cary. He had taken Holy Orders, and there is an amusing story about the comments that Clare made to him on parsons at dinner one night, but the poet's dislike of the race did not prevent his having a sincere affection for the individual.

> And there sits Cary, the translator of Dante, one of the most quiet, amiable and unassuming of men. He will look round the table in a peaceful silence on all the merry faces, in all the vacant unconcernment imaginable, and then he will brighten up and look smilingly on you and me and our next-hand neighbour, as if he knew not which to address first—and then perhaps he drops a few words like a chorus that serve all together. His eyes are not long on a face. He looks you into a sort of expectation of discoursing, and starts your tongue on tiptoe to be ready in answering what he may have to start upon, when suddenly he turns from you to throw the same good-natured cheat of a look on others. He is a tallish, spare man, with a longish face and a good forehead; his eyes are the heavy-lidded sort, whose earnest look seems to meet you half closed. His authorship and his priesthood sit upon him very meekly. He is one of those men which have my best opinions and of whom I feel happy with every opportunity to praise.

Then there was Allan Cunningham, who "when the company's talk is of poetry, he is ready to talk two ways at once, but when puns are up his head is down over his glass, musing and silent", and Wainewright, who "wears a quizzing-glass, and makes an excuse for the ornament by complaining of bad eyes".

During the two days which Clare spent with Cary at Chiswick, they visited Richmond together to see the grave of Thomson, whose *Seasons* had delighted Clare at an early age. Cary described a dinner at his house which Lamb and Kelly attended:

> . . . With the cheese had been placed on the table a jug of prime ale imported for the especial use of Clare. As the servant was removing the glasses, Clare followed him with his eye, let his own glass go without a sign of displeasure; but when the jug was about to follow, it was more than he could bear and he stretched out both his hands to stop it; the tankard was enough for him and he could dispense with the refinement of a glass.

Clare left London sooner than he had intended, as he received disquieting news from Helpston, where Patty, who was expecting another baby, was very far from well. He had a last carousal with Bennion on the Sunday night, and then got the coach back to Stamford.

The visit had been a tremendous experience for him and had brought him into contact with several very fine intellects; he had made a lot of acquaintances and a few friends, and took back to Helpston much that he could ponder over.

The "Londoners", although many of them had but an imperfect understanding of him, seem to have felt that here was a rare being whose simplicity was a pearl of great price—in which, indeed, they were perfectly right—and they were afraid that too much company of a more sophisticated kind would spoil him.

Wainwright wrote:

> One word at parting, John Clare. . . . I have known jovial nights, felt deeply the virtues of the grape and the barley-corn . . . and yet I say to thee visit London seldom, shutting close thy ears in the abounding company of empty scoffers; ever holding it in thy inmost soul that love and perfect trust, not doubt, is the germ of *true* poetry.

And C. A. Elton said in a verse letter written some time later, which he called "The Idler's Epistle to J. Clare":

> I would not have a mind like thine
> Thy artless childhood tastes resign,
> Jostle in mobs, or sup and dine
> Its powers away,
> And after noisy pleasures pine
> Some distant day.

14

HELPSTON AGAIN

CLARE ARRIVED HOME TO FIND that another daughter had been born on 13th June. Patty was so ill as to cause considerable anxiety for a few days, and Mrs. Emmerson, who was to be godmother to the baby, wrote in some alarm after receiving a letter from Clare, "I hope in God for your sake, and for the sake of your dear Children, that all danger is over and that she is now in a fair way to be speedily restored to you." The baby was christened Eliza Louisa after her god-mother, who sent her a silver cup and other presents, and Lord Radstock offered himself as the other godparent.

We learn a little more about Clare's stay in London from letters written in the latter half of June. On the 19th, Taylor wrote to his father:

> I have only just lost my visitor Clare—he went back last Sunday evening,—apparently very much gratified with his visit.—He was excellent Company while he staid, but a little too much elated with a glass of Ale if you indulged him in it.—He saw all our literary Ac-quaintance, and kept his ground with all of them. He could not pun, but then he had such a Fund of Good Sense and so many shrewd Remarks to make on what anyone said,—besides his Judgment of Books was so very sound,—that let what would be the Subject of Conversation he was always well worth listening to.

On the 28th, Bennion—the porter at Taylor and Hessey's, wrote to Clare:

> . . . I hope my dear fellow you got safe home, as the sunday night we parted we where both quite fresh, and hope you felt no ill effects from what we had the day we parted.

He followed this, on 21st July, with an epistle which made up in entertainment what it lacked in grammar:

> I received your letter and was happy to hear you got safe home, as i was very uneasy till i heard from Mrs E——, you know who i mean;

she told me she had heard from you and that you had got a daughter. She commenced her conversation in the usall Theatrical Manner respecting you, first by enquiring if you had not disgraced yourself very much the night you dine with the contributer of the London Mag, and if you had not given great offence to the Revd. Mr. C——by saying you wished the churches where all in ashes and the parson's sent to beg their bread. I told her i did not hear you say it, and if you did some excuse was to be made for you, as you might be a little fresh; i told her that Mr C was on very good terms with you so i was sure that he was not offended. She said she heard you was very D—; i told her it was not so, you was very Merry. She said she had heard all this from a friend that you had told, and that she was very sorry to think you was so strong a deist; i told her you was but a very little inclined to deisem. I found out who this friend was before i left her—its Mr R——. You'll know who i mean, so you'll be on your guard, if you write to him, of what you say, as its sure to go to her. . . . i have a goodeal to say when we meet again, but let me beg on you to be cautious what you say to Mr R——, for it will go to Mrs E—— and L—d R——, so mind your Ps and Q.

But, before Clare read Bennion's cryptic references to Rippingille's disclosures, he had confessed to Mrs. Emmerson about his carousal on the night he left London, and she had already written to reprove and to beg him "for your own and your dear Children's sake arm yourself with a determination, a fortitude which would do honour to your excellent heart and good understanding, to fly from such mode of consolation, from a poison that will quickly destroy you".

Clare was corresponding with several of the Londoners during the autumn; he sent copies of his books to Charles Lamb, who wrote back:

I am an inveterate old Londoner, but while I am among your choice collections, I seem to be native to them, and free of the country. [He thought Clare was too liberal with his provincial phrases:] Now and then a home rusticism is fresh and startling, but where nothing is gained in expression, it is out of tenor. [He sent Clare two of his own volumes, and concluded his letter:] Since I saw you I have been in France, and have eaten frogs. The nicest little rabbity things you ever tasted. Do look about for them. Make Mrs. Clare pick off the hind quarters, boil them plain, with parsley and butter. The fore-quarters are not so good. She may let them hop off by themselves.

Towards the end of August, Clare again fell into low spirits, which continued throughout the autumn and winter. A fever of some sort was raging in the fen country, and he and all his family were attacked by it. He was also worrying about his financial affairs and wanted an account from Taylor and Hessey which the firm were too dilatory or too unbusinesslike to produce. On the back of a letter from Hessey in October he wrote:

> Mem: My sallaries from Lord Spencer and the Funds have not been separately mentioned this year from the other monies I asked for and it has puzzled me which to account for as those sums, but I have had not a single farthing more than is here mentioned in these letters from which my sallaries must be deducted.
>
> Mem: Never had anything for the writing for the Magazine as yet accounted for, tho' a year and a half, and to prevent mistakes I have set down the money sent for independant of the fund money and sallary as "Credit", from which the Magazine money must be deducted.

In fact, Clare never did receive payment for his contributions to *The London Magazine*, although each number, at that time, contained several of his poems.

One that he wrote during the winter was a sonnet dedicated to Bennion, but the latter wrote to him on 13th January, 1823:

> . . . i must now thank you for the honour conferd on mee by wishing to see mee in print; this i new nothing off till a short time ago i chanced to see a Sonnet dedicated to me from you, i suppose it to be intended for the pages of the L—— Mag, but i must never think of its making its appearance, that will be too great a honour for me of course.

Apparently Bennion had, on occasion, tried his hand at verses, but he said, "i can never satisfy myself with what i doo, so that I commit them to the fire in their young days".

Taylor and Hessey were late in paying Clare the dividend from the Fund money, and consequent straitened circumstances encouraged the "blue devils" that troubled him. He evidently wrote to Mrs. Emmerson in despairing tones, for a letter from her, written in January, bids him to "Suffer not these fantasies of the brain to induce you, even in jest, to speak of self-annihilation".

But, in spite of poverty and depression, Clare was still hard at work; among other things, he was engaged, just then, on "The Parish", a long satirical poem, and also on "The Recruiting

Party". Of the former, which was not finished until considerably later, Clare said:

> This poem was begun and finished under the pressure of heavy distress, with embittered feelings under a state of anxiety and oppression almost amounting to slavery—when the prosperity of one class was founded on the adversity and distress of the other. . . . But better times and better prospects have opened a peace establishment of more sociable feelings and kindness and to no one upon earth do I owe ill will.

He saw Henderson fairly frequently, with whom he enjoyed discussing botanical questions and problems of his garden, and he visited him and Artis at Milton about Christmas-time, but for the most part he was confined to the society of the villagers, and found them a poor exchange for the lively intellectuals in whose company he had passed his time while in London. At the end of January he wrote to Taylor:

> I am windbound in my sooty corner, drinking now and then a pot of misnamed medley as nigh Ale as shadow is to substance, small beer's sad reality, or now and then seeking the "Bell" to be cheered up with the silence of company who sleep all day with their eyes open or only [wake] to howl about the times. Books and authors are as dark and unknown things as if they inhabited the bottom of the sea.

In February, *The London Magazine* published a feature called "The Literary Police Office, Bow Street", written by Reynolds, in which various writers of the day were reported as having been put on trial for absurd offences. Clare received a paragraph in it:

> John Clare (a comely-looking man, in a smock frock, and face to match) appeared to resist an order of filiation, made on the affidavit of one of the Muses with whom he had kept company, and who appeared to have been too liberal of her favours to him. The oath being persisted in, his innocence stood him in no stead; and he was ordered to set apart half-a-crown, out of sixpence-a-day, to support the child. He pleaded poverty; but the magistrates explained to him that a poor soldier had been known to have managed such an allowance, and therefore they resisted his plea. Clare is said to have a wife and ten little children all under the age of four years, which makes his case more reprehensible.

9

But *The London*, though it might twit Clare so good-naturedly, was not proving a friend to him, for it not only published his poems without payment, but it took up so much of Taylor's time, that he had little left in which to attend to Clare, and although he had now written a fair number of the poems for his next book, nothing had as yet been done about editing them.

This neglect, together with another reason, caused Lord Radstock to take up the cudgels again, and on 12th March he wrote to Clare:

> You have long known my opinion of T—— The more I hear of him the more am I convinced that opinion was well founded—in a word that it is his determined resolution to keep you in Bondage and Obscurity so long as he has the power of so doing. Now if these vile and ignominious chains be not speedily broken the fault will not be mine.

Radstock's other grievance was that the Revd. W. Allen, whom he had met while staying with Lord Kenyon, had written a critique on Clare's poetry, in the form of four letters which had been sent to Taylor with the proposal that they might be published in *The London Magazine*, and Taylor, after keeping them for several days, had returned them to Lord Radstock with a polite refusal; it would be pointless, he said, as the letters would only be read by those who already had the poems.

The Admiral was determined that Allen's very excellent and discerning articles should be published, and he and Mrs. Emmerson, after approaching John Murray without success, paid the cost of having them published in book form by Hatchard and Son. Apparently Taylor refused even to mention the book among the new publications which were listed in the magazine, which makes it evident, if it was not so already, that he was merely being obstructive out of pique with Lord Radstock. Hessey wrote to Clare some time later and said that Taylor's refusal to publish the letters was due to the fact that he felt it would have looked too much like puffing their own productions, and would have done more harm than good; but the publisher had had no such feelings with regard to his own article on Clare in October, 1821, which might easily have been criticised on the same grounds.

Cary wrote in April and paid a sincere tribute to Clare's poetry: "You must surely have something better than fenny flats about you; or else where do all the fine things come from that get into your verses. Do not wish for a residence near London. You would ere long have cause to wish yourself away again."

Clare still received letters from a number of strangers who wrote to praise his poetry, though he was not now troubled, as he had once been, by curious visitors. One letter that he received about this time must have given him some amusement; it came from a man called Roberts, of Moulton, near Spalding, and eight pages were written in the most pompous style imaginable. It began:

> Out of the abundant store of your inimitable condescension graciously deign to pardon the bold assurance and presumptuous liberty of an animated mass of undistinguished dust, whose fragile composition is most miraculously composed of congenial atoms so promiscuously concentred as to personify in an abstracted degree the beauteous form of man, to convey by proxy to your brilliant opthalmic organs the sincere thanks of a mild gentle and grateful heart for the delightful amusement I have experienced and the instruction I have reaped by reading your excellent poems in several of which you have exquisitely given dame nature her natural form, and delineated her in colour so admirable that on the perusal of them I was led to exclaim with extacy "Clare everywhere excels in the descriptive".

The letter ended with an invitation to Clare to go and stay, which, if his "opthalmic organs" ever got to the eighth page, he cannot have felt any great urge to accept.

In the spring of 1823 Clare, full of remorse for past excesses, was resolving to shun the temptation of strong ale, for he realised the harm that it was doing to his weak constitution as well as the distress it caused his family and the drain on his purse which he could not afford.

In April or early May he wrote to Mrs. Emmerson about quite a different matter that had been troubling him—an affair of the heart, though whether it was his abiding love for Mary or some new and transient affection there is no means of telling; his letter has never come to light, and there is only Mrs. Emmerson's reply to tell us of it:

> And so you have been love-sick of late!—at variance with the world about a silly fickle woman—What says your dear Patty to this? but she need have no fears of your integrity of heart towards her—I honour your sentiments upon this point—And for all else she must

be liberal towards you and remember that her husband is a poet and that he must have his idols of the mind as well as of the heart! besides first impressions will linger about us even after the spell be broken: —and thus it is, we remain the slaves of feeling, tho' but in degree; for there are shades in love as there are in colours. You tell me you are now "recovering apace"—I am happy to hear it and pray do be content with one fair she—and leave all the rest of our sex to wander where they will except it be the loves of your imagination.

Certainly Clare knew that his love for Mary was something of an entirely different nature from that which he felt for Patty, and Mrs. Emmerson's startlingly percipient letter, with its remarks about "idols of the mind" and "shades in love", may well mean that Clare had made one of his very rare references to that hidden love. The loss of his letter arouses tormenting speculations as to the valuable information that it might have contained, for we know that he was still writing poems to Mary and that over the years his love for her was undergoing a change, was being transfigured into something ethereal, so that she eventually became for him an image of perfection far above and beyond mere woman; but he never spoke of her until years afterwards when she became the centre of his delusions, and so the course of his love during these middle years can only be traced by a hint here and there, by his later writings, and by the tone of his poems.

In June, Mrs. Emmerson wrote to tell Clare that Allen's critique was out, and also to say that she was sending "a few trifles for the dear Children" which she hoped Patty would make up at once.

There are four pieces of coloured muslin for 4 frocks—and a bit of striped white muslin for 2 more for Sunday ones—also a little cambric muslin to make them 4 petticoats—My dear Clare will also find in the parcel a couple of waistcoat pieces and the lining for them— which I beg him to accept and wear for my sake, wishing him health to set him off to advantage.

In July, Clare's elder child, Anna, became very ill with measles, and he, who was the fondest of fathers and could not bear to see a child suffer, was beside himself with anxiety. He relieved his feelings, as always, with a poem, which he addressed "To Anna Three Years Old", and in it he pictured her in health, running about in the fields, as happy and carefree as the bees and butterflies.

Thou'lt leave my hand with eager speed
The new discovered things to see—
The old pond with its water weed
And danger-daring willow tree,
Who leans an ancient invalid
O'er spots where deepest waters be.

In sudden shout and wild surprise
I hear thy simple wonderment,
As new things meet thy childish eyes
And wake some innocent intent. . . .

But thou art on the bed of pain,
So tells each poor forsaken toy.
Ah, could I see that happy hour
When these shall be thy heart's employ,
And see thee toddle o'er the plain,
And stoop for flowers, and shout for joy.

For three days the child's life was in grave danger, and when she showed the first signs of some improvement Clare, still under the shadow of the fears that he had felt for her, wrote to Taylor "my heart cannot forget aching tho' this morning has found her so much better".

In the same month, Clare lost a good friend by the death of Gilchrist, who was only forty-four. There had always been a hearty welcome for the poet at his house at Stamford, and he was one of the few people in the neighbourhood with whom Clare could talk over his work and the things he was reading. Drury had lately moved to Lincoln, and Clare was thus bereft of two of his literary friends within a short time.

Taylor, whose letters had lately become very rare, wrote:

Poor Gilchrist! I was indeed much shocked when I heard of his Death—for I never thought him in so very dangerous a State, and when I called upon him last January I encouraged him to hope for a perfect Recovery this Summer. He is recovered, I hope, for he has lost now all taint of human Infirmity. You say you have no very clear Notions on this point. I confess that I am satisfied—for I cannot persuade that Spirit which I feel within me that we die utterly when we go hence—and if not, where do we go? Somewhere to be either more happy or more miserable than we are here.

Towards the end of July, Clare faltered in his resolution to avoid the alehouse, but he wrote afterwards to Mrs. Emmerson in a

state of remorse, and she praised his honesty but reminded him
of the harm that he would do his health.

Bennion sent news from Fleet Street of the "Londoners'"
dinners, which, he said "are perfectly harmless i can assure you,
for i don't think their as been so much mirth prevaild among
them as when you was in London".

Taylor managed to tear himself away from his editorial duties
long enough to write to Clare that he would be agreeable to the
publication of another volume that winter, in which they could
include the poems that had been printed in the magazine. He had
been discussing it with Hessey, and they thought that it would be a
good idea to call it "The Shepherd's Calendar" and arrange it
according to the months of the year.

15

TREATMENT BY DR. DARLING

CLARE WAS BUSY IN THE HAR-
vest fields during August and September, and had little time for
writing. He heard from Hessey the news that Bloomfield was
dead, and bitterly regretted that he had never been able to make
the journey to see him, for he admired him both as poet and man.
He wrote three sonnets to his memory, one of which was published
in *The Rural Muse*.

In the same letter Hessey sent a more cheering piece of news. A
rich West Indian, Sir Michael Benignus Clare, had sent five
guineas to the publishers to be passed on to the poet who shared
his name.

Clare was hard at work with his poetry again as soon as the
harvest was over, and in October he sent to London the MS.
volume of poems for the proposed "Shepherd's Calendar".
Hessey liked some of them, but said that others would not do as
they were too much like what he had written before. He thought
they were deficient in human interest, and suggested a number of
subjects which Clare might write upon—the country festivals,
customs, and superstitions—into which little stories might be
woven. Hessey added to this rather crushing reception of the
poems a complaint that Clare did not take enough pains over "the
mechanical operation of writing".

Clare was not in a state to take rebuffs lightly, and the attitude
of his publishers towards the new volume discouraged him so
much, that he talked of abandoning the project, but Hessey, who,
since Taylor had taken on his editorial work, had been doing most
of the business correspondence for the firm, wrote that he must not
think of giving up.

It was evidence of Clare's distressed condition that he, who had
always been courageous in the face of difficulties, should contemplate surrendering to them. He was once more in the grip of a
terrible depression, and in November Mrs. Emmerson was writing
to sympathise with him for his "fiery torments" and for "this

'troublesome nothing which haunts you', this abiding shadow of misery".

On 6th January, 1824, Clare's first son was born and was christened Frederick. Mrs. Emmerson wrote: "May he indeed be ignorant of his father's cares and too tender feelings—but may he be bless'd (as his brightest dower) with his father's genius."

The New Year saw no improvement in Clare's health. Taylor consulted his own physician, Dr. Darling, who had attended Keats and a number of other poets and artists, and from the description of the symptoms he prescribed some pills. Lady Milton told Henderson to communicate with Mr. Walker, an apothecary of Peterborough, and send him to see Clare, and he was also visited, a few weeks later, by Dr. Arnold of Stamford, who had treated him for his fits some years before.

Taylor wrote on 24th February to suggest that Clare should come to London again and see Dr. Darling, or that, if he preferred, he should get the advice of a local man whose fees Taylor expressed himself willing to pay. He had not yet read through the MSS. which Clare had sent up four months before, but he was "getting forward with them". If Clare remembered that Taylor had once talked of publishing the book this winter he was probably beyond feeling either disappointment or exasperation.

At about this time Clare wrote a long letter to Taylor, telling him of the spiritual troubles that he had met with, and overcome, and the faith to which, after much thought, and many doubts, he had found his way.

I have felt as bad as ever since I wrote you but now I think I feel improving again. I think the doctors none of them know the real cause of my complaint; I feel now a numbness all over me, just as I should suppose a person to feel when bitten by a serpent, and I firmly believe I shall never get over it. Be it as it will, I am resigned for the worst; my mind is placid and contented, and that is something, for when I was first took, God forgive me, I had hard work to bare up with my malady and often had the thought of destroying myself. From this change in my feelings I satisfactorily prove that Religious foundation is truth and that the Mystery that envelopes it is a power above human nature to comprehend, and thank God it is, for if a many uneasy discontented minds knew of the bargain they should gain by being good they might still be discontented and I might be one of them. Besides, there is little merit in undergoing a hardship for a prize when we know what it is. . . . True Religion amounts to this—if a man turns to God with real sincerity of heart, not canting

and creeping to the eyes of the world, but satisfying his own conscience so that it shall not upbraid him in the last hours of life, that
touch-stone of faith and practice, careless of what the world may say
either for him or against him, that man, in my opinion, is as certain
of Heaven in the next world as he is of death in this.

Convinced, now, of the existence of a future world and the hope
that all men may hold because of the mercy of God, Clare sought
to find answers to some of the lesser problems that troubled him,
and he wrote sometimes to Taylor or to Hessey about passages
of the Bible which he found difficult to understand. He found that
St. James on the subject of 'Faith and Works' introduced new ideas
to him and overturned his former notions, so he questioned Hessey,
who replied that he "thanked St. James for undeceiving" Clare
if he had previously thought that "a man might do what he pleased
so that he did but believe".

At this time he was seeking, too, to find a religious community
to which he might belong with more enthusiasm than he was able
to feel for the Church of England, whose members he considered
too prone to cant and humbug. He contemplated joining the
Ranters,[1] and Taylor advised him that he did right "to get real
practical Religion wherever it can be found". Clare said that he
believed them to be simple and sincere Christians, with more zeal
than knowledge; "Their affection for each other, their earnest
though simple extempore prayers, puts my dark unsettled
conscience to shame."

Clare's long illness was marked by that periodicity to which the
spirit of man—and particularly of the artist—is subject, and there
were days when his despair ebbed from him and he was able to
look to the future and think about his work. In such a mood he
wrote to Taylor that he had decided it would be best if he published nothing for eight or ten years, during which he intended
to try "the Drama in pastoral and tragic pictures" and a hundred
sonnets as a set of pictures. In these days of respite from illness
and depression he turned, too, to his great love, Nature, and
Martin tells how he would disobey the doctor's injunctions by
going for long walks in the fields and woods which exhausted
what little strength he had and several times caused a relapse.

But soon afterwards Clare was again writing about his conviction that death was near, and he asked Woodhouse to send him
a will form; this he filled up, making provision for his wife and

[1] Primitive Methodists who had seceded from the Wesleyan Methodists.

children by the interest from the Fund-money, and leaving £10 to his sister (who was now married), and four shillings a week to his parents out of the copyright of his works. He expressed the wish that Taylor should edit his remains, for "he was one of the first friends I met, and I wish to leave him one of my last".

Mrs. Emmerson, who was herself suffering from depression and nervous disorders, wrote frequent long letters in which she made every effort to cheer and encourage Clare, telling him that his illness was nothing serious, that perhaps it resulted from "some slight obstruction of the Liver", and that "all these sad feelings may have been induced by your late anxietys in the service of your darling Muse".

Bennion also wrote in March to send Clare an account of the latest dinner for the contributors of *The London*, which had been attended by only two of the party with whom Clare had dined—Reynolds and Phillips.

> Those two where the chief sport of the party, indeed i may say the verry life and soul of it after dinner, and you was mentioned twice or thrice during the night. Your old friend Elia was prevented from being one of the party thro' being ill, but he is better, but there wanted him and you and then there would have been more mirth among them.

Although Dr. Arnold sent Taylor an encouraging report of Clare's health, the poet wrote desperately to Hessey in April that he was no better, indeed that his memory was "worse and worse, nearly lost", and that his sight was very bad. The sensation "as if cold water was creeping all about my head" was, he said, less frequent, but it came on sometimes in the evening when he was usually at his worst. He wanted Dr. Darling's help but hesitated to go to London in case it did him no good; he had already spent so much on doctors at home that he did not like to spend more, and he was fearful of becoming worse on the journey and not reaching his destination. He reiterated his opinion that he was suffering from an incurable complaint, but, he added, "life is sweet and I would feign get better".

Encouraged by both the Fleet Street partners and by Mrs. Emmerson, Clare at length decided that he must try Dr. Darling's treatment as the last hope of recovery, and he wrote to announce his intention of coming to town.

Towards the end of May he made the journey by the Stamford

coach—now quite familiar—and was met at "The George and Blue Boar", Holborn, by Tom Bennion, who conducted him to Fleet Street.

Clare remarked that, this being his third visit to London, "the vast magnitude of that human ant-hill that strikes every stranger with wonder had lost its novelty", but he still derived as much entertainment from watching the stream of passers-by as he had done when the sight was new to him. He would sit in the window of a ground-floor room in the Fleet Street house to watch the traffic, and it was a source of amazement and delight to him that there were so many beautiful women to be seen. De Quincey tells us that Clare was particularly fascinated by "the French style of beauty, as he saw it amongst the French actresses in Tottenham Court Road".

Dr. Darling undertook the treatment of Clare with enthusiasm and much kindness; he recommended rest, and ordered Clare not to read or write much and to abstain from anything that might cause him undue excitement. By following these directions Clare soon found an improvement in his health, but he was still in a very nervous state, and his overwrought imagination filled him with terrible fears if he went out alone at night—fears of such fiends and hobgoblins as the old women of Helpston loved to talk about, and from which, as a boy of fifteen or sixteen, he had sought refuge by telling himself stories on his journey home from Maxey with the bag of flour. He went quite frequently to dine with Mr. and Mrs. Emmerson, and this meant that to reach his bed he must go from Stratford Place to Fleet Street alone in the dark.

> I used to sit till very late because I was loath to start, not for the sake of leaving the company but for fear of meeting with supernatural [agents] even in the busy paths of London. Though I was a stubborn disbeliever of such things in the daytime, yet at night their terrors came upon me tenfold, and my head was as full of the terrible as a gossip's. Thin, death-like shadows and goblins with saucer eyes were continually shaping on the darkness from my haunted imagination; and when I saw anyone of a spare figure in the dark, passing or going on by my side, my blood has curdled cold at the foolish apprehensions of his being a supernatural agent, whose errand might be to carry me away at the first dark alley we came to.

Clare had a particular dread of the dark and narrow Chancery Lane, and one night, convinced that he would "meet death or the devil" if he went down it, he tried to reach Fleet Street by some other way and got hopelessly lost in the attempt. He offered a watchman a shilling to show him the way, but the man demanded half a crown, which Clare gave him.

Mrs. Emmerson wrote to Patty on 31st May to tell her that she had seen Clare and that his health had gradually improved since his arrival in London: "His poor head is still at times much oppressed—but I have no fears that under the skill of Dr. Darling he will ere many weeks be quite restored to the blessing of perfect health and to his family."

On 14th June she wrote again. Clare's spirits, she said, were "on the whole much better—he sleeps more comfortably, and his appetite and digestion are much improved".

In this letter she said:

> I am requested by your dear Husband to beg of you to go to the drawers upstairs and get my Portrait in the red Morocco case, if you do not find it in the drawers you must open the Bookcase to look for it as Clare is not certain in which of them he put it:—You will be so good as to let the Portrait be very carefully packed up in brown paper and get some friend to direct it to my [address] as below—as I am going to have it framed by your Husband's request that it may hang up in your cottage.

It would be interesting to know what Patty thought of this idea, but her opinion on this and many other subjects is unfortunately lost to us because, although she could read a little, she never learned to write. There *is* a letter at this time, written for Patty by some neighbour, but it only reported that Clare's garden was "very prosperous" and that they were all well except Anna, who had a bad eye.

As Clare's health improved he was able to go farther afield and to take an interest in seeing new people and places. He sometimes accompanied Bennion on his errands about the city, and he renewed his acquaintance with some of the "Londoners" and met others for the first time.

While visiting with Hessey one day at a house at the corner of St. Paul's Churchyard, he met William Etty, the painter, who, he says, "was a man of a reserved appearance and felt as awkwardly situated, I dare say, as myself when Mr. Vowler proposed healths and expected fine speeches in reply. For though Etty replied, he did it very shortly, and when mine was drunk I said nothing; and though the company's eyes were expecting for some minutes, I could not say a word, though I thought of some several times, and they were wishes that I was out of the house."

At Taylor's, Clare met De Quincey, "a little, artless, simple-seeming body, something of a child overgrown, in a blue coat and black neckerchief", who stole gently among the company "with a smile, turning timidly round the room"; and Coleridge, "with a venerable white head", whose words "hung in their places at a quiet pace from a drawl, in good set marching order, so that you would suppose he had learnt what he intended to say before he came".

Clare saw a good deal of Charles Elton, classical scholar and contributor to *The London Magazine*, whom he had met on his previous visit and who afterwards wrote "The Idler's Epistle to J. Clare" which has already been mentioned; and he also saw Charles Lamb, visiting his house at Islington one evening in company with Taylor and Hessey. He made the acquaintance of George Darley, the Irish poet and dramatist, some of whose work was so much imbued with the spirit of the seventeenth century that Palgrave, when compiling the *Golden Treasury*, placed a lyric of his between poems by Milton and Carew. Another literary man whom Clare now met for the first time was Harry Van Dyk, the author of a book of poems called *Theatrical Portraits*, who later undertook the work of editing *The Shepherd's Calendar* which Taylor was too busy to do.

A companion of Clare's former visit, Edward Rippingille, arrived in London while he was there, and although, on this occasion, he refrained (probably on the instructions of Mrs. Emmerson) from taking Clare to taverns and alehouses and keeping him up all night, he conducted him round certain other amusements of London, and introduced him to a number of people.

One of the entertainments to which he took Clare is of particular interest because of the profound impression that it seems to have made on him and the part that it played years afterwards when Clare was suffering from strange delusions. They went to see a fight at the Fives Court:

It was for the benefit of Oliver, and I caught the mania so much from Rip for such things that I soon became far more eager for the Fancy than himself. I watched the appearance of every new hero on the stage with as eager curiosity to see what sort of fellow he was as I had before done the poets. I left the place with one wish strongly uppermost, and that was that I was but a Lord to patronise Jones the Sailor Boy, who took my fancy as being the finest fellow in the Ring.

With Rippingille and Elton, Clare went to visit Deville, the phrenologist, who fingered the bumps on his head and told him he had a talent for poetry. "His predictions", Clare said afterwards, "are so cautiously uttered, with so many causes for the likelihood of failures in nice points, that even failings themselves in his lectures strike as convictions." He made a cast of Clare's head, and Martin tells a story, which is amusing but apocryphal, that Clare, not liking to be buried in plaster, "ran away in the midst of it with the loss of a portion of his skin".

Rippingille also took Clare to the house of Sir Thomas Lawrence, whom the poet thought "a very polite, courteous and kind man". Prince Leopold was going in to sit for his portrait when they arrived at the door, so they walked about in the Square until they saw him depart. Rippingille then sent in his card, and they were taken up to the gallery where, after a few minutes, Lawrence joined them. He shook Clare by the hand and asked him several questions about himself, and he then complimented Rippingille on his picture "Breakfast at an Inn", telling him in a friendly manner what he thought to be its faults. He showed them his pictures, and talked for some time, and when they were leaving he took them into another room to show Clare "a brother poet"— a head of Walter Scott.

> I left his house [Clare said] with the satisfied impression that I had never met with a kinder and better man than Sir T. L. and I dare say Rip was highly gratified with the praise he had received; for Sir T. told him that the Royal family, at a private view of the Exhibition before it opened to the public, took more notice of his picture than all the rest. But Rip would not own it, for he affects a false appearance in such matters.

On two or three occasions Rippingille, who seems to have been intent on playing the role of an energetic guide to London, took Clare to the French Playhouse, in Tottenham Court Road, and Clare's humorous comment is a dig at himself as well as his companion:

> None of us understood a word of French and yet we fancied ourselves delighted, for there was a very beautiful actress that took our

fancies. Rip drew a sketch of her in pencilling for me, something like her, though he stole none of her beauty to

The death of Byron had occurred at Missolonghi in A his body was brought back to England in July for b Nottinghamshire. It chanced that Clare was walking Oxford Street on his way to Mrs. Emmerson's, and saw the small crowd that had collected to watch Byron's funeral cortège as it passed through London; he was unable to discover whose funeral it was, but he guessed that it was someone very famous, and he waited with the other spectators, who by now numbered about a hundred. As the procession of some sixty carriages came into sight, a young girl who was standing beside Clare, gave a deep sign, and said: "Poor Lord Byron."

> I looked up [Clare says] in the young girl's face. It was dark and beautiful, and I could almost feel in love with her for the sigh she had uttered for the poet. It was worth all the Newspaper puffs and Magazine mournings that ever was paraded after the death of a poet. . . . The common people felt his merits and his powers, and the common people of a country are the best feelings of a prophecy of futurity. They are the veins and arterys that feed and quicken the heart of living fame; the breathings of eternity and the soul of time are indicated in that prophecy. . . . They felt by a natural impulse that the mighty was fallen, and they moved in saddened silence. The streets were lined on each side as the procession passed, but they were all the commonest of the lower orders.

Clare was deeply moved by this evidence of the regard in which the common people held Byron, and his metaphor of the "veins and arterys" shows clearly his attitude towards them. Clare was no arrogant intellectual to scorn the opinion of the great mass of ordinary men and women. In 1820 he had written to Taylor about one of his poems which was under discussion:

> . . . it [has] undergone the Criticism of my father and mother and several rustic neighbours of this town, and all approve it. You will agree that they beat you polite Critics in that low nature which you never prove but by reading.

He was always mindful of his own origin in the peasantry, and his good sense was such that he never saw cause for shame or regret in that, although his poetic gift and his superior intellect separated him from those neighbours among whom he lived all his life. Fame was not a thing that he ever coveted, but he desired passionately that his poetry might be appreciated by his own people, that some among the great multitude whose spokesman he was might hear his melodies and approve.

Clare was not a man who was ever jealous of the success of others—perhaps because of his own humility—and he did not grudge to Byron the fame which he believed that he richly deserved. He added to the many others his own tribute to Byron's "mighty genius" in the form of a sonnet—"A splendid sun hath set!"—and he ended his account of the funeral procession by saying:

> I believe that his liberal principles in religion and politics did a great deal towards gaining the notice and affections of the lower orders. Be [it] as it will, it is better to be beloved by those low and humble for undisguised honesty than flattered by the great for purchased and pensioned hypocrisies.

But it is difficult to account for Clare's preoccupation with Byron's life and work at this time, and for the part which the author of *Childe Harold* played in his delusions of after years, unless it be that Clare was—perhaps subconsciously—mortified by the contrast between Byron's fame and his obscurity. They had never met, and their lives had but touched briefly in 1821 when Byron, as a participant in the dispute between Gilchrist and Bowles, had referred to Clare in a published letter as "a deserving poet". It was strange then, that of all the men of genius whom Clare admired it should be Byron who was constantly in his troubled mind in the years of his insanity, and it is perhaps only in that note of contrast that an explanation can be found. There can hardly have been, in all the annals of literature, two men of one generation who were so wholly different.

Soon after he went home, Clare began an *Essay on Popularity*, in which he wrote about Byron, and in another brief passage on criticism he called his exploits in Greece those of an actor playing the part of hero, yet said that his infirmities were but as spots on the sun. When he heard that Byron was not to have a monument in Westminster Abbey, he wrote angrily:

> Time is his monument, on whose scroll the name of Byron shall be legible when the walls and tombs of Westminster Abbey shall have mingled with the refuse of ruins, and the sun, as in scorn, be left free again to smile upon the earth so long darkened with the pompous shadows of bigotry and intolerance.

After nearly two months in London, Clare's health and spirits were much improved and he was anxious to get home, but Dr. Darling wanted him to remain until he was entirely satisfied with his condition. On 31st July Hessey wrote to Patty:

> You need have no fear of your excellent husband having forgotten you—for many weeks past he has been very anxious to return home and nothing but the positive orders of his Doctor could have kept him in London. . . . I am happy to assure you that he is now so much better that the Dr. has given him leave to go home in the course of the next week if he continues as well as he is now. He has requested me to write for him and to enclose the sum of Fifteen Pounds which he supposes will be sufficient to pay all the Bills which he owes to the end of the last half year: but if it should not be enough he wishes you to pay a part of each, as far as it will go, and when he returns he will settle the remainder.

Clare left London on 8th August, after giving Dr. Darling his promise, that he would in future take ale or spirits only in the strictest moderation, and, if possible, would give them up entirely. He had been away from Helpston for about ten weeks, and it was with a lifting heart that he saw again the familiar church spire above the trees and the friendly landscape which was coloured with ripening corn, soon to be harvested.

> Light tawny oat-lands with a yellow blade;
> And bearded corn, like armies on parade;
> Beans lightly scorched, that still preserve their green;
> And nodding lands of wheat in bleachy brown.[1]

Whatever regrets Clare may have felt for the wit of the "Londoners" and the amusements of the city, it was here that he belonged and here that he was happiest, and as he came home at evening along the road to Helpston, far removed from the noise and bustle of Fleet Street, his keen eye and ear would have delighted in the sights and sounds of closing day, when

> Cooing sits the lonely dove,
> Calling home her absent love.
> With "Kirchup! Kirchup" 'mong the wheats,
> Partridge distant partridge greets.[2]

[1] "Summer Tints."   [2] "Summer Evening."

16

AUTUMN DAYS

From clare's letters, written after his return home, we learn that the improvement in his health was not a lasting one and that he began once more to have days of sickness and depression, alternating with periods when he was cheerful and reasonably well.

He wrote to Allan Cunningham (whom he addressed as "Brother Bard and Fellow Labourer") sending him Bloomfield's autograph and comparing the latter with Crabbe. Bloomfield he considered "our best Pastoral Poet", but "Crabbe writes about the peasantry as much like the Magistrate as the Poet. He is determined to show you their worst side: and as to their simple pleasures and pastoral feelings, he knows little or nothing about them compared to the other, who not only lived amongst them, but felt and shared the pastoral pleasures with the peasantry of whom he sung." In this letter he said: "I can scarcely tell you how I am, for I keep getting a little better and a little worse, and remaining at last just as I was. I was very bad this morning, but have recovered this evening as I generally do, and I really feel that I shall never entirely overset it."

To this Cunningham replied with some reflections on Bloomfield's work and the way it had been ignored and slighted by the public and the critics alike.

Learned men make many mistakes about the value of learning. I conceive it is chiefly valuable to a man of genius in enabling him to wield his energies with greater readiness or with better effect. But learning, though a polisher and a refiner, is not the creator. It may be the mould out of which genius stamps its coin, but it is not the gold itself. [He concluded with words of encouragement.] Keep up your heart and sing only when you feel the internal impulse, and you will add something to our poetry more lasting than any of the Peasant Bards of old England have done yet.

To Thomas Inskip, a friend of Bloomfield's, Clare wrote that he was very little better: ". . . a numbing pain lies constantly about my head and an aching void at the pit of my stomach keeps sinking me away weaker and weaker." He spoke of trying what sea air would do for him if he was no better in a few weeks' time.

On 18th September Clare wrote to Cary:

I am ill able to write or do anything else. I thought I was getting well once, but I've not a hope left me now. I have employed myself when able, since I came home, at writing my own life, which, if I live to finish it, I should like to trouble you to read it and give your opinion of it; for my own judgment in such matters is very often faulty.

Mrs. Emmerson's first letter after Clare's departure from London told of the sad end of the cast which De Ville had made of Clare's head, and which the poet had apparently given to her:

On Monday evening I was returning some books into my bookcase on the top of which I had placed your cast from "De Ville"; on shutting the door of the bookcase the bust suddenly fell upon my poor shallow pate and made a severe cut on one side of it, luckily it bled freely but I have suffered at times ever since very distressing pains inside my head. However I may regret the wound you have given me I still more regret the destruction of the cast for it was shivered to atoms by the fall.

Clare kept in close touch with Dr. Darling during the autumn, writing to him about his symptoms and receiving from him pills, prescriptions, and injunctions as to his diet.

In addition to his anxiety about his health, Clare was worried about his financial affairs, and it was a constant struggle to manage on his slender income. The dividend from the Fund-money, which had at first amounted to £18 15s. per annum, had fallen in 1823 to £15 15s. which meant that when the payments from Earl Spencer and the Marquis of Exeter were added Clare still had only £40 a year. In order to keep his parents, wife, and three children, he must augment this sum either by his poetry or by field-labour, but for nearly a year he had been prevented by illness from doing any manual work and he had had additional expenses in the way of doctors' bills. His payment for his poems still came to him in the form of an occasional £5 from Taylor when things were particularly difficult, and he had had no account either for *Poems Descriptive* or *The Village Minstrel*, so that he did not know whether he had a credit or a debt outstanding with his publishers.

But Clare's anxieties did not impair his creative energy, and the phase of being almost unable to write, of which he had complained in his letter to Cary, passed quickly. He worked furiously during the autumn and winter, reading, writing poetry, and working at his autobiography; he also wrote a number of essays, some literary criticism, and a natural history of Helpston in the form of letters to Hessey, as well as keeping a diary in which he noted down his opinions of what he read, his day-to-day activities, and the thoughts that occupied his busy mind.

The autobiography, which Clare asked Cary to read, has unfortunately disappeared, and there only remain certain fragments which are probably part of the original draft, but the letters on natural history, which are beautifully written and of great interest, remain and must surely be published one day; the diary, too, is luckily intact, and gives a very detailed account of the year from September 1824 to September 1825.

In the journal entries for early September, Clare mentions that he has read Foxe's *Book of Martyrs*, and Walton's *Compleat Angler*. On the former he comments:

> The great moral precepts of a meek and unoffending teacher were: "Do as ye would be done unto", and "love those that hate you". If religious opinions had done so, her history had been worthy praise.

Of Walton's book he says that the descriptions are

> simply true, and like the Pastoral Ballads of Bloomfield, breathe of the common air and the grass and the sky. One may almost hear the water of the river Lea ripple along and the grass and flags grow and rustle in the pages that speak of it.

> Friday 10 Sept. My health would permit me to do nothing more than take walks in the garden today. What a sadly pleasing appearance gardens have at this season. The tall, gaudy hollihock with its melancholy blooms stands bending to the wind and bidding the summer farewell, while the low Asters in their Pied lustre of red white and blue bend beneath in pensive silence as tho' they mused over the days gone by and were sorrowful. The swallows are flocking

together in the sky, ready for departing, and a crowd has dropt to rest on the walnut tree, where they twitter as if they were telling their young stories of their long journey, to cheer and check their fears.

Sat. 11 Sept. Written an Essay today "on the sexual system of plants" and began one on "The Fungus tribe" and "Mildew, Blight, etc." intended for "A Natural History of Helpston" in a series of Letters to Hessey, who will publish it when finished. I did not think it would cause me such trouble or I should not have begun it. . . .

In subsequent entries Clare recorded that he had been reading the Book of Genesis, the poems of Chatterton, and the sonnets of Shakespeare, "which are great favourites of mine".

On 16th September, he had a visit from Henderson, who brought him Byron's *Don Juan*.

I was very ill and nursing my head in my hand, but he revived me and advised me to read *Don Juan*. We talked about books and flowers and Butterflies till noon. . . .

On the 20th, Helpston was the scene of a gipsy wedding, which Clare had never known before, and he wrote a song for the occasion as Israel Smith and his bride were both old friends—doubtless from the days when Clare, just back from his militia service, had sought the company of the gipsies in preference to that of the villagers, and had gained a bad name for it.

Wed. 22 Sept. Very ill and did nothing but ponder over a future existence and often brought up the lines to my memory said to be uttered by an unfortunate nobleman when on the brink of it, ready to take the plunge:

> "In doubt I lived, in doubt I dye,
> Nor shrink the dark abyss to try,
> But undismayed I meet eternity."

The first line is natural enough, but the rest is a rash courage in such a situation.

Thurs. 23 Sept. A wet day; did nothing but nurse my illness— could not have walked out had it been fine. Very disturbed in conscience about the troubles of being forced to endure life and dye by inches, and the anguish of leaving my children, and the dark porch of eternity whence none returns to tell the tale of their reception.

Sunday 26 Sept. Took a walk in the fields; heard the harvest Cricket and shrewmouse uttering their little clicking Songs among the crackling stubbles. The latter makes a little earpiercing noise not unlike a feeble imitation of the skylark.

Friday 8 Oct. Very ill and very unhappy—my three children are all unwell. Had a dismal dream of being in hell—this is the third time I have had such a dream. As I am more and more convinced that I cannot recover I will make a memorandum of my temporal concerns, for next to the Spiritual they ought to come and be attended to for the sake of those left behind. . . .

Clare's memorandum contained instructions, that if any of his letters were published after his death the names of people still living should be left blank and all objectionable passages should be omitted. Mrs. Emmerson might, if she wished, publish any of his manuscripts which were in her possession, and he expressed his intention of making Mr. Emmerson an executor of his new will.

I wish to lye on the North side of the Churchyard, just about the middle of the ground where the Morning and Evening Sun can linger the longest on my Grave. I wish to have a rough unhewn stone, something in the form of a mile stone, so that the playing boys may not break it in their heedless pastimes, with nothing more on it than this Inscription: "Here rest the hopes and ashes of John Clare." I desire that no date be inserted thereon, as I wish it to live or dye with my poems and other writings which, if they have merit with posterity, it will, and if they have not it is not worth preserving.

On Sunday, 10th October, Clare was reading the life of Savage in Johnson's *Lives of the Poets*, and commented on it:

It is a very interesting piece of biography, but the criticisms are dictated by friendship that too often forgets judgment ought to be one of the company. To leave this and turn to the Life of Gray— what a contrast! It almost makes the mind disbelieve criticism and to fancy itself led astray by the opinions of even the wisest of men. I never take up Johnson's *Lives* but I regret his beginning at the wrong end first and leaving out those beautiful minstrels of Elizabeth —had he forgot that there had been such poets as Spenser, Drayton, Suckling? But it was the booksellers' judgment that employed his pen and we know by experience that most of their judgments lye in their pockets; so the Poets of Elizabeth are still left in cobwebs and mystery. Read in the afternoon Erskine's *Evidence of Revealed Religion* and find in it some of the best reasoning in favour of its object I have ever read. . . .

The books that Clare comments on in his diary during the latter half of October are evidence of how wide and varied was his reading, and his discerning criticisms show that he read with perception and attentiveness. He read the poems of Tannahill, Elton, Coleridge, Lamb, Lloyd, Pope, and Wordsworth, and essays by Hazlitt, Knox, and Bacon. Of the latter he said: "What beautiful Essays these are! I take them up like Shakespeare and read them over and over and still find plenty to entertain me."

He read *A Midsummer Night's Dream* for the first time, and expressed the wish that he might not die before he had read all Shakespeare's plays. He wrote some more of his autobiography, gave arithmetic lessons to a lame boy in the village, worked in his garden and wandered in the fields. He noted with loving care the blooming of flowers, both wild and cultivated.

Wed. 20 October. Worked in the garden at making a shed for my Ariculas. The Michaelmas daisy is in full flower, both the lilac-blue and the white, thick-set with its little clustering stars of flowers.

Thurs. 21 Oct. . . . Took a walk in the fields—gathered a bunch of wild flowers that lingered in sheltered places as loath to dye. The ragwort still shines in its yellow clusters, and the little heath bell or harvest bell quakes to the wind under the quick banks of warm furze. Clumps of wild Marjoram are yet in flower about the mole-hilly banks, and clumps of meadow-sweet linger with a few bushes yet unfaded. . . .

Saturday 30 Oct. Received a present of two Volumes of Sermons "On the Doctrines and practice of Christianity" from Lord Radstock —he is one of my best friends and not of much kin with the world. The chrysanthemums are just opening their beautiful double flowers. I have six sorts this year—the claret colored, the buff, the bright yellow, the paper white, the purple and the rose-color; lost one—the chocolate or coffee color. Promised more from Milton. . . .

Monday 1 Nov. Took a walk to Lolham Brigs to hunt for a species of fern that used to grow on some willow tree heads in Lolham lane when I was a boy, but could find none. Got some of the yellow water lily from the pits, which the floods had washed up, to set in an old water tub in the garden and to try some on land in a swaily corner, as the horse blob thrives well which is a water flower.

Listened in the evening to Glinton bells at the top of the garden.
I always feel melancholy at this season to hear them, and yet it
is a pleasure. . . .

On 3rd November, Hessey wrote to say that he was greatly
concerned to hear that Clare was no better and was going to give
up the assistance of Dr. Darling and try other methods. Hessey
was convinced that with perseverance Clare would have entirely
recovered under the treatment of the London doctor, and he urged
him, if his own plans did not produce good results, to put himself
once more in Darling's care.

On the subject of *The Shepherd's Calendar*, Hessey said that he
and Taylor were engaged in reading through the MS. poems, but
they would have to be considerably altered before publication, as
they had been written too hastily and carelessly. He added that
they "abound too much in mere description and are deficient in
Sentiment and Feeling and human Interest". He sent a batch
of the poems for Clare to correct, with suggested amendments.

Clare noted the arrival of this letter in his diary for 7th
November:

> Received a packet from London with the Magazine and some
> copies of MSS. that come very slowly and a letter very friendly
> worded; but I have found that saying and doing is a wide difference,
> too far very often to be neighbours, much less friends. . . .

Van Dyk was also at work on the poems, but his assistance did
not seem to make the editing any quicker; it was now more than
a year since Clare had sent the MS. volume to London.

Clare had contemplated writing a life of Bloomfield with a
critical estimate of his work, and had begun to make some
inquiries as to the possibilities of it, but on 11th November he
wrote in his diary:

> Received a letter from Inskip, the friend of Bloomfield, full of
> complaints at my neglect of writing. What use is writing when the
> amount on both sides amounts to nothing more than waste paper?
> I have desires to know something of Bloomfield's latter days, but
> I can hear of nothing further than his dying neglected so it's of
> no use enquiring further, for we know that to be the common lot
> of genius.
> Monday 15 Nov. Went to gather pootys[1] on the roman bank for a

[1] Snail shells.

collection; found a scarce sort of which I only saw two in my life—one picked up under a hedge at Peakirk town-end, and another in Bainton meadow. It's color is a fine sunny yellow, larger than the common sort, and round the rim of the base is a black edging which extends no further than the rim. It is not in the collection at the British Museum. . . .

Friday 19 Nov. Had a visit from my friend Henderson, and I felt revived as I was very dull before. He had a pleasing News to deliver me, having discovered a new species of Fern a few days back, growing among the bogs on Whittlesea Mere, and our talk was of Ferns for the day.

On 22nd, Hessey wrote again to say that Clare would shortly receive

another portion of the Poems—they have been copied and are only waiting to be read over carefully with the Manuscript by Taylor and myself and then they shall be forwarded. I hope the last parcel reached you safely and that you have been well enough to revise the Manuscripts and to make such alterations as may have occurred to your Judgment. The poems which are next to be sent John tells me are better than the former and that we shall not have to propose to you so much correction.

He had seen Dr. Skrimshire, who had apparently been in London, and had discussed Clare's case with Dr. Darling. He had given "a very tolerable account" of Clare, and the two physicians had agreed in their idea of treatment.

Let me hear from you soon [Hessey continued]. I am anxious to know how you and all your little family are, and how the Poems go on, and how your Spirits are and to know something more about the snipes and the kingfishers and the lapwings and the wild fowl of the fens and meres.

There had been a fire in Fleet Street, and six or seven houses to the left of No. 93 had been burned, but after they had removed all the account books and paper and the more valuable part of the stock, the wind abated and the flames, meeting the resistance of a strong party wall, luckily came no farther.

But even this long and friendly epistle did nothing to dispel Clare's present mood of disillusionment.

Received a letter from Hessey. I have not answered his last and know not when I shall. The world's friendships are counterfeits and forgeries. On that principle I have proved it and my affections are sickened unto death. My memories are broken while my confidence is grown to a shadow. In the bringing out of the second edition of the "Minstrel" they were a twelve-month in printing a title-page.

On 27th November, Henderson sent some ferns with a boy called John, who probably lived at Helpston and worked at Milton, as he frequently carried messages between the two friends. With the ferns was a note begging Clare to come to Milton:

> It would really be an act of charity under the present circumstances —Lord Milton and family have returned from Wentworth and neither Artis nor any of the *Male* upper servants are with him, so I am entirely under pettycoat government.

Nearly three weeks elapsed before Clare paid this visit, and by then Artis had returned and was busy with his fossils and Roman antiquities. Henderson showed him his collection of ferns, and the talk was mostly of botany; Clare saw "a fine edition of Linnaeus's *Botany* with beautiful plates" and also a book on insects by Curtis.

Christmas, judging from Clare's diary, came in mild weather.

> Gathered a handful of daisies in full bloom: saw a woodbine and dogrose in the woods putting out in full leaf, and a primrose root full of ripe flowers. What a day this used to be! When a boy, how eager I used to attend the church to see it stuck with evergreens (emblems of Eternity), and the cottage windows and the picture ballads on the wall all stuck with ivy, box and yew.—Such feelings are past and "all this world is proud of".

Mrs. Emmerson, who had just returned from France, wrote at the end of December that her husband and Van Dyk were both of the opinion that Clare should have a clear statement of accounts from Taylor and Hessey, and a more definite arrangement about the publication of the new book. She advised Clare to think things over carefully and then write to the publishers, and she added that if Mr. Emmerson's intervention would do any good he would gladly do all in his power to help.

On 5th January, 1825, Clare noted that "Jillyflowers, Poly-anthuses, Marigolds, and the yellow yarrow are in flower, and the double scarlet Anemonie nearly out—crocuses peeping out above ground, swelling with flower", and two days later he was buying cakes of colour with the intention of making sketches of any rare flowers, butterflies, or snail horns that he might meet with.

On 23rd, after entering in his diary that he had been to Hilly Wood and brought home a plant of white maidenhair fern, he wrote: "Finished my 'two ballads to Mary' which I intend to send to the *Literary Gazette*, as also my three Sonnets to Bloomfield, and I am weary of writing."

17

DELAY CARRIED INTO A SYSTEM

EARLY IN 1825, CLARE BROKE
his resolution to avoid drink and indulged in a carousal with the
Billings brothers and other friends, but the usual fit of remorse
followed, and he evidently confessed to Mrs. Emmerson, for she
wrote to him:

> You tell me that you have "played the fool"—no small proof of
> your wisdom that you have done it "only once in the last twelve
> months".

It was only a brief lapse, and subsequent ones were very rare;
Clare had virtually conquered the temptation.

On his wanderings in the woods and fields Clare saw the first
signs of spring, and noted them in his diary:

> Monday 31 Jan. Went to Simon's Wood for succor of the Barberry
> bush to set in my Garden—saw the Corn tree putting out into leaf—
> a yellow crocus and a bunch of single snowdrops in full flower. The
> mavis thrush has been singing all day long. Spring seems begun—
> The woodbines all over the wood are in full leaf.

He was also busy with his natural history letters:

> I always admire the kindling freshness that the bark of the different
> sorts of trees and underwood assume in the forest—the "foulroyce"[1]
> twigs kindle into a vivid colour at their tops, as red as woodpigeons'
> claws, the ash, with its grey bark and black swelling buds, the birch,
> with its "paper-rind", and the darker mottled sorts of hazel; black
> alder, with the greener hues of sallows, willows, and the bramble that
> still wears its leaves, with the privet of a purple hue; while the strag-
> gling wood briar shines in a brighter and more beautiful green even
> than leaves can boast at this season. Odd forward branches in the
> new-laid hedges of whitethorn begin to freshen into green before the
> arum dare peep out of its hood, or the primrose and violet shoot up
> a new leaf through the warm moss and ivy that shelter their spring
> dwellings.

[1] Dogwood.

Early in February, he received a letter from Hessey, full of excuses for the delay that had held up publication of the book.

> In regard to *The Shepherd's Calendar*, it is I assure you a fact that Taylor has been so occupied by his various editorial duties that he has not been able to go regularly through the MS. and make the requisite selections for the press. But he has not forgotten you, and he is very anxious to have it put in a train for publication.

Hessey had also something to say on the subject of the Peterborough apothecary, who, he said, had sent the firm "an exorbitant bill" for medicines prescribed by Dr. Skrimshire. The apothecary had attended Clare by order of Lady Milton, but he did not feel justified in charging to her the medicines that had been ordered by Dr. Skrimshire, whom Taylor and Hessey had requested to visit Clare. "By the way," Hessey added, "I hope you have dispensed with the Dr's visits. I had not the remotest idea of his intending to charge you for attendance."

The broad hint that more doctors' bills would not be welcome did not come at a good time. The children, it seems, had not been well, Clare's own health, though better, was by no means good, and on 13th February he noted in his diary, "My Anna taken very ill." He evidently wrote to Dr. Darling for advice, and the kindly Scotsman replied at once, prescribing both for the child and for Clare, though even before this letter arrived Clare was able to record "My Anna is something better".

Meanwhile a letter came from Van Dyk, reporting that all the poems except "January", which had been overlooked, were now ready for the press, and Clare might expect the first proof sheet very soon. The book, Van Dyk thought, would probably be out in six weeks, but, in fact, it was a month before the promised proof-sheet arrived, and it was just two years later that the book was published. Clare had learned, by bitter experience, to be wary of promises, and he was no longer surprised by delays and prevarication, but had he guessed at that time how long he would have to wait for the appearance of the book the load of disappointment and anxiety would have been heavy indeed. The entry in his diary for 9th March shows with what eager, yet fearful, expectation he was looking forward to the publication:

> I had a very odd dream last night and I take it as an ill omen, for I don't expect that the book will meet with a better fate. I thought I

had one of the proofs of the new poems from London, and after looking at it awhile it shrank through my hands like sand, crumbling into dust. The birds were singing in Oxey Wood at 6 o'clock this evening as loud and various as in May.

Taylor's letter, written on 18th March, was not calculated to hearten Clare:

> The Fact is this [the puplisher wrote], my Heart has not been in the Business from my Conviction that I could not make such a Volume from the whole Collection, answering to the Title of *The Shepherd's Calendar,* as would surpass the others or equal them in the Estimation of the public—and you were too ill to make perfect those parts which I should have found it necessary to cut away. Not but that I think there are many Poems of as great Merit as any you have written, and in some places perhaps greater; but the whole Collection would I felt be regarded as inferior. However I will do my best and if the Result is not successful as I could wish you must not hold me responsible.

In his last letter Clare, encouraged by Mrs. Emmerson and Lord Radstock, had evidently spoken rather plainly about the behaviour of his publishers over the new volume, and Taylor referred to this further on in his letter:

> I would gladly pass over the Allusions you have made in your Letter to certain Hints and Cautions you have received, because I think you wrote in a State of Irritation which perhaps might result very justly from my long Silence and apparent Inattention to your Work; but you know me pretty well by this Time, and you cannot be in much Doubt whether I am to be considered your Friend or not— If you or any of your Correspondents think you can put your Poems into the Hands of any one who is more likely to do you Justice, I will part with them willingly, and this I have often told you before. Let those therefore who gave you these Hints and Cautions take the MSS. if you please and deposit them in the Hands of Persons whom they have more Confidence in. But if not, if you and they cannot find a Publisher who is more disposed to serve you let us not have any Feeling of Dislike created by the Mention of such Things. I can see no Good likely to accrue from it, and some Harm may. At all Events, it is better to terminate the Connection at once than to continue it in Distrust.

From the injured tone in which Taylor reproves Clare it might be supposed that the poet had been guilty of some terrible injustice to his publisher rather than that he had remonstrated with him for a state of affairs which most people would not have endured for nearly as long as he had done. Taylor's letter was, in fact, an ultimatum that Clare must either accept unquestioningly everything that he did (or failed to do), or he must take his poems elsewhere. He knew quite well that Clare had no wish to adopt the latter course, for the poet recognised Taylor's ability and had, besides, a sense of loyalty to him and a personal affection; all of which Taylor understood, and in the circumstances it was extremely unfair to silence his protests with the threat of severing their connection entirely.

On 29th March, Van Dyk wrote to say that the copying of the poems was not, after all, complete, as he had found that Taylor had still in his possession quite a number of them which he had forgotten to give him.

It was probably at about this time, when he was sore and discontented at the treatment he had received, that Clare wrote a description of Taylor:

Taylor is a man of very pleasant address, and works himself into the good opinions of people in a moment; but it is not lasting, for he grows into a studied carelessness and neglect that he carries into a system, till the purpose for so doing becomes transparent and reflects its own picture while it would hide it. He is a very pleasant talker and is excessive fluent on paper currency and such politics. He can talk on matters with a superficial knowledge of them very dexterously, and is very fond of arguing about the Latin and Greek poets with the Reverends and the Cambridge [wits] that drop into his Waterloo house. He assumes a feeling and fondness for poetry and reads it well—not in the fashionable growl of mouthing spouters but in a sort of whine. He professed a great friendship for me at my first starting and offered to correct my future poems if he did not publish them. So I sent all my things up as I wrote them, and neither got his opinion or the poems back again—his only opinion being that he had not time to spare from other pursuits to revise and correct them for the press: and when I sent for the poems agen he was silent. He wrote the Introduction to both my volumes of poems. His manner is that of a cautious fellow who shows his sunny side to strangers.

He has written some pamphlets on politics and *The Identity of Junius*, a very clever book; and some very middling papers in *The London Magazine*, and some bad sonnets. Gilchrist told me that he first displayed the schoolboy prodigy of translating some of Horace's odes into rhyme, which he sent to the *Mirror*, that hotbed of Indications.

He wished me to correspond with him, which I did very thickly, as I fancied he was the greatest friend I had ever met with: but after he had published 3 vols. of my poems, his correspondence was laid by, and I heard nothing more from him.

He never asks a direct question or gives a direct reply, but continually saps your information by a secret passage, coming at it as it were by working a mine—like a lawyer examining a witness. And he uses this sort of caution even in his common discourse till it becomes tedious to listen or reply. He sifts a theory of truth, either true or false, with much ingenuity and subtilty of argument, and his whole table talk is a sort of *Junius Identified*. But his patience carries it to such length in seeming consistency till the first end of the ravelled skein which he winds up at the beginning is lost again and unwound in looking for the other. To sum up, he is a clever fellow and a man of Genius: and his *Junius Identified* is the best argument on circumstantial evidence that ever was written.

In the meantime there was still sickness in the cottage at Helpston to add to Clare's worries. On 18th March, Mrs. Emmerson wrote that she was sorry to hear of Anna's continuing indisposition: ". . . is it consumption or may it not originate in *worms*? . . . My poor little namesake too is under the visitation of a Malady, but have you not chosen a very unseasonable moment to have her innoculated? 'Beware the ides of March' is an old proverb."

In April came another letter from Darling on the subject of Clare's own illness which had lately shown signs of recurring:

> You are right in believing that its origin is not mental but you are wrong if you suppose that anxiety about your wife and children and any other cause will not materially aggravate it and retard your recovery.

On 15th April, Clare learned from Lord Radstock that Van Dyk was going out of London, which would mean a further delay in the work of preparing the poems for the press, and he wrote to Hessey two days later, expressing his dissatisfaction in stronger terms than he was accustomed to use. The letter was not written impulsively or without thought, and was both courteous and reasonable, but the procrastination over *The Shepherd's Calendar* was not Clare's only grievance, for he had also been trying, without success, to get the publishers to send back some MS. poems which he wanted to work on, and which they had had for four years.

I do not wish to hurt the feelings of anyone [Clare wrote], nor do I wish they should hurt mine; but when delay is carried into a system its cause must grow a substitute for a worse name. I will go no further, but I will just ask you to give a moment's reflection to my situation, and see how you would like it yourself.

He entered in his diary: "Wrote to Hessey in a manner that I am always very loath to write, but I could keep my patience no longer."

A week later, Mrs. Emmerson was writing about investigations that she had made to try and ascertain the real position about the book. She had seen Van Dyk who was unwell and could not write or apply himself to anything. "On the subject of your MSS. I could only learn that Mr. T. was not pleased with V. D. cutting out so much, and that it did not depend upon him, as to the delay that exists in publishing your new Vol."

Clare was fortunately well enough to be out of doors a great deal, and he sought refuge from his troubles in the company of his early love, Nature. Years afterwards he was to write a poem that expresses the mood that possessed him then and many times during his life, when he turned his back on home and books and letters and the troubles of a literary life, and was able, for a few brief hours, to forget everything except the absorbing study of what materials the whitethroat was using for her nest, or which flowers the bee was visiting for honey.

> I'll lay me down on the green sward,
> Mid yellowcups and speedwell blue,
> And pay the world no more regard,
> But be to Nature leal and true.[1]

The knowledge that he acquired from these patient hours of watching and listening was far greater than what he could have learned from books; in fact he mistrusted the majority of natural history books and relied only on his own observation. In his own natural history notes he said, that he would "insert nothing but what has come under my notice", and in a letter about the "two sorts of the willow wrens," he said, ". . . as for naturalists you must not let them go before your own observations for some of them are 'naturals' indeed".

His diary for April and May is full of the records of what he saw on his wanderings:

[1] "I'll dream upon the days to come."

Sat. 16 April. Took a walk in the field, birds nesting and bota-
nizing, and had like to have been taken up as a poacher in Hillywood
by a meddlesome, conceited keeper belonging to Sir John Trollop.
He swore that he had seen me in act more than once of shooting game,
when I never shot even so much as a sparrow in my life. . . .

Sat. 23 April. I saw the redstart or Firetail today and little Willow
wren. The black thorn tree in full flower that shines about the
hedges like cloaks hung out to dry. . . .

Thurs. 28 April. Hedge sparrow finished her nest in Billings's
Box-tree and laid one egg. Wallnutt showing leaf—Sycamore and
Horse chestnutt nearly covered. I observed a Snail on his journey
at full speed and I marked by my watch that he went 13 inches in
3 minutes, which was the utmost he could do without stopping to
wind or rest. It was the large Garden snail. . . .

Friday 6 May. Could not sleep all night. Got up at three o'clock
in the morning and walked about the fields—the birds were high in
their songs in Royce wood and almost deafening. I heard the
Cricket-bird again in full cry in Royce wood—it is just like a child's
screecher. . . .

Tues. 10 May. Saw a male and female of the Tree-Sparrow (as I
supposed them) in Royce close hedge next the lane. The cock bird
had a very black head and its shades of brown were more deep and
distinct than the house sparrow; the female when flying showed two
white feathers in her tail. They seemed to have a nest in the hedgerow but I could not find it. Saw a Pettichap[1] in Bushy close—its note
is more like "Chippichap"; it keeps in continual motion on the tops
of trees, uttering its note. . . .

Thurs. 26 May. I watched a Blue cap or Blue Titmouse feeding
her young, whose nest was in a wall close to an Orchard. She got
caterpillars out of the Blossoms of the apple trees and leaves of the
plumb—she fetched 120 Caterpillars in half an hour. . . .

By the beginning of May *The Shepherd's Calendar* seemed no nearer
to making its appearance, and Clare wrote a long and earnest
letter to Taylor:

I had hopes when I received your last that your resolves to get on
with the poems were in earnest—it is not for the mere gratification of
seeing it out that makes me urgent, but it is for more substantial
reasons which I shall not lengthen the letter to explain. . . . I have
waited and hoped for the best and as I hate offensive correspondence
I pass over the unpleasant part[s] of ours as well as I can. I might be
under a mistake, and if so the feelings they excited would be irritating,
yet I feel now that the negligence in getting out the poems would

[1] Chiff-chaff. Clare used the same name for the willow warbler.

make anyone complain, and, whatever harm may come from complaining of matters that appear to claim no commendation I am
sure no good can come from speaking in their praise. When I feel
anything I must speak it. I know that my temper is hasty, and with
that knowledge of myself I always strive to choke it and soften hard
opinions with reasonable interpretations—but put yourself in my
place for a minute and see how you would have felt and written yourself, and if you feel that you should have acted otherwise, then I will
take it as an example and strive to correct my failings and be as perfect in an imperfect world as I can. I have no desire to seek another
publisher, neither do I believe any other would do so well for me as
you may do—much less better—but when obligation is sought or
offered it kills kindness, therefore I will go no further on that head.
If you want to get out of the job of publishing my poems, you may
tell me so, and I will seek another and trust to providence, but, if you
have no desire to turn me adrift, the speedy publication of my poems
will gladly convince me that I was mistaken and I shall be happy to
prove that you are my friend as usual.

Taylor evidently felt the justice of Clare's remarks, and he wrote
back:

> Putting myself in your Situation I dare say I should have com-
> plained as you did—and yet I could think that if you were in mine
> you would see that I was less blameable than I seemed to be. . . . As
> for quarrelling I am sure that it ought to be far from you and me, for
> I could never say one Word to give you Pain which would not re-act
> with tenfold Fury on myself—and you, I am sure, desire not to speak
> harsh things to me. Let these differences now be forgotten.

This letter contained the news that he and Hessey were to
dissolve their partnership in midsummer; in future Taylor would
manage the publishing business at the house in Waterloo Place,
and Hessey the retail trade in Fleet Street.

At the end of May, Clare's younger daughter, Eliza, was ill
again with a fever and caused some anxiety for a few days, and on
2nd June he wrote in his diary: "This is my darling Anna's birthday
who is five years old, a weakling flower fast fading in the bud—
'withering untimely.' . . ." Patty, too, whose health was much
more robust than that of her husband or children, was ill at that
time with "a painful malady in her neck", and probably Dr.
Skrimshire or the apothecary who had sent Hessey "an exorbitant
bill" had to be called in.

Clare visited Milton in July, and talked about birds and Roman remains with Henderson and Artis. He was there on his birthday, and wrote in his diary: "This day I am thirty two, and my health was drunk at Milton by two very pretty girls—Mrs. P—r and Mrs. B—n—who wished I might treble the number. I had my wish in turn, but I did not drink it in return. . . ."

On 21st August, Clare received from Mrs. Emmerson the news that Lord Radstock had died the previous day after an attack of apoplexy.

> He was the best friend I ever met with [Clare wrote]. Tho' he possessed too much of that simple heartedness to be a fashionable friend or hypocrite, yet it often led him to take hypocrites for honest friends and to take an honest man for a hypocrite.

Hessey wrote to Clare about Radstock's death in a letter of September 6th:

> You have of course heard of the death of poor old Radstock and have lamented his loss as that of a kind well-meaning old friend. He was taken ill at Mrs. E's house and was safely taken home but he never spoke after.

Taylor had been very ill, and Hessey said that he was delirious for ten days but was now recovering. Despite the dissolution of their partnership, the two men continued in close touch with each other, and Hessey still wrote fairly frequently to Clare to give news of the book or advise him about his MSS.

In July they had disposed of *The London Magazine* to Henry Southern, who edited it until 1829, when it was absorbed by *The New Monthly*, and Hessey, in telling Clare the news, had remarked that: "It may perhaps cause something like a sigh at parting", but the work involved had been too much for them. In fact, the once glorious *London* had fallen off sadly, and some of its best contributors had drifted away. As long ago as September, 1823, Lamb had written of it: "I linger among its creaking rafters, like the last rat. It will topple down, if they don't get some Buttresses."

What Taylor and Hessey actually lost or made by their four years' connection with the magazine is not known, but they showed their good business sense by getting rid of it when they did, and if payments to the other contributors were forgotten as completely as those to Clare, they probably made quite a good profit.

In September, Clare wrote to Taylor:

I have been much better these last two months than I have ever
been since I was first taken, and the last prescriptions that I had from
Dr. Darling set me up as I had hoped in earnest, but this last five or
six days I have been alarmed with fresh numbness and stupidness in
the head and lightness in the skull as if it were hooped round like a
barrel.

But, although Clare's letters during the autumn and winter of
1825 mention the discomfort and anxiety that he felt from these
and other symptoms, he does not seem to have been troubled with
such dark and abysmal gloom as he had experienced in the
previous winter. It is probable that under-nourishment was
materially affecting his condition at that time, and Martin tells a
story of how Clare fainted from hunger when he was out with
Artis one day in a search for Roman antiquities; the butler,
Martin says, after taking Clare home, went back to Milton, and
told the French chef, with whom Clare was a great favourite, that
he was worried about the poet, whereupon the chef asked Lady
Milton's permission to go himself to Helpston with some nourish-
ing broth and thereafter went several times with soups and stews
which he thought would do good.

Clare felt acutely his responsibility for his family, and it was
agony to him to see his children hungry, so that he developed
the habit of going without things himself and even, it is said,
deliberately going out at meal-times so that the others might
have a larger share. In earlier years, the nourishment that he
failed to get in food was to some extent provided by the ale
that he drank, and it is possible that Darling, when he ordered
Clare to give it up, was not aware of the useful purpose that it
thus served. The problem, however, was insoluble, for the two
alternatives were both equally good and equally bad; if he drank
ale it gave him nourishment, but a very little intoxicated him,
which was harmful to his nerves and constitution generally, and
if he did not he avoided injurious excitement but came nearer to
starving.

No doubt the proverbial "hope deferred" was also a factor in
Clare's condition while *The Shepherd's Calendar* dragged on from
month to month and seemed as though it would never be published, but he went on courageously with his work and found a
new market for his poems in the Annuals, which were then both

umerous and fashionable. Contributing to them was an unsatis-factory business, as Clare soon found, although he started off in the summer of 1825 full of hope. Many of the editors were unreliable in their payments, either delaying for a year before making them, or else not making them at all; some considered that a free copy of the Annual should be sufficient remuneration, and they were all apt to alter contributions drastically and without reference to the author. By December, 1825, Clare was already driven to saying in a letter to Hessey:

> . . . as to the poetical almanacks they may all go to Hell next year for me, for I can get nothing by them and my contributions are so mutilated that I do not know them again.

Another activity upon which Clare was engaged during 1825 and 1826 was that of writing poems in imitation of the Eliza-bethans. He had always had a strange delight in playing such "literary tricks", as when he read aloud his own poems to his parents and pretended they were another's, or when, in later years, he sent a poem to Taylor for criticism under the name of "Percy Green". It amused him to try his hand at imitating another man's work, and the mild deceptions may also have arisen from the desire to see how much his situation in life influenced people's judgment of his poetry. He had read widely among "those beautiful minstrels of Elizabeth", and it seems that the idea of imitating them occurred to him in the winter of 1824–5.

On 19th January he wrote in his diary:

> Corrected the poem on the "Vanitys of the world" which I have written in imitation of the old poets on whom I mean to father it and send it to Montgomery's paper *The Iris* or the *Literary Chronicle* under that character.

In the letter which he sent with the poem to James Mont-gomery of Sheffield, the editor of *The Iris*, he said:

> I copied the following verses from a MS. on the fly-leaves of an old book entitled *The World's Best Wealth, a Collection of Choice Counsels in Verse and Prose*, printed for A. Butterworth, at the Red Lion in Paternoster Row, 1720: they seem to have been written after the perusal of the book, and are in the manner of the company in which I found [them]. I think they are as good as many old poems that have been preserved with more care; and, under that feeling, I was

tempted to send them, thinking they might find a corner from oblivion in your entertaining literary paper, *The Iris*, but if my judgment
has misled me to overrate their merit, you will excuse the freedom I
have taken and the trouble I have given you in the perusal; for, after
all, it is but an erring opinion that may have little less than the love
of poesy to recommend it.

Montgomery printed the verses with Clare's story of their origin,
but he evidently suspected that they were not a genuine product
of the Elizabethan age. In May, 1826, more than a year after
their publication, he considered including the verses in a chrono-
logical collection of "Christian Poetry", and he wrote to Clare to
inquire if they were really copied from an old book and, if so,
whether he might borrow it as it probably contained other poems
that he could use in his collection.

> Now though I suspected [he wrote] from a little ambiguity
> in the wording of your letter, that these verses were not quite so
> old as they professed to be, and that you yourself perhaps had
> written them to exercise your own genius and sent them to exercise
> my critical acuteness, I thought that the glorious offence carried
> its own redemption in itself, and I would not only forgive but
> rejoice to see such faults committed every day for the sake of such
> merits.

Clare replied at once with a full confession of his forgery, and
explained to Montgomery how he had come to do it:

> I have long had a fondness for the poetry of the time of Elizabeth,
> though I have never had any means of meeting with it farther than in
> the confined channels of Ritson's *English Songs*, Ellis's *Specimens* and
> Walton's *Angler*; and the winter before last, though amidst a severe
> illness, I set about writing a series of verses in their manner, as well
> as I could, which I intended to pass off under their names, though
> some whom I professed to imitate I had never seen. As I am no judge
> of my own verses, whether they are good or bad, I wished to have the
> opinion of some one on whom I could rely; and as I was told you
> were the editor of *The Iris* I ventured to send the first thing to you with
> many "doubts and fears". I was happily astonished to see its favour-
> able reception.

During the year following his first attempt at literary deception,
Clare had a poem on "Death" published in Hone's *Everyday Book*
under the name of Andrew Marvell, and *The European Magazine*

published "Thoughts in a Churchyard," ascribed to Sir Henry Wootton, "The Gipsy's Song" to Tom Davies, and "A Farewell to Love" which was said to be by Sir John Harrington. After his suspicions had been confirmed, Montgomery published another of Clare's imitations, this time an "Address to Milton" by William Davenant.

18

"THE SHEPHERD'S CALENDAR"

Towards the end of 1825 Clare was again writing to Dr. Darling for medical advice. He was evidently worrying himself about his children's weak constitutions, and Darling wrote on 3rd December to reassure him: "Make your conscience easy respecting your children, for however much they may suffer it will not be from any voluntary fault of yours." Later in the month he sent some new medicine for Clare to take, and advised him: "Above all do not lay-a-bed or give way to low spirits or abstain from exercise which negatively does you more mischief than you can well imagine."

Mrs. Emmerson, now bereft of the energetic help of Clare's other patron, Lord Radstock, continued to do all that she could for the poet, and to write to him frequently and at length. In September she and her husband had come down from London, and Clare had spent three days with them at the New Inn at Market Deeping; in November she sent plants for Clare's garden, which her father, who lived near Bath, had obtained for her—polyanthus, carnation, and auricula roots, with some stocks and wallflowers. A few weeks later, she was writing about "The Grasshopper", a new poem for children, which Clare had addressed to Anna and which Mr. Emmerson had been trying, without success, to sell for him. He had also, Mrs. Emmerson said, called on Taylor for a long talk about Clare's affairs, and had found the publisher most friendly and anxious to help.

Mrs. Emmerson's letters at that time refer to certain confessions which Clare evidently made to her about a love-affair. On 22nd December, she wrote:

> You have in your letter mentioned a subject in which I feel more than a common interest and anxiety—you promise in a "few days to write more fully to me about it"—I shall wait with much solicitude your unreserved and free explanation of what may have taken place since I was at "Deeping"—half confidence will not on the present affair allow me to say more than to entreat you will not forget what is

169

due to yourself and, need I add, to others who are deeply inter-
woven in all that can touch your honour and happiness. . . . Be
cautious, I beseech you, not to indulge during the Xmas in anything that may affect your Head—for it is on its strength alone you
can rely—your poor heart is alas! too yielding for your general
good!

Clare, with that terrible, self-accusing honesty which lacerated
him in his fits of remorse, told the whole story to Mrs. Emmerson,
and she replied on 11th January, 1826:

But you account in your letter which I received yesterday for your
long silence—you have been wandering from home, from yourself,
and alas! from happiness:—and much do I fear that my influence as
your attached and true friend, will have little power to win you back
to tranquillity and to domestic peace—and, above all, to your dear
Children, for it is them I feel the most for, on the present occasion! I
deeply regret "the cause of your late outbreakings from propriety"—
but why, my dear Clare, will you allow the temper or injudicious conduct of others to harry you away from your own reason, and induce
you to do such things as can only bring upon you the loss of health,
the expenditure of money, and that wretchedly disturbed mind of
which you complain so forcibly, and with so much just reasoning. . . .
I am not a "prude" nor a "moralist" but I would be enough of the
philosopher and friend to prevail on you by every gentle, kind, and
reasonable entreaty to give up your acquaintance with ——; it is an
unworthy connexion, and can only bring you a train of miseries! I
cannot enter further upon the subject than to thank you, my dear
Clare, for the confidence you have reposed in me, and to beseech you,
as you value my esteem and affectionate regard, that you will
(having returned again to your home and family) that you will call
forth all your Social and parental feelings to induce you to be as
happy as possible and to remain with your dear Children and your
aged Parents; and I hope —— will do all in her power to make your
mind more contented, and to enable you to pursue your literary
labours. . . . I never wrote to you, my dear Clare, with such reluctant
feelings as on the present occasion: I love to speak only in your
praise—to extol your genius, to make others feel your worth. How
painful, then, is it to have the task of writing upon matters of weakness
in a character where strength only should be found?"

On 13th May, she wrote:

I hope all the causes for your late uneasiness will be so settled as
to leave you perfectly free to once more enjoy peace in your own

cottage, and in the bosom of your own little family. I would have you master of your own passions and feelings, and I would have your Muse the only object to engage your fancy.

Three weeks later Clare received a letter containing another allusion to the matter:

I rejoice to hear other disagreeables are in the fair way of settling— but do not lose your own firmness in this event of folly. Keep your own station, and do not be hurried away by undue delicacy or fear in this unfortunate event. It will no sooner be whisper'd abroad than the sound will pass away and mingle with the thousand discordant notes produced by similar causes. Without meaning to glorify errour or to espouse the frailtys of human nature, I should say the noblest way is to meet and to face our actions, and by a steady daring to conquer the weaknesses we have committed.

From this we may conclude that the affair was ended and a measure of domestic peace restored to the cottage at Helpston, but Clare's conscience continued to trouble him, and two years afterwards he was seeking the advice of Hessey as to how he might make his peace with God.

The preparation of *The Shepherd's Calendar*, meanwhile, dragged on at the usual snail-like pace. In December, 1825, Taylor wrote that he would soon be sending proofs and hoped to get on with the publication now that his health had improved. He hoped to send Clare a statement of account in a few days, and thought that there was about £40 due to him on the sale of the poems.

The *Poems* and *Village Minstrel* have neither of them sold much of late, but the former have very nearly cleared the Expenses of the Reprint, and the latter have paid their Expenses and left the Profit to which I have alluded.

The statement of account, needless to say, did not come, and in January Clare wrote to Taylor in much agitation about his financial troubles, and the long delays over *The Shepherd's Calendar*. This drew forth a long letter from the publisher, written "more in sorrow than in anger", and expressing his sense of injury at the charges of promise-breaking which Clare had levelled at him.

I have desired to serve you in this Matter as I did at first, from no Hope or Expectation of Gain, but with a single Wish to your individual Interest: and if all were known that has been done in the

Business by Hessey and myself, and in what Manner we have been recompensed for our Trouble, our greatest Enemies would not think we had profited too much by the Speculation. . . .

Heretofore I have submitted, and apologized, and taken Blame to myself, because I was resolved, if possible, to complete my Undertaking, whatever Pains it cost me: but your frank Censure has at last relieved me from my irksome situation, and I must now as frankly tell you, that for the principal part of the Delay and for the present total Stop again you are alone responsible.

The poems, Taylor complained, were so badly written that he was the only person who could read them, and it was useless to employ anyone to transcribe them, for "not three words in a line on the average are put down right" and many had to be omitted.

The Poems are not only slovenly written, but as slovenly composed, and to make good Poems out of some of them is a greater Difficulty than I ever had to engage with in your former works—while in others it is a complete Impossibility.

There was, no doubt, some justice in what Taylor said about the illegibility of the MSS.—Clare's hand, which was open and very easy to read when he wrote carefully, could be difficult in the extreme and *was* so in many of these poems—but it was unnecessary for the publisher to keep the MSS. nearly three years before he made his complaint. If in the beginning he had returned the difficult pieces to Clare for transcription, as he did now, the poet would gladly have copied them all with care and the work of publication could have gone forward; but Clare forbore to point this out and merely admitted his fault, saying that he would now do his best to remedy it. Nor, it seems, did he make any protest when Taylor wrote in March, and again in April, about poems which had got lost either in his office or at the printer's.

The new drafts of the poems met with Taylor's approval. Clare had taken pains with them, and in writing poetry he now took more trouble in other ways, for he had developed a certain selective power which, although it was never his strong point, greatly improved his work.

I do assure you [he wrote to Taylor] all that I now write undergoes severe discipline, for if a first copy consists of a hundred lines its second corrections generally dwindle down to half the number, and I heartily wish I had done so at first.

At this time Clare was in correspondence with Elizabeth Kent, sister-in-law of Leigh Hunt, and author of *Flora Domestica* and *Sylvan Sketches*. She had written to Clare in May, 1825, to ask if he would help her by giving some information on ornithology for a *History of Birds* which she was preparing. Clare was annoyed by the brevity of her letter, and wrote in his diary: ". . . if my assistance is not worth more than twelve lines it is worth nothing and I shall not interfere", but he afterwards relented and promised to help her in any way he could.

In January, 1826, she wrote to ask if he could tell her where the different species of wren made their nests; she was sure that she had seen one, which she supposed was a willow-wren, visiting its nest in a hole very high in the trunk of a tree.

Clare replied that she was quite right as to the nesting site, and added:

> I only know of two sorts of the willow wrens, one larger than the other and of a lighter green. The smaller one, I believe, comes first.

In subsequent letters they discussed migration and the fascinating mysteries attaching to it. Clare also wrote to her about the blackcap, and she answered in May, 1826:

> The Blackcap which you speak of, I am well acquainted with; its song has, in some parts of England, obtained for it the name of the Mock Nightingale. This species is very numerous at Ham, a little village about 12 miles from Town, where we have a cottage. . . .

Of these little grey-green birds Clare spoke when he wrote one of his most beautiful lines which glows with the magic and indefinable essence of poetry. He remembers the trees and hedges, quickening to new life:

> Where little blackcaps in their early song
> Do calm the March winds with their merry throats.

In 1826 the market for poetry had declined considerably and the booksellers were suffering and growing consequently more cautious. Early in the year Mrs. Emmerson had told Clare that the bankers of a certain firm of publishers had "return'd Bills upon them to the amount of 25000£ and that the concern had stop'd payment for thrice that sum", and towards the end of May,

Mrs. Gilchrist, widow of Clare's old friend Octavius, wrote to ask if it was true that Taylor's name was in the bankrupt list.

Clare, much alarmed, wrote at once to Mrs. Emmerson, who replied with a welcome reassurance:

> Not a breath of what you mention relative to T—— has met my ear—and if affairs were such as Mrs. G—— mentions I certainly should have learned it and told you immediately.

On 16th June, Patty gave birth to another son, who was christened John. Mrs. Emmerson said the poet was to "tell dear Patty she must not bestow any more dear little Johns upon you——

> Two little girls—two little Boys
> Are quite enough for Wedded joys."

Clare's younger daughter, Eliza, was starting school, and Mrs. Emmerson had given Patty a sum of money for the school expenses of both the girls when she visited Clare's cottage in September, 1825. In the autumn of 1826, she wrote promising a further amount for the coming year, having undertaken to meet all the expenses of her god-daughter's education.

Hardly had the false alarm of Taylor's bankruptcy died down when Clare was perturbed by another anxiety which, unfortunately, could not be dispelled by Mrs. Emmerson. This came in the form of a letter from Edward Drury, dated 27th June, 1826, making a claim upon Clare for £41 9s. 3d., "for cash advanced to you whilst writing the V[illage M[instrel] and for other expenses, viz. supplying you with Goods, procuring Medical advice for your Mother, Binding your Books and other particulars."

Taylor, in the process of winding up the affairs of the firm at the dissolution of the partnership, had evidently been attending to some ancient accounts still outstanding, and he had sent Drury a claim for over £100 which the firm had apparently advanced by paying off certain debts of his in the days when they were partners in the publication of Clare's work. Drury had then sent *his* account for the money which he said Clare owed him, but Taylor declined to put this in the book account and said that Drury and Clare had better settle it between them.

It was, of course, quite impossible for Clare to find £40; things were difficult enough in any case, and he had been at field-labour most of the summer to get a little money which would help in the perpetual struggle to make ends meet. He was very much worried and upset by this new financial trouble, and when Drury wrote again on 25th July, pressing for payment, he wrote to Taylor asking for help in dealing with the matter.

Taylor replied:

> Never mind Drury. He has made his Claim, and as far as it seems to be right we must allow it—I am sorry for his own sake that he should so far forget what is right as to urge his Claim with the threat of putting you to Trouble. He has much Cause for Shame at having written such a Letter. We are trying now to get the old Account settled, and when that is done I shall be glad to have no further Dealings with him.

Hessey then took a hand in the matter and wrote, early in September, to tell Clare that they had settled the bill after deducting three items which had already been paid, and the sum had been placed to Clare's account with the firm.

The anxiety over his money troubles made Clare feel, for a time, ill and depressed again. In July, when Taylor sent him a cheque for £20, being the dividend from the fund-money and his payments from Earl Spencer and the Marquis of Exeter Clare wrote that he would try to manage on £15:

> I do assure you that I live as near as ever I can, and, though I did not tell you, I have been out to hard labour most part of this summer on purpose to help out my matters. But the price of labour is so low here that it is little better than parish relief to the poor man, who, where there is a large family, is literally pining.

The wages of a married agricultural labourer were then somewhere between 4s. and 9s. a week, varying according to the parish. The standard of living had fallen sharply since 1795, when the Speenhamland system was introduced, a fact which is clearly shown by the comparison between the amount of food thought necessary for a working man then and in subsequent years. In 1796 the allowance was three gallon loaves a week for a man, and one and a half for his wife and each member of his family; in 1816 the Northamptonshire magistrates fixed the allowance at just over three gallon loaves for a man *and* his wife—in other words two were to eat little more than one had eaten before. By 1831 the generally accepted ruling was that a labourer should have one loaf weekly for each member of his family, and one over. The chief constituents of their diet were bread and cheese, tea, potatoes, and porridge.

But Clare was better by August, having once more risen above his anxieties, and was busy with his reading and writing which, for a time, he had given up. Taylor was holding out hopes of producing the new book in October, and we learn from a letter of Mrs. Emmerson's that the slight coolness between him and Clare was now over.

> And now, last but not least, your re-union with your friend Mr. T——. I heartily rejoice that your good opinion of him is restored— that he shows himself still anxious in your literary affairs and general welfare.

In September, Hessey wrote to suggest that Clare should write the preface for the new book himself, and should "account for the long delay in the coming out of the Volume on the score of ill health". It seemed hard, after all that had happened, that Clare should be asked thus to take the blame before the public. De Wint, for whose work Clare had a great admiration, agreed to do a frontispiece for the book, but the first drawing that he did was unsatisfactory, and although Clare received six advance copies of the book in November, it was not until April, 1827, that the engraving was finished, and the book ready for publication.

In March, Clare received a letter from Darley, with whom he had become friendly during his last visit to London. He was busy with mathematical works and did not know when he would continue with his critical work for which he had now little taste, believing that criticism was "fit only for the headsmen and hangmen of literature, fellows who live by the agonies and death of others". He had heard from Taylor that Clare was in poor health.

> What *can* be the matter with you, so healthfully situated and employed? Methinks you should live the life of an oak-tree or a sturdy elm, that groans in a storm, but only for pleasure. Do you meditate too much or sit too immovably? . . . Poetry, I mean the composition of it, does not always sweeten the mind as much as the reading of it. There is always an anxiety, a fervour, an impatience, a vaingloriousness attending it which untranquillizes even in the sweetest-seeming moods of the poet. Like the bee, he is restless and uneasy even in collecting his sweets.

At the end of the month, Taylor wrote:

I am very much disappointed that I cannot yet send you the perfect Copies of the New Work—Though De Wint and I have done all
in our Power to force the Engraver to get his Work done, it is not
finished. He says he has met with an Accident, which has delayed
him, and that he wants to do it in a very superior Manner.

But at last, at the end of April, the long and troubled course of
the preparation of Clare's third book came to an end, and *The
Shepherd's Calendar* was published. Taylor wrote on 1st May to say
that the finished copies should by now be in Clare's hands:

Great and vexatious Delay took place in the plate, but now it is
done I think you will like it, and agree with me that our Friend De
Wint, who has made the Drawing for nothing, out of Friendship for
the Author, deserves a line or two of Thanks for his Kindness.

19

SORROW AND SICKNESS

FROM A FINANCIAL POINT OF view *The Shepherd's Calendar* could hardly have been a more complete failure, for in two years it sold only 425 copies. It was not really surprising, for everything was against its success; the fashion for poetry, which had been at its height a few years earlier, had gone, and the book trade generally was at a low ebb; works of literary merit found no purchasers and the craze was for the Annuals and Almanacks, with their gilt-edged pages and luscious illustrations. These circumstances were against all the poets of that time, but Clare was further handicapped by the length of time that had elapsed since his last volume; the public memory is proverbially short, and in six years his name was forgotten, or remembered but dimly as a literary phenomenon that had excited interest long ago and was no longer worth bothering about. The form of the volume was not a good one, either, for the necessity of arranging the poems in calendar form fettered Clare to the disadvantage of the work, and tended to encourage the slightly pedestrian element which had sometimes marred his early poems, but which his ripening genius was now overcoming.

The volume, however, showed a distinct advance on the previous ones, and contained some beautiful things. The twelve long poems of the months gave a full and fascinating picture of the happier side of village life at that time—the tales told round the fire on winter evenings, the decorating of the cottages at Christmas-time, carol-singing and dancing, the whistling of the ploughboy and the song of the milkmaid as they go to work in the early mornings, the children gathering wild-flowers and searching for birds' nests, the heat and stillness of July, when

> Scythes tinkle in each grassy dell,
> Where solitude was wont to dwell.[1]

[1] "July."
178

Then harvest and ploughing and sowing again, until winter comes,

> And stops the plough, and hides the field in snows.[1]

Although many of these poems had been written in sickness and want, the hunger and poverty and unrest of that troubled time are not reflected in them at all; rather are they the product of those hours when Clare escaped from the darkness of present and future, either into the separate and absorbing world of Nature, or backwards into his childhood, when the village festivals and the lonely wanderings in the fields filled his life. His picture of high summer when

> . . . green wood-fly and blossom-haunting bee,
> Are never weary of their melody.[2]

suggests a very paradise, where men went happily to their work until the evening, then drank their ale and slept; where there was peace and leisure to tend their gardens and play with their children, and search the field and hedge for

> Large bind-weed bells, wild hop, and streak'd woodbine,
> That lift athirst their slender throated flowers.[3]

No hint there of the labour beyond his strength that a man must undertake for a few shillings a week so that his children will not starve, nor of the three gallon loaves that he must share with his wife, nor of the meat that he rarely sees.

There was only one poem in the book which reflected the terrible darkness of the despair that sometimes weighted Clare down and almost broke his spirit; it was the account of a dream that he had had, in which he thought the end of the world had come and knew that hell was his doom.

> And days mis-spent with friends and fellow-men,
> And sins committed,—all were with me then.[4]

But, in the midst of his terror, he awoke to the blessed sight of early morning, and heard the cock crow, and knew that it was but a dream.

There were some shorter poems in the book, and these included

---

[1] "November."   [2] "June."   [3] "June."   [4] "The Dream."

several of the imitations of the old poets. The volume was offered for sale at 6s., and was dedicated to the Marquis of Exeter, who bought ten copies. The reviews were few, and mostly condescending rather than appreciative—*The Eclectic Review*, *The Morning Chronicle*, *The Monthly Magazine*, *The Literary Chronicle*, and *John Bull* published notices. *The Literary Gazette* found things to praise in the poetry, but considered that it would not be romantic enough for the public taste, a fact which the reviewer thought was due to the regular routine of comfort in the life of the English peasantry.

Meanwhile, at Helpston, Clare's hopes for the new volume faded slowly, but he said little of his disappointment.

In June, Patty gave birth to another child which died before it was baptised.

In July, Clare was visited by Henry Behnes, a sculptor and friend of Mrs. Emmerson's, whom he had probably met on one of his visits to London. Mrs. Emmerson wrote when their mutual friend was back in town:

> Harry B told me of your welcome, of the pleasant hour he spent with you, of your harvest, or rather Botanical pursuits, of your delightfully rustic attire, your "unshaven" chin and all the etcetera that are so peculiarly the attributes and habits of the genius of solitude.

With characteristic kindness she enclosed a little gift for Clare, and wrote a postscript: "You will find a *sovereign* remedy for thirst this hot weather—use it for your comfort and say nothing about it."

But Behnes was evidently distressed and shocked by Clare's indigence, and he wrote on 10th July to tell the poet as kindly and tactfully as he could, that the world must be made aware of the true state of things.

> Your Poetic Fame is abroad far and wide and riots on the Lip of rank and Beauty. But yet Rank and Beauty and in short the world as it goes imagines that Poets live immediately upon the conjurations of their own wonder-working imaginations—you can and must undeceive it. Patty and the little ones say you must, they are all eloquent and from their decision can even a genius appeal? The recluse must throw off his cowl for a season and his enquiry into the differences of the "Bee and [spider] orchis" must be changed for the

The bust of John Clare by Henry Behnes, 1828

study of that wasp orchis man. His point gained—merely the independence of himself and Family—he may reabstract as speedily and as quickly as he please.

In August, Taylor wrote enclosing £5 and telling Clare to "keep your Expenses within bounds". He found that he must pay the late firm of Taylor and Hessey between £70 and £80 for advances made to Clare and for the bill that had been settled with Drury on his behalf, and he thought that there was no hope, now, that the sale of the books would reimburse him.

> Of Profit I am certain we have not had any, but that I should not care for—it is to be considerably out of Pocket that annoys me, and by the New Work my Losses will probably be heavy.

He spoke, in the same letter, of the lack of understanding and appreciation for works of merit at that time:

> Sometimes I think the reading Public don't know what true Poetry is, and that it would be a good deed to inform them by selecting the best passages from the true Poets and commenting on them. Since the old Belief in Rhymes and regular recurring Emphases has been determined not to include all the characteristics of Poetry, the poor Folks who were accustomed to count Syllables and look at the Exactness of the Clink at the end of Popeish Couplets for a Test of Excellence, are all thrown out, and nowadays they really do not know what to pin their Faith in.

Clare was hurt and distressed at being set down as a sort of literary liability, and he voiced his feelings both to Mrs. Emmerson and to Henderson. Taylor was evidently feeling injured, too, and a silence ensued between them which lasted for about three months.

Clare continued to see Henderson quite frequently, and we hear of them going on an expedition to look for bee and spider orchis during the summer. Artis had left Milton the year before after some "misdeeds" whose nature is not known, but he remained in the neighbourhood, for a time at any rate, and worked on a book, which he hoped to publish, on the subject of the Roman remains that he had discovered round Castor, and Clare sometimes saw him.

Other acquaintances of whom Clare saw a good deal were the Bishop of Peterborough and his wife, Mrs. Marsh, and although the poet was doubtless not as much at his ease with them as with Henderson and Artis he received much kindness from them. Herbert Marsh was that same bishop to whom Clare had been introduced by Lord Radstock in 1820, and to whom the old Admiral had read extracts from one of Clare's letters to convince him of the purity of the poet's political principles. Mrs. Marsh, a German by birth, took a particular interest in Clare, and in all that she did to help him in the years of sickness showed a tact and lack of condescension that warm the heart towards her. Clare dined at the Bishop's Palace in the summer of 1827, but there is unfortunately no account of the visit, and we learn of it only from a reference in one of Mrs. Emmerson's letters. In October, her letters again provide the sole information as to a meeting between Clare and the Bishop, but this time it is of a different nature and the incident is sufficiently intriguing to make the absence of any further allusion a matter for disappointment.

> The visit of the Bishop was very kind, and his gift to you well suited, I should think, to your tastes—but it was certainly not a little "Malapropos" that you could not ask your noble visitor to enter your cottage, in consequence of the door being lock'd against you.

Had Patty, one wonders, gone out for the day and taken the key, or was a matrimonial quarrel in progress, which had led her to punish her husband by the indignity of being locked out?

In November, Clare broke the long silence with Taylor by sending a friendly letter in which he said that before their correspondence withered away completely, he would "kindle up the expiring spark that remains, and make up a letter by its light". The relationship between poet and publisher was thus restored to a footing of friendliness and mutual regard, having survived another period of coolness. Taylor talked of coming down with Darley to see Clare at Christmas-time, but the plan was never carried out, as Darley was too busy to get away. However, he sent Clare a copy of his new work, *Sylvia*, and expressed the hope that the visit might be made in the spring, although, he said, it would be more for his pleasure than Clare's, "for I have no faculty at conversation—dull as a signpost".

The news that Taylor and Darley would not, after all, be seen at Helpston that Christmas was followed by other and more startling news from London: Taylor had been appointed publisher and

bookseller to the University of London, and Clare must look elsewhere for someone to publish the next volume of poetry, on which
he was now at work.

Christmas found Clare in a state of deep depression again, and
suffering from nervous disorders and pains in the head. Mrs.
Emmerson sent the money for the year's schooling of Eliza, and
also a sovereign with which Patty was to buy some roast beef and
plum pudding for their Christmas dinner; she was, she said, in
poor health herself, and doubted whether another year on earth
would be allotted to her.

Early in January, Clare heard from Dr. Darling in answer
to a request for help and advice over his malady. Darling said
that he could "see no cause for the gloomy tone of your epistle,
but the excitable and consequently depressible nature of the
Poet's feelings. You generate bad humours in your corporeal
frame because you eat more and work less than you used to
do." Clare was worried about an eruption of the skin, and
was evidently not reassured by Darling's letters, for the London
doctor wrote again towards the end of January to suggest that
it might be wise for Clare to consult a local man who could
see him.

Clare wrote to Hessey, too, about the fears which were torturing
him, not only of disease but also of damnation; his thoughts were
on the transgression which he had confessed to Mrs. Emmerson
nearly two years ago.

Hessey replied with a long letter of advice.

> I am very glad to find that the alarm which you entertained when
> you wrote your last letter but one has not so serious a foundation as
> you then supposed—but as there is reason for the suspicion you enter-
> tained, from the character of the person concerned with you, I think
> you should not be content without taking the Opinion of a Medical
> man on the case unless you actually find that all the symptoms have
> entirely disappeared. On your wife's Account (whose name I am
> ashamed to couple with yours in speaking on such a subject) this is
> proper and your duty, and I trust you will think with me and act
> accordingly. . . . You ask for my advice as to what you should do to
> make your Peace with God. Alas, my dear Clare, I am a poor Coun-
> sellor, but I will tell you what David did, when he, who was distin-
> guished by so many marks of the Divine favor, had been led by his
> evil passions into the Commission of the double crime of Adultery
> and Murder—he said "I have sinned against the Lord"—he humbled

himself before the God of Purity, in whose sight he had polluted himself—and if you will read the 51st Psalm you will see in what Language he poured forth the agony of his Soul. You have sinned like him in the first instance, and in intention have been guilty of the second—but it pleased God to frustrate your rash design upon your own life and to afford you time for Repentance. . . . Look to the sacred Book which you have perhaps hitherto too much neglected— see how he encourages sinners to come to him. In almost every page of the Gospels you will find encouragements—"Him that cometh to me I will in no wise cast out". . . . Pray to God for forgiveness and for an Humble heart.

In February, Clare was invited again to the Bishop's Palace, but he was not well enough to go, and told Mrs. Marsh that he had not much hope of recovering. The good lady wrote from Cambridge, whither she had gone with her husband, to recommend some remedies for rheumatism, which she seemed to think was the cause of Clare's illness. He must wear flannel next the skin, and Patty should make him a couple of flannel shirts without delay.

The common thick brown paper, picked of all the little rough-nesses which are generally on its surface is an excellent thing to be worn next the skin, and I recollect one instance where a gentleman had something like a "jacket" of that brown paper tacked together and wore it for more than a month and was cured by it. But there is a plaister which . . . adheres very tightly to the Skin and has in most cases a wonderful effect on rheumatic pains. If I can procure some today you shall have it with this letter. . . .

If poor Clare was able, at that moment, to smile at all, he may well have done so at the idea that an illness such as his could be cured by brown paper.

Mrs. Emmerson wrote on 14th February, begging him to come up to London.

Now, my dear Clare, let me, instead of listening to (or rather acting upon your melancholy forebodings) entreat you to cheer up, and in the course of another week make up a little bundle of clothes, and set yourself quietly inside the Deeping Coach for London. I will get your "sky chamber" ready to receive you, or my niece Eliza shall yield to you her lower apartment, the Blue room. We can then, in "council met", talk over "Wills", and "New Vols of poems", and all other worldly matters relating to yourself, myself and posterity.

Patty and Clare's parents were all anxious for him to go, and he would have the double benefits of Dr. Darling's attendance and a change of scene, so when a second letter came from Mrs. Emmerson, telling him to come on the following Saturday, he yielded to persuasion and went.

He spent about five weeks in Stratford Place and received treatment from Dr. Darling, which included sulphur baths; he spoke afterwards of the relief which these afforded him, and no doubt the journey, and the different company and surroundings helped to cheer him somewhat and distract his thoughts from their gloomy channels. How much Dr. Darling understood of the nature of Clare's illness it is impossible to tell, but he certainly realised that its origin was not physical and he could not do very much more than treat Clare symptomatically and prescribe the rest and good food which he could not have. The evidence of the course of the disease is not very complete, but it is possible to trace the alternations of furious creative activity and black and terrible despair, which latter state gave rise to numerous physical symptoms, such as pains in the head, numbness, and sleeplessness. Darling certainly helped Clare more than any of the other doctors that attended him, and his task was made easier by the fact that his patient had great faith in his skill.

The visit to London might have proved even more beneficial had Clare been able to consort more with his old friends, but their circle was now broken, and he did not, in any case, feel well enough to do much visiting. Rippingille was out of town, Van Dyk was seriously ill, and was to die some three months later, after struggling against terrible poverty; Reynolds, De Quincey and the rest of the "Londoners" had lost touch with Taylor since the magazine dinners had ended. Darley, alone of them all, had remained a close friend of the publisher, and Clare saw him, as also Allan Cunningham. He visited Cary at the British Museum and was shown round the library, which astonished and delighted him, and he saw a good deal of Henry Behnes, who then and afterwards showed him great kindness.

During this visit, Behnes, who had now added Burlowe to his name to distinguish him from his brother, did a bust of Clare in bronze, which was said to be a very good likeness. Clare's head must have been an interesting one to the sculptor, with its clean-cut features and high forehead. S. C. Hall, editor of one of the

Annuals, who met Clare in 1828, noticed particularly that remarkable feature:

> He was short and thick, yet not ungraceful in person. His coun-
> tenance was plain but agreeable; he had a look and manner so
> dreamy, as to have appeared sullen—but for a peculiarly winning
> smile; and his forehead was so broad and high, as to have bordered
> on deformity.

Clare, of course, saw Taylor during his stay in London, and the publisher proposed to him that he should take a number of copies of the poems at a rate below the normal price and try to sell them in the neighbourhood of Helpston. The exercise and employment of carrying the books round from house to house would, he thought, be helpful to Clare's health, and it might also result in the sale of books which were otherwise doomed to remain on his hands. Clare readily agreed to the plan, and seems to have been quite enthusiastic about it; he spoke of it to Cunningham who was indignant that Taylor should expect a poet to submit to a scheme so derogatory to his dignity, and Mrs. Emmerson at first said the same thing, but Clare's hope and confidence in his ability to make a success of it overcame her doubts, and she ended by encouraging him in the venture.

Towards the end of March, Clare began to long for home. Martin tells how he went for a walk through Regents Park and past Primrose Hill towards Hampstead where he found some early violets; the sight made him so homesick that he rushed back to Stratford Place and told Mrs. Emmerson that he must go, which he proceeded to do in less than twenty-four hours. If this was so, he must have abandoned his earlier plan, for he wrote to Patty on 21st March to announce that "next Wednesday night will see me in my old corner once again amongst you". He had presents for all the children:

> . . . I am anxious to see you and the children and I sincerely
> hope you are all well. I have bought the dear little children four
> books, and Henry Behnes has promised to send Frederick a wagon
> and horses, as a box of music is not to be had. The books I have
> bought them are *Puss in Boots*, *Cinderella*, *Little Rhymes*, and *The Old
> Woman and the Pig*. Tell them that the pictures are all coloured and
> they must make up their minds to choose which they like best ere
> I come home.

On the same day he wrote to Allan Cunningham to say that he had meant to see him to say good-bye, but "as you are aware of my ignorance in travelling about your great Babel, being insufficient to do so in most cases without a guide, which is not always to be procured, you must allow me to make up for the omission by a shake of the hand on paper, as hearty as your imagination can feel it".

So Clare turned his back upon the "great Babel" and went home to Helpston.

20

THE STRUGGLE FOR INDEPENDENCE

M<small>RS. EMMERSON'S FIRST LETTER</small>
after Clare's return home suggests that, even if his departure was not as sudden as Martin would have us believe, it was somewhat hurried and created a certain amount of chaos at Stratford Place. She said that his "goods and chattels were so numerous to assemble together upon your departure from me, that I might naturally be expected in my nervous state of feeling and absence of mind to forget the packing up [of] a portion of them—your 'greatcoat' should have been remembered most particularly for your own comfort's sake". But she promised to send the coat, with some books which had also been forgotten, by coach to the Bull Inn at Market Deeping, where Clare could collect them.

The poet, who was much improved in spirits and whose mind was now once more freeing itself from the weight of despair under which it had laboured all the winter, prepared to start on his new venture as a travelling bookseller. He was full of hope that it would prove a means of making some money, and setting him up in less straightened circumstances.

> I do assure you [he wrote to Taylor] I have been in great diffi-
> culties and tho' I remained silent under them I felt them oppress my
> spirits to such a degree that I almost sunk under them, for those two
> fellows of Peterboro' in the character [of] doctors have annoyed and
> dunned me most horribly by times, and tho' one's claims are unjust I
> cannot get over him by any other method than paying. But my
> coming up to town has alleviated me a little, and by the next latter
> end of the year I hope to be half set up.

He was also going to write for various of the Annuals, which he disliked but regarded as a possible source of money and could not, therefore, afford to ignore. In his present mood of increasing cheerfulness he did not lack resolution or courage to face his diffi-culties, and he was even able to feel to himself fortunate in the possession of a happy home, and superior to the Londoners in the nearness of his well-loved fields; ". . . thank God," he said, "I am once more in my old corner, and in freedom I am as great as her Majesty, so a fig for the Babelonians".

On 15th April, Taylor sent him six complete sets of the four volumes, and an extra half-dozen of *The Shepherd's Calendar*, and wished him all luck in his "new Business of Bookselling". But the venture begun with such high hopes was not a success.

According to one story, Clare went on the first day to Market Deeping and, after meeting with a chilling reception from the rector, who disapproved of poems being "hawked about" in this manner, took shelter from the rain in the covered yard of an inn. There he met with a party of horse-dealers who, to his astonishment knew and admired his work; they offered him brandy which he refused, treated him to a good breakfast, and bought all the books he had with him, for which some of them paid more than the full price.

This seemed a good beginning, but Clare could not forget the snub that he had received at the rectory, and wondered uneasily whether the other people that he was to visit would take after the rector or the horse-dealers. He went the next day in the direction of Stamford, visiting a number of houses on the way, but he did not succeed in selling a single volume. Many of the people knew his name and had heard of his poems, but most of them expressed shocked surprise that he should descend so low as to "go through the country with a bundle on his back", and poor Clare, who could see nothing undignified in being a pedlar of books, began to realise the project was a dismal failure.

On 29th April, 1828, another son was born to Clare and Patty, and was christened William Parker. No doubt Clare regarded the event with mixed feelings. He loved his children too well to feel that any of them were unwanted, yet his very affection for them made him feel more keenly the lack of money with which to provide food and clothes and an education; each new life added to the burden of responsibility upon his shoulders, and he was fearful of their future, wondering what would happen to them if he died or became permanently ill.

In May, Mrs. Emmerson wrote that she had seen the bust of Clare by Behnes Burlowe, and was more than delighted with it, "not only as a Work of Genius—but for its faithful, at the same time highly poetical resemblance to our modern Shakespeare!" Clare, evidently irritated by this piece of fulsome praise, crossed out the last two words and wrote above them "too bad, Eliza".

The good lady was busy with a scheme to get Clare a better cottage and a little land, which would make him independent, and she had hoped that her friend, Henry Ryde, who was probably agent to Lord Spencer at Burghley, would be instrumental in arranging it. He apparently expressed himself able and willing to do this when she saw him in London, and she wrote several times to Clare about it, but nothing came of Ryde's promises.

In September, Clare went to Boston for a few days at the invitation of Henry Brooke, editor of the Boston *Gazette*, and was there given a great welcome by many admirers of his work. The Mayor gave a dinner for him of which he wrote an account to Taylor:

> He [the mayor of the town] was a very jolly companion, and made me so welcome, while a lady at the table talked so ladily of the Poets, that I drank off my glass very often without knowing it, and he as quickly filled it with no other intention than that of hospitality and I felt rather queer and got off almost directly after finding myself so, but I was nothing like disordered; yet it was wine, and I was not used to the drink, and tho' it made me ill for two days—or at least helped to do so, for I had a sort of cold at the same time—it was nothing of that kind that caused my illness after my return.

Clare was delighted with the kindness and sincere admiration of the people of Boston, but the role of a literary lion was not one that he enjoyed playing. Following on the mayor's dinner came news of a plan, formulated by a party of young men, to give a supper at the inn where Clare was staying, and to persuade him to make a speech.

> But as soon as I heard it [Clare said] I declined it, telling them if they expected a speech from me they need prepare no supper, for that would serve me for everything. And so I got off. . . . Really this speechifying is a sore humbug, and the sooner it is out of fashion the better.

Clare sold quite a number of books while in Boston, which he autographed for his admirers, so that the visit was a financial help to him as well as a pleasing reminder that there were still plenty of people who remembered his name and appreciated his work. It was also the first, and in fact, the only occasion on which he saw the sea; he was deeply impressed by its immensity and majesty, and we are told that the thought of it kept him awake on his first night in Boston, and that "when he fell asleep, towards the morning, the white-crested waves of the sea, stretching away into infinite space, hovered in new images over his dreams."[1]

He was invited to visit three other Lincolnshire towns where people were anxious to do him honour—Grantham, Tattershall, and Spalding—as well as King's Lynn in Norfolk, but he had had enough of social occasions and did not feel equal to any more, so he went straight home. It is said that when he got back to Helpston he found £10 which had been placed in his wallet by the young men who had tried to give a supper for him, and he was deeply touched and filled with regret that he had been so ungracious as to refuse to make a speech for these kind friends.

Clare was taken ill after his return with a fever which he had doubtless caught in Boston, for there was always a great deal of ague and fever in the fen country at that time of year. He gave it to all his family, and it was consequently some time before the household was free of the unpleasant and lowering sickness.

As soon as he was better, Clare was at work again; he had now a considerable number of poems, written in the last five years or so, and he was anxious to publish another volume, but he did not know whom to approach on the subject. Taylor was now established in Upper Gower Street and was busy with such publications as Darley's *Popular Algebra*, and *Popular Geometry*, and a series of Interlinear Translations, which were the works of Latin and Greek authors interlined with the English version. This was the man who had championed Keats against a hostile world, introduced a peasant poet to the public, and edited a magazine which numbered among its contributors Hazlitt, Lamb, and De Quincey, and one is tempted to wonder how, after the glory of those former days, he could be content to publish nothing but educational books. But content he was, and he gave no sign of regret for the cessation of the bold ventures and noble risks that he had once undertaken in the name of literature. Perhaps under the circumstances it was but natural; Taylor was now a man of middle age who had tired both mind and body with overwork for many years, and had lately been through a severe illness. The fire of youth had gone out of him, and with it the desire to champion lost causes or risk losses on the work of young poets; he wanted

[1] Martin's *Life of Clare*.

security and an absence of adventure, and the safe haven of London University provided him with both. He continued to correspond with Clare and to take a friendly interest in all that concerned him, but he could make no suggestions as to a possible publisher for Clare's work, and his only advice was that in view of the flatness of the market it was best to be content with contributions to the Annuals.

At Christmas, the kindly Behnes Burlowe sent presents for Clare and Patty, and accompanied them with a cheerful letter:

> I send two Bottles of the Best Blood of the Grape for Mrs. Clare and as all of us great and small are more or less under petticoat government I have sent some Flannel to "Patty" to render this "ruling power" as tolerable and comfortable for both parties as possible. To render it to you, my Boy, still more Bearable I send something in the shape of a bottle of kind Brandy, enough to make any Job modern or ancient bid defiance to—even to his wife.

In January, Clare was writing cheerfully to Taylor:

> I don't think I have drunk a pint of ale together this two years; in fact I can drink nothing strong now in any quantity, and as to spirits I never touch [them] and yet without them I feel hearty and hale and have quite recovered from my last ailments and hope to prolong the lease of life for a good season, tho' I don't think I am much qualified for an old man.

In this hopeful mood Clare was not only writing furiously but was seeking to turn his work to good account. Meeting with no helpful advice as to his poems from Taylor, he occupied himself with another scheme which was to publish a volume of the imitations of the old poets. Taylor thought that if he did so he should offer them as his own work, but Clare still clung to the idea of a literary deception, and wrote to ask Cary his opinion on the subject.

He replied that he thought it would be a mistake, and might injure Clare's reputation; his "own natural guise", Cary thought, was better than the borrowed trim of the Elizabethans.

> What you most excel in is the description of such natural objects as you have yourself had the opportunity of observing, and which none before you have noticed, though every one instantly recognises their truth.

Clare then wrote to Darley about a long descriptive poem on which he was engaged and which he had called "The Pleasures of Spring". Taylor had not been encouraging about it, and Darley was hardly more so.

> There have been so many "Pleasures of so-and-so" that I should almost counsel you against baptizing your Poem on Spring the "Pleasures" of anything. Besides, when a poem is so designated it is almost assuredly forejudged as deficient in action (about which you appear solicitous).

He thought, however, that Clare could "infuse a dramatic spirit" into the poem, and that it was most essential that he should do so; he might take as a model Thomson's *Lavinia*, spread out into a longer story, "incidents and descriptions perpetually relieving each other." He mentioned, also, Allan Ramsay's *Gentle Shepherd*, but said that he lacked "imagination, elegance, and a certain scorn of mere earth, which is essential to the constitution of a true poet. You want none of these; but you want his vivacity, character, and action: I mean to say you have not *as yet* exhibited these qualities."

Having given up the idea of publishing a volume of the imitations, Clare saw no prospect for the moment but that of continuing with his contributions to the Annuals. Among those that published his poems in 1829 were *Friendship's Offering* edited by Thomas Pringle, *The Amulet*, edited by S. C. Hall, Hood's *Gem* and Cunningham's *The Anniversary*. In the three previous years he had contributed to Alaric Watts's *The Literary Souvenir*, and others in which he was represented several times over a course of years were *Friendship's Offering*, Ackermann's *Forget Me Not*, and Marshall's *Pledge of Friendship*. But, although quite a number of Clare's poems were printed, it was not much help to him financially, for some of the Annuals never paid him for his work and others only paid after repeated visits from Clare's friends. Pringle was punctilious in making his payments, and so was Allan Cunningham, who was one of the few editors for whom Clare was glad to write, knowing that his poems would be appreciated. So far from having to importune Cunningham for money, as he was obliged to do with certain others, he wrote in February, 1829, to point out that he had been paid too much; evidently he suspected that this was due to Cunningham's kind heart, and his pride was roused.

I do not expect pay by the foot or page, but I like to give good measure and throw in an extra gratis. You gave me too much for my last, and I hope you will keep that in mind next year and not do so; for I never feel the loss of independence worse than when I cannot serve a friend without knowing that I receive a recompense in return far more than the labour is entitled to.

One of the poems that Clare sent to *The Anniversary* was addressed to Mrs. Emmerson, under her initials, E. L. E. Cunningham, having apparently read it hurriedly or inattentively, took the letters to be L. E. L., which was the signature used by Miss Landon, the poet, and wrote to Clare: "Your verses to Miss Landon are the very best you ever composed. After all, a flesh and blood muse is best, and Miss Landon I must say is a very beautiful substitute for these aerial mistresses. I shall show it to her."

Clare was embarrassed by this mistake but he did not like to write to Cunningham about it himself, so he asked Mrs. Emmerson to put things right. If she felt the matter "too delicate to write upon" she was to tell the Miss Frickers, sisters-in-law of Coleridge and Southey, who would explain it for her.

Clare also had poems published in a few newspapers and magazines of that time, and *The European Magazine* printed his essay on "Popularity in Authorship".

In February, 1829, Clare went to Northampton to visit George Baker, who worked for many years on a History of Northamptonshire which was never finished.

In April he was writing to Taylor about his attempts at bookselling; he persevered by means of advertisements in the *Stamford News*, but although these brought a few visitors there was rarely a purchaser among them. He pressed Taylor again for a statement of account:

> For if there is anything owing to me it will be acceptable at any time, and if there is nothing I shall be content. The number printed of the first three volumes I have known a long while by Drury's account; but whether I have overrun the constable or not since then, I cannot tell, and that is what I should like to know at the first opportunity.

In May, Hessey's name appeared in the register of bankrupts; Clare wrote: "Poor Hessey's failure astonished me. . . . I always thought him a cautious monied man."

During the summer Clare worked in the fields, and he wrote to Mrs. Emmerson that he was "right heartily in good health".

In August the long-awaited accounts came at last. They covered the whole period of Clare's association with the firm of Taylor and Hessey, and were divided into Accounts A, B, C, D, and E.

A, which was the general account, showed, on the debit side, the various sums paid out to Clare between 1820 and 1829, the bill of Drury's which the firm had paid on his behalf, and a sum of £24 for books. On the credit side were profits on his books, and dividends and annuities that were paid through Taylor. The account showed that Clare owed the firm £140.

Account B showed the list of subscribers to the Fund which Lord Radstock had raised, and C gave details of the four editions of *Poems Descriptive of Rural Life and Scenery.* Rather over 3,600 copies had been sold in all, but no profit to Clare was entered on the account; Drury and Taylor and Hessey had a half profit each on the first three editions, and Taylor charged a 5 per cent commission for his work as editor, while £20 was entered as having been paid to Clare for copyright per Drury. The £100 which the firm had contributed to the Fund for Clare in 1820 was entered to the debit side of the account. In the Introduction to *The Village Minstrel,* Taylor had said that the sum was "advanced" by the firm, but in a letter to Clare dated 18th April, 1820, he had clearly said that it was a gift.

In Account D, which was concerned with *The Village Minstrel,* there was a profit of £56 on the 1,250 copies sold. Half of this was entered to Drury and the firm, and the other half to Clare. On the debit side appeared 15 guineas for Hilton's portrait of Clare which had been painted by Taylor's wish and not by Clare's, although it seems that at one point there had been some discussion as to whether the poet should pay for it. As some of the transactions now under review dated back nine years, it is not surprising that both parties had rather forgotten what they said at the time.

Account E showed that only 425 copies of *The Shepherd's Calendar* had been sold, and the book had failed to pay expenses by £60.

Clare, having studied the accounts carefully, wrote his comments:

> In this cash account there is nothing allowed me for my three years' writing for *London Magazine.* I was to have £12 a year and this

with £7 given to them for me by Duchess and never sent me makes
my 3 years writing for Mag £36

Duchess Subscription   7
                            ———
                £43 never yet accounted for.

Who the Duchess was, we are not told, but she may have been
the wife of one of the three Dukes who subscribed to the original
Fund.

Elsewhere Clare commented on the £20 copyright said to have
been paid for his first poems.

> How can this be? I never sold the Poems for any price. What
> money I had of Drury was given me on account of profits to be
> received: but here it seems I have got nothing and am brought in
> minus twenty pounds of which I never received sixpence. . . .

Clare was busy with the harvest when the accounts came, and
he took no action in the matter for some weeks, except to write to
Mrs. Emmerson and tell her of his dissatisfaction. She replied:

> The claims brought against you, appear very unjustifiable, and I
> should think will be greatly modified by your own clear and simple
> statement of facts:—Mr. Taylor is surely a just man, and will not
> attempt to enforce that which cannot be well substantiated, viz, the
> £20 for the copyright—the 15 guineas for the Portrait (of course,
> this Picture is, in such case, your own property and you will claim it!).

Clare's letter to Taylor was evidently written with considerable
reluctance, and he apologised for pointing out the errors in the
account. He felt that this last revelation of the state of his financial
affairs dealt the final blow to his hopes of earning a living by his
writing, but he said that "in losing hope I have cleared the prospect to see a little further as to how I must proceed for the future".
It was now his idea to try and get a cottage with some land and
concentrate his energies on gaining a living from that.

Taylor did not take offence at Clare's letter, but he did not
answer it until January. He had consulted Hessey, who, since his
bankruptcy, had moved to Regent Street and set up as a book and
print auctioneer, and they had agreed that some of Clare's corrections should be admitted. "You need never expect any Difference
of Feeling in me from the candid Declaration of your own Views
and Opinions."

Meanwhile, Clare had written to Drury on the subject of the £20 which Taylor and Hessey had paid to him but which *he* had never paid to Clare. Drury replied on 18th November, 1829:

> In the first place, in respect to the sum of £20, which you suppose has not been paid to you, I beg to say that at the identical time of your executing the instrument intended for my protection, I paid you a Balance which with some previous payments made to you and by your direction, made up this sum of £20. [He added:] I must now beg to be excused for declining to take any interest in by-gone concerns, which indeed afford me small reason for congratulation.

Clare commented that his loss was £40, for not only had he never been paid the £20, but had in fact been charged it for his own property. "I could hardly bear patience to contradict such a barefaced lie—and when I did it was to no purpose—so there the matter rested."

During the winter, Clare went on with his work, and corresponded spasmodically with his London friends. His contributions to the Annuals continued, and in the spring he was trying to exact payment from S. C. Hall, but without success. His old friend Sharpe, a Northamptonshire man who worked in the Dead Letter Office, tried to get an interview with the editor to demand Clare's money, but he had to report: "Hall is as hard to catch as a little eel."

21

THE CLOUDED MIND

In the summer of 1830 Clare's parents left the cottage and went to live elsewhere; the removal was doubtless necessitated by lack of space, for besides Clare and Patty there were now five children and another one expected.

Clare was apparently still in good health and spirits during the spring and early summer, and was busy with his writing and his natural history observations. But on 14th July occurred an incident which marked the end of this period of happiness and the beginning of the descent into an abyss of sickness and misery. He was invited by the Bishop and Mrs. Marsh, whom he had visited at frequent intervals during the summer, to dine with them and attend the theatre at Peterborough. According to Martin, who misdated the incident by six years and whose account is therefore not to be regarded as wholly reliable, the play was *The Merchant of Venice*, and Clare, after listening in silence to the first three acts, sprang up during the scene where Portia delivers judgment, climbed on to his seat, and began shouting abuse at Shylock. He was apparently led out of the theatre and went home to Helpston in a state of great agitation.

The next day Mr. Mossop, the vicar of Helpston, asked Clare to come to his house, as he had a friend staying with him who was anxious to meet the poet. In an account which he wrote years afterwards, he said that Clare "had not been long seated in the room ere he showed aberrations of intellect by variety of fancies; among the most prominent was that of appearing to see spirits of a hideous description moving about in the ceiling of the room". Mr. Mossop was so much alarmed by his appearance that he insisted on getting medical advice and communicated with Lord Fitzwilliam, who sent Dr. Skrimshire.

Clare's mind seems to have become quite clear again within a short time, but his physical symptoms persisted for several months—violent pains in his head, indigestion, and feelings of numbness about his body. There remained also the acute melancholy and strange and horrible fears which gave him no peace.

Whether he afterwards remembered the incident at the theatre, or whether he only knew of it from others, we do not know, but four days after it had happened, Frank Simpson, nephew of Mrs. Gilchrist and a good friend of Clare's, wrote to say that he had heard of the affair from a clergyman named Heycock and was too fond of Clare to remain silent or indifferent. He advised him to lose no time in writing an apology to Mrs. Marsh.

> It was your frailty not your viciousness which was uppermost, and the (tho' warm yet unwise) conduct of your Companions which hurried you into Error—Let your Confession whether in prose or verse (and either is sure to do honor to your heart and extraordinary understanding) breathe only your real feelings and the Charity of your good patroness will be sure to receive it with pleasure and admiration. . . .

It seems rather as though Simpson thought that Clare had been drunk, and as the neighbourhood knew of his old failing in that direction it is quite probable that such was the story being told in Peterborough and Stamford. Certainly Simpson had not, at that point, any idea of how ill Clare was or he could not have imagined that it was possible for him to write his letter of apology straight away.

The news that reached London, however, was plainly of a mental collapse and not of intoxication. Behnes Burlowe was visited at the beginning of August by a friend from Stamford, who told him the story, and he at once sent a note to Mrs. Emmerson. She wrote to Patty on 4th August to express her concern: "I hope in God! the account of his illness and the *mental* part of it is without foundation." If so, she hoped that Clare would write to reassure her without delay, but if it was unhappily true Patty was to get someone to write her particulars of his illness.

By the beginning of September, Clare was recovering, and Simpson wrote to him on 9th: "It gives me the greatest possible satisfaction to see how much you are recovered by the friendly and clever letter you have this day written to me."

Simpson's mother, too, was full of kindly concern for Clare, and we find her writing on 17th September to echo her son's sentiments of pleasure that his condition was improving.

I now think you may keep yourself well if you do but study your stomach. I have not the least doubt but that all your depression arises from a weak digestion and I recommend you very earnestly when you feel more uncomfortable than usual to take if it was even two or three times a day—or night if necessary—as much as would lay on a shilling of powdered Rhubarb and the same quantity of carbonate of soda mixed in a wine-glass of water.

As soon as Clare was well enough to write, he had sent his apologies to Mrs. Marsh, and she replied on 9th October, expressing her relief at the news that he was better.

We were so soon informed of your illness that whatever there had been of alarm has long vanished, and I must request you from us all that you will try to obliterate it from your Memory. . . . I recommend you to eat a few of our grapes, which though not so sweet as in a more genial summer, are still very pleasant and I hope they will be beneficial to your health. Therefore I must request you to eat them *all yourself* by degrees, and to make that the easier, I send some ginger-bread for the children.

The children now numbered six, and the youngest was much too small to eat gingerbread, for another daughter had been born on 24th July and christened Sophia.

Clare had also written to Taylor as soon as he was strong enough to do so, and had evidently given him a detailed account of his illness, for the publisher's reply gives some idea of what Clare had suffered during the first severe phase when his mind was affected. Taylor thought that it must have been a more severe form of the kind of attack that he had had when he was so ill in 1825:

I had not your Imaginations of unreal sights and sounds, but I had the same suspicions of those around me, and the same convictions (I am happy to add) of the indestructible Nature of my own Soul—It seemed to glow like a Spark of Fire beneath a pile of Mountains, and nothing would extinguish or injure it—had the whole world been heaped together over it I felt as if it was impossible to be crushed. . . . I was heated in Mind, and under some false Impressions, but not quite unable to form a tolerably correct Judgment of what was going on around me, and herein your Illness surpassed mine in the violence of its Effects.

He had communicated with Dr. Darling, who had promised to write instructions to Clare and did not doubt that he would soon be better.

To Hessey, too, Clare wrote at this time about his illness, about his faith, the happiness of his home and his thoughts of the future.

As for religion, my mind is completely at rest in that matter. My late deplorable situation proved to me that I had read the Bible successfully, for it was an antidote to my deepest distresses and I had not the least doubt on my conviction of its truth.

He spoke of the good health which Patty enjoyed, and how she was

so seldom ill that she forgets from time to time what illness is and I have heard her declare that she never knew what the headache was in her life until within these last few years. She has been of much comfort to me, both in illness and health, and I always feel happy that I met with such a fortunate accident that brought us together, for "an honest woman is the honour of her husband". . . . My children are comforts in their kind, but the thoughts of their future welfare often makes me uncomfortable about them. I wish to make them all good common scholars, and wish also to instill into all their minds the inestimable value and the upright integrity of common honesty. Mr. Mossop, our vicar, has been uncommonly kind to me in my illness, and he wrote as kindly while I was ill to Mrs. E to ask her to get my eldest boy, Frederick, into a school—and he has told me to mention it again to Mrs. E but the shock that his success will give [me] in being obliged to part with him (if the attempts of his friends are successful) will be so great that I never have had the courage to allude to it.

The school was Christ's Hospital, and the Emmersons and Behnes Burlowe made several attempts to get a place there for Frederick, but without success.

Clare's mood is reflected in a poem called "Recovery" which he wrote after one of his serious attacks of illness and desperate melancholy:

> The storm is past, a weary storm,
> And, like a broken tree
> Whose fragment still with hope is green,
> So do I turn to thee.
>
> I come before thee like a child,
> Unknowing if I sin;
> I come with every hope beguiled
> And think thou'lt take me in.

In November he wrote to Taylor about the fears that troubled him whenever he was depressed: "I feel as if haunted by evil spirits sometimes, of the evil kind, who chanted incantations in rhymes. . . . I believe spirits both evil and good are existing."

But a month later he was in a happier mood, and wrote to Mrs. Emmerson in such cheerful vein that she thanked him for his "charming picture of *real* comfort, of chimney-corner enjoyment, of winter delight, of social and sweet cottage love".

Taylor wrote on 12th January, 1831, promising to send by the coach the next day the balance of Clare's half-yearly dividend, and a copy of Chaucer's works. "Take care of the Chaucer," he said, "it was Keats's copy." He made a strange suggestion about paying the dividend money; he sent Clare an account for Drakard and Wilson, of Stamford, for books to the value of £5 7s. 4d. which they had owed to Taylor and Hessey since 1827, and Clare was to collect the money and keep it as part payment of what was due to him. The poet, not unnaturally, refused. He owed money to Drakard and Wilson, so he could hardly present a bill and demand payment. Anyway, he did not want to fight the publisher's financial battles for him, and was in no fit state to do so. He was not so well again at that time, and in a letter to Taylor he sadly remarked that he could not help "often wishing I had never been known beyond 1818".

On 5th February, Frank Simpson sent a note by Patty, who had been to Stamford, saying that they were all much concerned to hear of Clare's ill health. He had been negotiating for him with a Mr. Nell, who wished to publish one of his poems set to music. The letter ended with a nice piece of advice: "Patty is urgent to go but I will conclude with advising you to keep *your Bowels open and the Fear of God before your eyes* not jocosely but seriously and sincerely."

Simpson acted for Clare in another literary negotiation later in the spring. A local paper called *The Bee or Stamford Herald and Country Chronicle* had been started in November, and Clare had been contributing to it without receiving any of the payment that had been promised him; in May he was desperate for money, and Simpson undertook to plead his cause with the editor, but it seems that he never got the money and he stopped his contributions. He was not sorry, for the paper was a product of the political unrest of that time and was very violent in its politics. Clare explained that he was not in sympathy with its sentiments any more than with those of the opposing paper, *The Champion*, for which he also wrote.

> I hate party feuds [he said] and can never become a party man, but where I have friends on both sides there I am on both sides as far as my opinions can find it right; but no further, not an inch.

At the time Clare wrote this, England was ablaze with "party feuds". In his immediate neighbourhood there had been, in the previous year, riots round Peterborough, Stamford, Oundle, and Wellingborough. In that year (1830), it will be remembered, Cobbett had published his *Rural Rides*, with its appalling revelations—for those who cared to read—of the sufferings of the peasantry. Of labourers near Cricklade, whose dwellings were "little better than pig-beds", he said: "I never saw human wretchedness equal to this: no, not even amongst the free negroes in America who, on an average, do not work one day out of four." If the case of which he spoke was a particularly bad one, there were thousands all over England whose plight was not much better, and the risings were an inevitable consequence of such a state of affairs. The end of 1830 and the beginning of 1831 saw a number of mass trials of the men who had taken part in them, and at the first of these, held at Winchester, 101 prisoners were capitally convicted, of whom 6 were executed, and 95 transported for life.

No one understood better than Clare the sufferings that caused these troubles, for he had watched them and shared them all his life, but his compassion and his desire to see reform did not overcome his innate hatred of violence, and he was convinced that it would do no good, for "as extremes must be met by extremes, the good is always lost like a plentiful harvest in bad weather". Intolerance in religion or politics was always repugnant to him, and he ascribed this view to "the little wisdom I have gotten", believing that had he not learned to read and write he would not have regarded such matters with the same unbiased outlook. Party politics, it seemed to him, were seldom free from profit-seeking or bigoted opinions, and he wished to keep clear of them.

> For I consider it nothing more or less than a game at hide and seek for self interest, and the terms Whig and Tory are nothing more in my mind than the left and right hand of that monster, the only difference being that the latter lies nearer the windfalls of success than the other; but that there are some, and many, who have the good of the people at heart is not to be doubted.

In a letter to Taylor in 1831, he gave his opinion of the troubles of the time. The farmer, he said, was always on the look-out for "high prices and better markets", the parson advocated lower taxes, so that his tithes and livings might be left untouched, and the speculator wanted a paper currency to help his cheating. He thought that a paper currency on sound principles would be a good plan, and that "a universal reduction of tithes, clerical livings, placemen's pensions and taxes . . . suitable to the present decreased value of money and property" was the only way to bring salvation to the country.

> I am no leveller, for I want not a farthing of any one's property. All I want is to keep the little fortune allowed me to call mine; but if the Government goes on taking a little from those who have little and leaving the wealthy untouched, I shall quickly be what I have been.

Clare's health, after the set-back in January, made no improvement, and in March, 1831, he wrote to Taylor in a state of acute depression. He had bad pains in his stomach, headaches, and prickly pains in his arms, head, and shoulders.

> Until last night I got tollerable rest but the pain at my stomach was more frequent in its attacks. I awoke in dreadful irritation, thinking that the Italian liberators were kicking my head about for a football. My future prospects seem to be no sleep—a general debility —a stupid and stony apathy or lingering madness.

He believed that the only person who could help him was Dr. Darling, and he wondered if he should sell out the Fund-money, and take a humble lodging in London to be near him.

The question of money was particularly acute just then; the value of the half-yearly dividend had fallen to £6 17s. 9d. which, added to the money from Spencer and Exeter, amounted to less than £20, and, while Clare was not well enough to work in the fields, this, and the uncertain payments from the editors of the Annuals, composed his income. He kept notes of some of his expenditure for this year; there was a school bill for Anna, Eliza, and Frederick, who were being taught by Samuel Williamson of Helpston, and there were several cobbler's bills for mending the children's shoes. The book in which he entered these was humorously labelled "For Matters of the first Importance and generally the last attended to."

Another sign of Clare's efforts to keep a tight rein on his expenses is a recipe for home-made ink which he entered in his notebook and used at about this time. Three ounces of bruised galls, $10\frac{1}{2}$ ounces of green copper, and a piece of stone blue were to be put in rain-water, soaked, and shaken every day until fit for use. The result may have been successful at the time, but in later years the ink ate into the paper and made great holes and smudges which rendered most of the writing illegible.

But sickness and anxiety did not stop Clare working, and he was busy on all sorts of literary activities—more poems, essays (of which he wrote sometimes three or four drafts), his long satirical poem, "The Parish", and a rather Dickensian Sketch called "The Bone and Cleaver Club". He was also writing an essay on "The Sublime and Beautiful in Poetry", in which he illustrated his remarks with selections; perhaps the idea had come to him as a result of Taylor's suggestion that it would be a good deed to tell the reading public the nature of true poetry.

22

NORTHBOROUGH

IN JULY, 1831, HENDERSON wrote to tell Clare that a cottage with a little land had become vacant at Northborough and to suggest that he should get Mr. Mossop to write to Lord Milton without delay and ask if Clare could have it. Lord Milton agreed to let Clare have a cottage, though not, it seems, the one Henderson had mentioned, but a new one that was being built and would be ready in January; it had five acres of land with it and was to be let at a rent of about £13 a year.

Clare was ill again at the end of the summer and evidently wrote few letters, for it was from Mr. Mossop that Mrs. Emmerson learned that the poet was, as she put it, shortly to become "Farmer John". She sent down a bundle of clothes at the end of July, which, she said, had seen better days but might usefully be cut down for the children. The piece of brown wrapper in which the things were folded would make Patty some scrubbing aprons. She enclosed some money with which Clare was to pay the village tailor for converting the clothes, and added a postscript: "You need *not* name *what* this letter contains in your next as I merely send it to pay 'Snip'."

A few days earlier, Taylor had written that he would like to sell the stock of Clare's volumes, and would willingly dispose of them at 1*s.* per copy in sheets to anyone who would take them all, but he did not wish Clare to adopt this plan unless he agreed that there was no hope of getting any more for them. It was a sad end to Clare's hopes, but they must already have been withered almost to nothing; in October, Mrs. Emmerson wrote that she learned from the pages of *The Athenaeum* and *The Literary Gazette* that "Poetry is in a Consumption, that it languishes upon the shelf and pines away from want of patronage".

In the same month, when Clare was recovering from his illness, he wrote tragically to Taylor; he was still too deep in the slough of despond, too battered from his late sickness, to show any of that courage and optimism with which he faced troubles when he was well. He felt lonely and neglected and without hope.

All I want to go on is a stimulus, an encouraging aspiration that refreshes the heart like a shower in summer. Instead of that, I have nothing but drawbacks and disappointments. I live in a land over-flowing with obscurity and vulgarity, far away from taste and books and friends. Poor Gilchrist was the only man of letters in this neigh-bourhood and now he has left it a desert.

In November, Taylor visited Mrs. Emmerson to discuss Clare's affairs, and the result was that they sent £10 to Mr. Mossop with which he was to discharge a doctor's bill which Clare owed. He also owed rent for two years, and his pride was deeply wounded, about this time, to learn that his landlord had been talking of it in the village.

. . . I thought that my honest intentions would have given him feelings of more delicacy towards me than throwing tokens of my poverty into the mouths of my neighbours for no other purpose than that of insulting me because he is offended at my going to leave the house to better myself—this hurt me in such a manner that I felt the truth of Solomon's advice as just: "My son it is better to die than to be poor."

In the autumn Clare's hopes, fixed upon the new venture, had soared high, and he seemed to be shaking off his depression. He would be sorry to leave Helpston, where "the very molehills on the Heath and the old trees and hedges seem bidding me farewell", and Northborough appeared to him a desert in comparison, where there was neither "wood nor heath, furze bush, molehill nor oak tree about it, and a nightingale never reaches so far in her summer excursions". Yet he was able to say that he felt as happy then as he had ever done in his life, for he was "looking at a sunny prospect".

. . . I think I shall yet live to see myself independent of all but old friends and good health; and as the best way to end well is to begin well, my desire is to start upon a new leaf, to get out of debt before I leave here and to keep out when I commence a cottage farmer.

If he was to do this and stock his little piece of land Clare could see no alternative but to sell out the Fund-money, and he asked for Taylor's advice on the subject but got no reply, although it seems that the publisher wrote to Mr. Mossop about the impossibility of doing as Clare had suggested.

Clare wrote again to Taylor:

> I was in hopes that I was at the end of my pilgrimage and that the shadow of independence, if not the substance, was won, as all I wanted was to use my own means to sink or swim as good luck or bad luck might hereafter allow me, and to free myself from talking and writing kindnesses that hang like a millstone about my feelings—I thought that one word to you would procure this and that I should launch into the broad ocean of liberty in my own boat. But no such thing. The conclusion of your letter to my neighbour came like a broad big wave, overpowering every struggle and throwing me back upon the shore among all the cold apathy of killing kindness that has numbed me for years. I am ready to start and not able, for I wish to start out of debt, and if two pence would do it I could get no such bond here.

Taylor wrote when he sent the dividend money on 13th January to say that he could do nothing about selling out the Funds until Woodhouse returned from Italy in May, as he was joint trustee, but he thought that it was impossible in any case; he could not, at present, find the Deed of Trust but he believed it did not empower the trustees to agree to the use of the capital in such a way.

Mrs. Emmerson then went to see Taylor on the matter, and was shown a letter from Woodhouse's brother who had found the Deed of Trust and confirmed that the capital was tied up and could not be touched; this had apparently been done with the idea of safeguarding it from creditors should Clare become bankrupt.

The cottage at Northborough was not ready by January, and Clare stayed on at Helpston for another four months. Early in the New Year, when he was in poor health and spirits, the kindly Mrs. Marsh sent him some cakes and made a joke of it in the accompanying letter, lest his pride should be hurt: "To show you how much I wish to cheer you, I am trying to make you laugh at sending you Cakes as one does to Children."

In February, Clare heard from Thomas Pringle, the editor of *Friendship's Offering*, who had found Clare "a man after his own heart" and had befriended him accordingly. He had been trying to find a publisher for Clare's new volume of poems, but he had been told on all sides that poetry was unsaleable and that even

John Clare's cottage at Northborough

such famous men as Wordsworth were having difficulty in finding a publisher for their work. Smith Elder and Co., whom he had approached, would only publish poetry at the author's risk.

Clare replied with an account of his writing which shows how he still regarded it as a thing to marvel at, a mystery which was at once a delight and a sorrow.

I became a scribbler for downright pleasure in giving vent to my feelings and long and pleasing-painful was my struggle to acquire a sufficient knowledge of the written language of England before I could put down my ideas on paper even so far as to understand them myself. But I mastered it in time sufficiently to be understood by others. Then I became an author by accident and felt astonished that the critics should notice me at all and that one should imagine I had read the old Poets and that others should imagine I had coined words which were as common around me as the grass under my feet. I shrank from myself with ecstasy and have never been myself since. As to profit, the greatest profits most congenial to my feelings were the friends it brought me and the names it rendered familiar to my fire-side, scraps of whose melodies I had heard and read in my corner. But had I only imagined for a moment that I should hold communion with such hereafter that would have been then to me "as music in mourning". But I wrote because it pleased me in sorrow and when happy it makes me happier; and so I go on, and when they please others whose taste is better than mine the pinnacle of my ambition is attained. I am so astonished that I can hardly believe I am myself, for nobody believed I could do anything here and I never believed that I could myself. I pursued pleasure in many paths and never found her so happily as when I sang imaginary songs to the woodland solitudes and winds of autumn.

With the spring Clare's spirits rose again so that he wrote cheerfully to his friends about the new house. Henderson went with him to visit it several times and helped him with planning the garden which was doubtless a pleasure to them both.

Early in May the move to Northborough took place. When the time came Clare was filled with a violent and disproportionate grief at leaving Helpston, and seemed to feel that he was going into some far exile instead of moving three miles. The poem which he wrote then, and which was subsequently published in *The Rural Muse*, expresses very beautifully the anguish which he felt. The hope of independence, the pleasure of a better house and a piece of land, the pride in his new garden—all were overshadowed and

14

forgotten beside the terrible home-sickness which, for a time, filled
his life.

> I've left my own old Home of Homes,
> Green fields and every pleasant place:
> The Summer, like a stranger comes,
> I pause—and hardly know her face.
> I miss the hazel's happy green,
> The blue-bell's quiet hanging blooms,
> Where envy's eye is never seen,
> Where tongue of malice never comes.[1]

This event did seem, in some strange way, to be a milestone on
the road of Clare's illness, although it is impossible to tell whether
his violent sorrow was the cause or the effect of the deterioration in
his condition, both mental and physical. That resilience which he
had once shown in rising from the depths of despair to face his
troubles with courage and even happiness had lessened, it seems,
after the illness which followed the incident at the theatre, and the
despair, when it attacked him, was proportionately deeper. Now
it was as though he once again suffered a change for the worse,
with darker melancholy and a less stubborn defence against the
world.

Yet the change of dwelling represented an enormous improvement in living conditions, and the new cottage was just such a
place as he had once dreamed of. It stood a little way back from
the road and faced towards the fields, with a little garden in front
of it, and, beyond that, an orchard. There was no door at the
back, which was towards the road, and the visitor approached by
a path at the side which could be seen from the window of the
room that Clare used as a study; he took advantage of this to slip
away when he saw unwelcome callers approaching, and was able
to vanish into the orchard before they reached the door. The
cottage was thatched, and contained three rooms upstairs and three
down. Beyond the orchard was the little field where Clare had
planned to keep his cow, but having, as yet, no stock, he was
obliged to let it for less than he paid for it.

In July, Mrs. Emmerson wrote that her husband had been to see
Taylor and they had decided to set on foot a private subscription
to enable Clare to purchase stock and tools. Of her own part in it,
Mrs. Emmerson said: "E. L. E. will give £10, which must be laid

[1] "The Flitting."

out in the purchase of a cow which she begs may be called by the poetic name of 'Rose' or 'Blossom' or 'May'." Taylor gave £5 for pigs, and she hoped that they would raise another £5 "to buy a butter churn and a few useful tools for husbandry".

Clare, though grateful for this help, felt vexed at having to accept it when he might have managed independently had he been able to get at the capital that was invested for him, and it seems that he felt also some indignity attaching to a system whereby he was not allowed to manage his own money. He complained of all this in letters to Mr. and Mrs. Emmerson, which Taylor saw, and the publisher wrote to Clare about it on 9th July.

> I . . . am sorry that what was done for you with the best Advice and the best Intentions is considered by you an Injury. As far as I am concerned I cannot see wherein I have erred, or done what I ought not to have done, having your Interest solely in View.

Clare had objected to the original subscription as a "Begging List", to the way Taylor had spoken of his poverty in the introduction to the second book, and to want of recompense for his works. Taylor, referring to these complaints, said that those who had subscribed to the Fund wanted to have their names mentioned and to know how the money was disposed of, and that, whereas there was no use in trying to conceal Clare's poverty, there might be some in speaking of it. "If you have not had sufficient Remuneration from your Works," he went on, "let it be recollected that I am out of Pocket by them, and that I do not carry on Business as a Publisher to have the Opportunity of giving that which I do not get. I can give Money without giving Time and Trouble also—and it will be so in future." He hoped that Clare would find a publisher more able to serve him, though he could not be more willing, and when Woodhouse returned he would, if possible, resign from his Trusteeship and put Mr. Mossop in his place.

> But I hope to be free soon from the odious Duty I have undertaken—And I will try to bring my Public Transactions with you to a Close. When I am like any other Friend, unconnected with you in Business, I shall not disappoint your Expectations, for nothing will be expected of me and our Correspondence will then be agreeable to us both.

Woodhouse, who was to have returned to England in May, was still in Italy where, like his friend Keats before him, he was slowly dying of consumption. Clare still had a dim hope that when he came back something might be done about the Fund-money, but in the meantime he was busy with another plan for raising some money and establishing his independence. He had composed a letter of proposals for publishing his new volume of poems, which he called *The Midsummer Cushion*, a title which he explained thus:

> It is a very old custom among villagers in summer time to take a piece of green sward full of field flowers and place it as an ornament in their cottages; which ornaments are called Midsummer Cushions.

In his address he gave what he described as "a plain statement of the facts". Difficulty, he said, had grown up "like a tree of the forest", and being no longer able to conceal it he met it in the best way possible by endeavouring to publish the poems for the benefit of himself and his large family. "It were false delicacy to make an idle parade of independence in my situation; and it would be unmanly to make a troublesome appeal to persons public or private like a public petition." The book would be offered for sale at a price not exceeding 7s. 6d. A printer in Peterborough printed 100 copies of the letter, and they were distributed during September and October among various people in London and in the neighbourhood of Northborough.

On 1st September, Clare wrote to Taylor about the proposal:

> I feel the situation in which difficulty places me dreadfully but as my stuff of independence is broken by that accident that nobody foresees viz. a large family—an accident that is as dear to me as happiness now—I must do as I can and I should think it is no shame to state the truth of my difficultys as the cause of wishing to make an attempt to get out out of them. . . . If Mr. Woodhouse is returned do your earliest opportunity to save me for I am as helpless as a child and everything is going wrong with me. . . . I have nothing as yet on the ground, neither cows nor pigs nor anything else and am in fact worse off than before I entered on the place.

Presumably Clare, having been obliged to let his pasture when he first took the house, had not yet got it back, as he would otherwise have been able to start stocking it with the money from Taylor and Mrs. Emmerson.

Clare's friends came readily to his aid in this new venture, and worked hard to collect subscribers; Mr. Mossop and his sister,

Mrs. Marsh, the Simpsons and Henderson all helped, and Mr. and Mrs. Emmerson, besides collecting subscribers, were investigating the possibilities of selling the copyright to a publisher as an alternative plan. Behnes Burlowe shared with them the opinion that this would be the more advantageous for Clare, as it would bring him a fixed sum without any risk or worry, and in November he wrote to tell Clare that he was negotiating with How, a member of the firm of Whittaker. The negotiations, however, did not lead to any definite agreement until more than a year later.

It is evidence of the change in the attitude of publishers towards poetry at that time that Clare should have had so much difficulty in finding a purchaser for his MS. Thirteen years before, Taylor had not hesitated to bring out the volume of his early poems which were written in such a way as to entail a good deal of work in editing them, while the new volume contained poems that were infinitely better and were copied neatly and carefully into a thick, firmly bound MS. book, needing few, if any, corrections.

Allan Cunningham was among those who gladly offered his assistance to Clare, and he placed his name on the list of subscribers. Clare wrote to thank him on 10th November, and told him that the impossibility of using the Fund-money had

> put my best intentions in jeopardy;—for the first volume brought me nothing, and the others, when I got some accounts which I cannot understand, seem to leave me in debt; so I thought there was neither sin nor shame in trying to escape my difficulty in the best way I could, and nothing but the publishing a volume by subscription seemed to make me certain of profit, so I wrote out a prospectus, and sent it to the printer before I had any inclination to waver, and sent one to Taylor telling him my intentions, and giving him the offer to print it if he chose, but he has not replied. I wish to hurt nobody, but I have those around me that make me turn to the practical matters of pounds, shillings and pence, and, though Mr. Taylor may have got nothing by the others to induce him to buy, I must turn so far a man of business myself as to make the best bargain I can. . . . I have a strong opinion of Taylor, and shall always respect him, and I think if the matter had been entirely left to business and I had sold them out and out even for a trifle I should have been better off and much better satisfied. . . . When the cow grows too old for profits in milk she is fatted and sold to the butchers; and when the horse is grown too old to work he is turned to the dogs; but an author is neither composed of the materials necessary for the profit of butchers meat or dogs meat—he is turned off and forgotten.

But meanwhile Clare was being vexed by other troubles which caused another coolness between him and Taylor almost as soon as the disagreement about the Fund-money had blown over. For some reason a rumour had been spread about at the time of Clare's removal to Northborough that Lord Milton had *given* him the cottage, and a paragraph to this effect appeared in *The Athenaeum* in August, 1832, and also in the Stamford paper, *The Bee*. Clare was very upset about it, as he feared that Lord Milton might think that the paragraphs had appeared at his instigation as a hint that he expected such a gift, and he told Clark, of the Stamford *Bee* that the story was untrue and that he expected to pay rent like his neighbours; he also wrote to London to have the matter put straight with *The Athenaeum*.

The result of these corrections was disastrous; certain of Clare's friends apparently felt that, as a false picture of comfort and prosperity had been given by the earlier articles, they must now acquaint the public in strong terms with the true state of affairs, lest it should be thought that no further help was needed by the poet. Who was actually responsible for the second crop of mis-statements is not certain, but it seems that Jacob, the Peterborough printer, told How (who was a relative of his) some very inaccurate facts about Clare's situation, which were passed on to the papers concerned.

One of the articles (in *The Athenaeum*) was written by Cunningham, but whether he drew his information from the same source or from elsewhere we do not know. Wherever the distorted facts came from, they were printed in *The Alfred* for October, 1832, in *The Athenaeum*, and in *The Bee*. The writers, after correcting the previous statements about the cottage, said that Clare had only £15 a year on which to keep his wife and family, that his publishers had robbed him of all his profits, and that certain noble patrons who lavished much praise upon him were content to let him starve.

Clare wrote at once to How to refute these mis-statements, and reaffirmed his belief in Taylor's absolute integrity. He wrote also to Simpson, who had had some connections with *The Bee*, and asked him to contradict the falsehoods which, he said, "not only hurt my feelings but injure me. . . . I am no beggar; for my income is £36, and though I have had no final settlement with Taylor, I expect to have one directly."

Mrs. Emmerson wrote early in November to express her disapprobation of the writers of these articles, who, she said, had made Clare "a pin to hang their own political and editorial *spleen* upon". But from Taylor, for the moment, there was only silence.

To a friend, probably Cary, at this time, Clare wrote of these difficulties and of the fierce, compelling force that drove him on to write, although he could feel no satisfaction with his work, which seemed to him too slight to merit that immortality that he so much desired. He spoke again of his "seeking independence and not asking charity"; yet independence seemed so impossible to attain.

> . . . Never mind, I must also write on, for ambition to be happy in sadness, as verses make me, urges me onward and if I have merit summer insects may annoy but cannot destroy me, and if I have not these buzzing authorities are nothings—they neither mar nor make me—and yet I am sadly teased and annoyed by their misrepresentations as they must come from enemies in disguise.

He mentioned his hopes for *The Midsummer Cushion*.

> If you laugh at my ambitions I am ready to laugh with you at my own vanity, for I sit sometimes and wonder over the little noise I have made in the world, until I think I have written nothing as yet to deserve any praise at all; so the spirit of fame—of living a little after life, like a name in a conspicuous place—urges my blood upwards into unconscious melodys, and, striding down my orchard and homestead, I hum and sing inwardly those little madrigals, and then go and pen them down, thinking them much better things than they are, until I look over them again, and then the charm vanishes into the vanity that I shall do something better ere I die; and so, in spite of myself, I rhyme on and I write nothing but little things at last.

23

"THE RURAL MUSE"

IT IS NECESSARY TO GO BACK A little to trace something of what was going on in Clare's mind while the struggle to bring out the new volume was in progress and the editors were printing extravagant stories about his misfortunes. It is only possible to tell with certainty a very little of what was happening inside the shell with which Clare protected his inmost thoughts from the world, but in his notebooks and his poems there are a few clues from which we may reconstruct the story.

In 1821, eleven years ago, Clare had told Taylor that he would write no more "doggerels" to "devoted Mary". He had not kept to his intention, but, since then, except for the poems that he continued to address to her, he had made no mention of her unless it was in the vanished letter to Mrs. Emmerson in 1823, which had caused her to reply that a poet must have his "idols of the mind as well as of the heart". In the intervening years Clare's mind was still occupied with the thought of Mary, and it seems that her memory grew slowly into something more good and more beautiful than any earthly woman. The image of perfect love and goodness which was thus born in Clare's imagination, became for him identified with all the things that his heart found most precious; she was a guardian angel who watched over his life and interceded for him in Heaven, she was a sublimation of earthly womanhood, and she was the spirit of Nature.

In one of his notebooks he wrote an account of a dream that he had on 13th October, 1832.

> That Guardian spirit in the shape of a soul-stirring beauty again appeared to me, with the very same countenance in which she appeared many years ago and in which she has since appeared at intervals and moved my ideas into ecstasy. I cannot doubt her existence.

In the dream, Clare was in a strange place among many people who paid him attention, but he was not happy until his guardian spirit came to him, gentle and smiling, and spoke some words which he could not remember when he woke.

Clare described two of the previous dreams in which she had appeared to him. In the first, which he had dreamed many years before, when he had not published anything, she had led him from home to a field nearby called Maple Hill, where there was an immense crowd of fine people; Clare, bewildered at being brought among them, when his only desire was solitude, asked her from his thoughts why it should be so. She answered, "You are only one of the crowd now", and hurried him away. Then they were in a book-shop, and Clare saw three volumes with his name on them, but as he turned to her in astonishment to ask what they were he woke up.

In a later dream, he was one of a crowd hurrying into Helpston Church to their final judgment. He was fearful and ill at ease until the spirit appeared "in white garments beautifully disordered, but sorrowful in her countenance". A brilliant light came from a corner of the chancel, and it seemed that from there came the judgment on all who were assembled in the church. Clare heard his own name called, and his guardian angel "smiled in ecstasy" and led him out into the open air, secure in the knowledge that all was well. In the poem which he wrote about this dream, Clare said that as he awoke, he heard the sound of her voice bidding him farewell, and the voice was Mary's.

In another notebook, Clare wrote a description of how the spirit comforted him in all his troubles.

I feel a beautiful providence ever about me as my attendant deity; she casts her mantle about me when I am in trouble to shield me from it, she attends me like a nurse when I am in sickness, puts her gentle hand under my head to lift it out of pain's way. . . . She attends to my every weakness when I am doubting, like a friend, and keeps me from sorrow by showing me her pictures of happiness and then offering them up to my service—she places herself in the shadow that I may enjoy the sunshine, and when my faith is sinking into despondency she opens her mind as a teacher to show me [faith] and give me wisdom. . . .

In one of the poems about Mary, Clare wrote:

When lovers part, the longest mile
Leaves hope of some returning;
Though mine's close by, no hopes the while
Within my heart are burning.[1]

[1] "Ballad."

So he spanned the distance of that "longest mile" in his imagination, and kept ever near to him the beautiful spirit whom he worshipped as he could never have worshipped Mary Joyce.

During this autumn and winter of 1832, Clare's health was bad, and he was often troubled with depression, with dark fears and forebodings. The instructions of a doctor (probably Skrimshire) which seem to refer to this time, include two leeches to each temple every third day, a blister applied to the nape of the neck, a shower-bath every morning, and a cloth applied to the head, soaked in brandy vinegar and rain-water.

At Christmas, Clare made a list of the presents that he had promised the children—books for them all, with *Dame Trott and her Cat* and *The House that Jack Built* for John and Sophy, the two youngest. No doubt he enjoyed reading them as much as the children, for he said that these little books "often give me more pleasure and more knowledge than many that are written for men".

On 4th January, 1833, Patty gave birth to another son who was christened Charles. Poor Clare had thus another life dependent on him when he knew not how to support those that he had already.

Taylor wrote on 9th January about the newspaper articles. He did not see why he should be exposed to this kind of treatment and supposed that Clare had been complaining of him to different people without considering the use they might make of it. He had commenced libel actions against the proprietors of *The Alfred* and *The Bee*. He was hurt with Clare for not having written to him on the subject, and had he not known that the articles contained manifest untruths would, he said, have been led by the silence to imagine that they had been published with Clare's approval.

The reply to this letter evidently contained news of Clare's sickness and fears, for Taylor wrote again on 19th February in a more friendly tone. "As for Evil Spirits, depend upon it, my Dear Friend, that there are none—and that there is no such thing as Witchcraft."

By July the publisher had abandoned his libel actions, and the relationship between him and Clare was once more quite friendly. In the same month Clare finished copying out his poems and sent the volume to Mrs. Emmerson, who promised that it should be forwarded to How. This was done, and in January, 1834, after a delay occasioned by the death of one of the partners in How's firm, the latter gave his promise to Mr. Emmerson that he would publish the poems in the spring under the title of *The Rural Muse* which Mrs. Emmerson had suggested.

Clare's land was now stocked, but his situation was not much improved; the children had been ill, the cow was not giving much milk, the debts had mounted to £35.

In February, Dr. Darling wrote in answer to a letter of Clare's, in which the poet had asked anxiously about the danger of small-pox to his children and had spoken of his own nervous fears. The doctor recommended him a "recipe" of the 23rd, 34th, and 37th Psalms, which, if he pondered on them and prayed frequently, would soon bring him peace of mind.

In March, Mr. Emmerson sent good news. He had concluded the bargain with How who paid £40 for the first edition of the poems, which were to be published by Whittaker. But this relief from immediate financial worry did little to banish Clare's dark fears. In May, Dr. Darling wrote again, telling him that they only arose from "a feverish state of body" and would be counteracted by the medicines he prescribed, and by keeping the head and body cool. But his advice did not help. Clare thought that if he could only see him, the doctor would be able to do more for him, and in July he contemplated a visit to London, but Mrs. Emmerson was going away and Taylor's house was full.

Clare was unable to write more than a few lines, and probably his London friends did not fully realise the extent of his sickness in mind and body and the weight of terrible despair under which he was sinking. Frank Simpson wrote for him to Mrs. Emmerson and to Behnes Burlowe to say that he was incapable of writing himself. But there had been other occasions when he could not write and when he had suffered from strange fears, and it was not unnatural that neither Taylor nor Mrs. Emmerson felt that there was cause for any undue alarm.

The publication of the new book, promised for the spring, had been delayed, but by August Clare had written the preface—a brief note of some twenty lines—and the volume was at the printers. How wrote that Taylor had consented to read the proofs, and that, as it would be impossible to get in more than about half of the poems, he had selected those that Mrs. Emmerson liked best.

Taylor, in the course of editing the proofs for Clare, wrote on 12th November: "In the last line of p. 31 'Heaven's eternal Peace is won', I have substituted for 'Death's long happy Sleep'". The last is good Atheism—the first is bad Divinity—I think it safer and better to give the incorrect religious Sentiment than the downright irreligious one—and I dare say you will agree with me."

How, who had now left Whittaker's but continued to take an interest in Clare, wrote on 6th December to suggest that he should apply to the Literary Fund for financial help. It was managed by a committee with the idea of relieving authors who were in great need, and Clare's application, which he made at once, resulted in his receiving £50 in the following month. This, with the £40 that he had been paid for *The Rural Muse*, freed him for the moment from all anxiety, enabling him to pay off his debts and still have a good sum in hand. There was a time when the lightening of this load would have raised Clare's hopes to the highest level and filled him with happiness, but it was now too late. It brought, certainly, a sense of relief, but it could do nothing to dispel his misery.

Clare wrote to Taylor at the beginning of January that he was so ill he could scarcely get across the house and had not been to Helpston for two years. Another child had been born and had died, and his old father had also been ill all the winter and under medical attention.

Taylor wrote on 9th January:

> Poor Charles Lamb is dead—perhaps you had not heard of it before. He fell down and cut his Face against the Gravel on the Turnpike Road, which brought on the Erisypelas, and in a few days carried him off. . . . Did I tell you that our good Friend Woodhouse was dead? He died in September last.

Clare's late trustee had left Taylor certain unpublished poems of Keats, and Taylor said that he would like to print a complete edition of the poems with some of the letters, but the world cared too little for Keats and he feared that he could not even sell 250 copies.

Clare, who would once have written at length on the death of these two old friends, could only reply, "I am sorry to hear your account of poor Charles Lamb, and the losses of our other friends."

Mrs. Emmerson, to whom Clare had sent a request some time before for a drawing-book for Frederick, wrote on 7th February to reprove Clare for the shortness of his letters and for the fact that he never asked after her health "even though I am as great an invalid as your poor self!"

Throughout the spring and summer Clare hardly wrote at all, and there is little indication of what was happening at Northborough. But on 10th July he sent a desperate appeal to Taylor:

> I am in such a state that I cannot help feeling some alarm that I may be as I have been. You must excuse my writing; but I feel if I do not write now I shall not be able. What I wish is to get under Dr. Darling's advice, or to have his advice to go somewhere. Yet I know if I could reach London I should be better, or else get to salt water. Whatever Dr. Darling advises I will do if I can. . . . I cannot describe my feelings; perhaps in a day or two I shall not be able to do anything, or get anywhere.

The Rural Muse appeared that month; it contained eighty-six sonnets and about fifty other poems, was dedicated to Lord Fitzwilliam,[1] and bore, as frontispiece, an engraving of Clare's cottage, with one of Northborough Church on the title-page. Most of the poems were taken from *The Midsummer Cushion*, but rather more than half of the MS. volume was left unpublished.

In the ten years since he had finished writing *The Shepherd's Calendar*, Clare had come to maturity; there is a beauty in the poems of *The Rural Muse* that transcends anything he had done before. It was not only that his genius had grown purer and stronger, his instinct for words more unerring, his sense of inward melody more perfect, it was also a reflection of the man himself and his changing philosophy. Clare had suffered as keenly as it is given to most men to suffer, he had talked with great intellects, read widely, thought much, and the result of all this was that he had worked out his own philosophy, his answer to that riddle of the universe that had puzzled him since childhood. He had doubted and wondered much in earlier years, and in his search for a key that would fit the lock he had tried a variety of theories, but when at last he found his philosophy it proved to be, like all really great things, infinitely simple. His wonder at the truths that he discovered was like his wonder at the mysterious gift of poetry, which made him "shrink from himself in ecstasy". As with everything that forcibly impressed him, he had to write about the things that he now believed to be of supreme importance, and because he was a greater poet than he had ever been before he sang of them in melodies of surpassing beauty. So *The Rural Muse* was the product both of his mature genius and his mature philosophy.

[1] The former Lord Milton who had now succeeded his father.

The thoughts that Clare comes back to again and again in these poems are the changeless quality of Nature and the nearness of God to earth, so that He loves all living creatures and His whole creation praises Him.

> All Nature owns, with one accord,
> The great and universal Lord;
> The Sun proclaims him through the day—
> The Moon, when daylight drops away;
> The very Darkness smiles to wear
> The stars that show us God is there!
> On moonlight seas soft gleams the sky,
> And "God is with us!" waves reply.[1]

In "The Eternity of Nature", which is one of Clare's most beautiful poems, we find that other thought which he expressed repeatedly—the mutability of man and all his works, which pass away and are forgotten, while the song of the robin, and the cowslip blooming in spring go on to the end of time.

> . . . Trampled under foot,
> The daisy lives and strikes its little root
> Into the lap of time; centuries may come,
> And pass away into the silent tomb,
> And still the child, hid in the womb of time,
> Shall smile and pluck them, when this simple rhyme
> Shall be forgotten, like a churchyard stone,
> Or lingering lie unnoticed and alone.

And

> . . . Cowslips of gold bloom,
> That in the pasture and the meadow come,
> Shall come when Kings and empires fade and die;
> And in the closes, as Time's partners, lie
> As fresh two thousand years to come as now,
> With those five crimson spots upon their brow.

Another of Clare's most beautiful poems, "Autumn", a slightly different version of which had first appeared in *The Anniversary*, was published in *The Rural Muse*, and so was "Summer Images", in which he joyfully recalls the delights of summer and everything that he sees and hears and touches in "the green woods and meadows summer-shorn".

[1] "Nature's Hymn to the Deity."

I love at early morn, from new mown swath,
To see the startled frog his route pursue;
To mark while, leaping o'er the dripping path,
His bright sides scatter dew,
The early lark that, from its bustle flies,
To hail his matin new;
And watch him to the skies.

To note on hedgerow baulks, in moisture sprent,
The jetty snail creep from the mossy thorn,
With earnest heed, and tremulous intent,
Frail brother of the morn,
That from the tiny bent's dew-misted leaves
Withdraws his timid horn,
And fearful vision weaves.

It was a part of Clare's great gift that he was able thus to express the love that he felt for the smallest of living creatures without a vestige of sentimentality but with infinite tenderness.

There were several charming ballads in the volume, and some poems addressed to Mary, and we find here once more that preoccupation with the inarticulate love which was perhaps a consequence of the things he had left unsaid when he courted Mary.

True love it is no daring bird,
But like the little timid wren,
That in the new-leaved thorns of spring
Shrinks farther from the sight of men.[1]

There were, too, several poems on birds' nests which Clare described with loving accuracy; the pettichap,[2] the yellowhammer, the nightingale. He had heard the thrush "sing hymns to sunrise", and he watched her building her nest:

And by and by, like heath-bells gilt with dew,
There lay her shining eggs as bright as flowers,
Ink-spotted over shells of greeny blue.[3]

It is perhaps logical to consider with these poems the others belonging to the same period that were in *The Midsummer Cushion*, and were excluded from *The Rural Muse*, but many of which have since been published. We find there another expression of the thoughts that were occupying Clare, a reiteration of his faith. In

[1] "Love."   [2] Willow warbler.   [3] "The Thrush's Nest."

"Song's Eternity" he compares the song of the blue-cap with the words of men—one so lasting, the other so transient.

> Dreamers, mark the honey bee;
> Mark the tree
> Where the blue cap "tootle tee"
> Sings a glee
> Sung to Adam and to Eve—
> Here they be.
> When floods covered every bough,
> Noah's ark
> Heard that ballad singing now;
> Hark, hark!

The note of absolute simplicity is there again, in the choice of words as well as in the thought from which the poem grew.

> Bird and bee
> Sing creation's music on.

In his prose writings—his essays and notebooks—over those ten years, we find the pattern of the universe taking shape for him.

We know [he wrote] that the world was made and we know its architect from no other book than the Bible. But, being a part of the architect ourselves, we cannot go to comprehend the whole. We know but little about the matter of which we ourselves are but a portion, and although new theories may entertain us by their novelty they seldom lead us to truth.

In his notebook he expressed his passionate belief in tolerance:

My creed may be different to other creeds but the difference is nothing when the end is the same—if I did not expect and hope for eternal happiness I should be ever miserable—and as every religion is a rule leading to good by its profession the religions of all nations and creeds where that end is the aim ought rather to be respected than scoffed at. . . .

24

HIGH BEECH

Such reviews as the new volume was given were all appreciative in tone; *The Literary Gazette*, *The Athenaeum*, and *The New Monthly* spoke well of it, and Professor Wilson in the August number of *Blackwoods* was enthusiastic in his praise. But the first edition was not nearly exhausted a year after publication.

Clare received letters from many old friends who expressed their admiration of the book—Montgomery, Sherwill, and Alaric Watts among them—but he was too ill to care very much for anyone's opinion. On 27th August he wrote to Taylor:

I feel anxious to get up to London and think I should get better. How would you advise me to come? I dare not come up by myself; do you think one of my children would do to come with me?

To Dr. Darling he wrote an account of his illness:

I write to tell you I am very unwell, and though I cannot describe my feelings well I will tell you as well as I can—Sounds affect me very much and things evil as well [as] good thoughts are continually rising in my mind. I cannot sleep, for I am asleep, as it were, with my eyes open, and I feel chills come over me and a sort of nightmare awake and I got no rest last night. I feel a great desire to come up but perhaps I shall not be able and I hope you will write down directly for I feel you can do me some good and if I was in town I should soon be well, so I fancy; for I do assure you I am very unwell and I cannot keep my mind right, as it were, for I wish to read and cannot.

He added a postscript:

I fear I shall be worse and worse ere you write to me, for I have been out for a walk and can scarcely bear up against my fancies or feelings.

Taylor had expressed himself very willing to have Clare at his house if he wished to come up for treatment, but the journey was never undertaken. Perhaps Clare felt that it would be too much for his strength, or perhaps he felt that the expense would be too great; letters at this date were few and there are gaps in the story.

On 18th December, 1835, Clare's mother died at the age of seventy-eight, and his father came to live at Northborough for the remainder of his life—another eleven years.

In February, Mrs. Emmerson wrote after a long silence to say that she had been very ill for the last three months and could not write but was now somewhat better. Her husband had lately bought a house near Bath and she hoped soon to be well enough to go there. A month later she sent Clare a waistcoat and a volume of Allan Cunningham's poems.

During the spring, it seems that Clare was physically better and began his walks in the fields again which he had discontinued for some time. Patty encouraged him to be out of doors, believing that it was good for him, and he found so much pleasure in renewing his old habits that he took to going off for the whole day and sitting alone under a hedge or in the woods. He spent some time in his garden, too, and possibly instructed his sons in tending the plants, for the story goes that in summer they clipped the two yews into their pattern of cones and circles while Clare looked on and gave directions from the garden seat. He had begun writing again in the winter, and had written several hundred short poems, most of them descriptive and many of them about birds and animals.

Rippingille wrote on 13th June: "When I look at *The Rural Muse* which I do often, and think of £40 as the poet's reward, I feel ashamed of the age in which I live and of the world of which I constitute a unit!"

In the late autumn, Taylor went up to Retford, and on his way back to London at the beginning of December he visited Northborough. His account of the visit makes sad reading.

The following morning at seven I set off to see Clare in a chaise accompanied by a medical gentleman of Stamford, who was to give me his opinion respecting poor Clare's health. We found him sitting in a chimney corner looking much as usual. He talked properly to me in reply to all my questions, knew all the people of whom I spoke, and smiled at my reminding him of the events of past days. But his

mind is sadly enfeebled. He is constantly speaking to himself and
when I listened I heard such words as these, pronounced a great
many times over and with great rapidity—"God bless them all",
"Keep them from evil", "Doctors". But who it was of whom he
spoke I could not tell—whether his children, or doctors, or everybody. But I think the latter. His children, seven in number, are a
very fine family, strongly resembling him; the youngest, a boy of three
or four years old; the eldest, a girl, sixteen. There are 3 boys and 4
girls. The medical man's opinion was that Clare should go to some
asylum. His wife is a very clever, active woman and keeps them all
very respectable and comfortable, but she cannot manage to control
her husband at times; he is very violent, I dare say occasionally. His
old father is still living with them. We went thence to see a clergyman who had always been kind to Clare for twenty years, and he has
promised to see Earl Fitzwilliam about an asylum.

The sequence of events during the next six months is difficult to
determine. It seems that Clare was to all outward appearance
quite normal and could talk rationally, but was most of the time
sunk in a brooding melancholy. At times he would break off in the
middle of a perfectly reasonable conversation and start talking
nonsense, and at other times he would grow violent, either from
the depths of his despair or from the uncontrollable agitation and
excitement which constituted the second of the two extremes
between which he alternated. Sometimes he did not know his wife
and children, and spoke of "John Clare" as someone separate
from his own identity.

It was probably during the winter of 1836 or the early spring of
1837 that the delusion was born in Clare's mind which was to
remain unaltered to the end of his life; it became his fixed belief
that Mary was his first wife and Patty his second, but he thought
that they were both living, and saw nothing strange in having two
wives, though he could not understand why one was kept from
him. It is said that Clare saw Mary from the window one day as
she walked along the road past his cottage, and that he was much
agitated by this happening which may have marked the beginning
of the delusion, but the sight of her was not in itself a sign of
derangement, for she was not, as Martin stated, dead by that time;
she lived until 1838 and it is quite possible that she *did* pass Clare's
cottage.

These months must have been a trying time for Patty, not only
because of the distress of seeing Clare in such a state, but because

the nature of his delusion was such that it may well have been hurtful to her and, at the best, called for great patience. The length of time that elapsed between the visit of Taylor with the doctor and the removal of Clare to an asylum may have been due to difficulty in finding a suitable place or to disagreement between those responsible as to where he should go, but it is also said that Patty pleaded for delay in the belief that she might yet succeed in nursing him back to health and sanity. Meanwhile he continued to work in his garden and roam about the fields, and the neighbours, though they apparently heard Clare calling molehills mountains, thought that nothing surprising from such an eccentric being as a poet and did not guess that his mind had gone.

He wrote a few letters, but they were brief and the writing slanted drunkenly down the page; there was a sort of incoherence about them, and a despair beyond words, as though he had cried for help too long and now could say no more.

On 5th May, 1837, he wrote to Taylor:

> I am scarcely able to write. I have got the drawing done here. You and Mrs. Emmerson are the best friends I have and just as you was . . . I should like to see Hilton and Cary. The Curate draws well and has made many sketches from the poems. God bless you all.

He clung still to his work, and even in these months when he was "at the world's end" he continued to write and had thoughts of making another volume of poetry for which he would use some of the MS. poems that had been excluded from *The Rural Muse*.

Meanwhile arrangements were being made for placing Clare in an asylum. Whether Mr. Mossop did approach Earl Fitzwilliam is not known, but if so the latter was evidently satisfied to leave things to Taylor. We do not know, either, how Taylor heard of Dr. Allen's asylum, though it may have been from Dr. Darling or through Thomas Campbell, whose son was a patient there. At any rate, Taylor arranged for Clare's admission to High Beech, Epping Forest, and in his peculiarly high-handed fashion did not inform any of the other people who were interested in the poet— not even Mrs. Emmerson.

On 13th June, 1837, he wrote a note which he sent down with the man who travelled from London to fetch Clare. Perhaps the publisher thought, as he composed those few brief lines, of all the letters that had passed between them in the eighteen years of their friendship—letters that spoke of great men and great things and the glory of poetry. And now it had come to this:

> . . . It is my sincere Hope that the Medical Care which is provided for you near this place will be effectual to your recovery. The Bearer will bring you up to Town and take every care of you on the Road.

Whatever the circumstances by which Taylor had become acquainted with Matthew Allen, he could not have placed Clare in better hands. Allen had been for five years medical superintendent at York Asylum, and had there established a system of treatment which was entirely new, and which he continued and perfected in his own private asylum which he set up in 1825. His theory was to allow the patients the maximum amount of freedom, to encourage them to occupy themselves with healthy work and amusement, and to establish between them and their attendants a relationship of complete confidence and friendship; he believed that if the patient was never deceived but was treated with honesty and frankness, he would give his trust in return, and the possession of that trust gave the doctor power to work on his mind and help his condition.

High Beech consisted of three separate buildings, which stood in extensive grounds on the borders of Epping Forest. Each house was divided into two parts, the back being given over to those patients who needed close care and attention, and the front to those who were well enough to lead a normal life. The latter groups were given as much domestic comfort as possible; they visited each other, played games together, and were mostly allowed out on parole. They were made to appreciate their privileges and to realise that normal behaviour was expected of them and that failure in this respect would mean banishment to the back of the house and to a life of considerably less freedom.

Clare was allowed much liberty, if not at the very beginning, at least within a month or two of his arrival. He was encouraged to write whenever he felt like it and, although a certain watchfulness was probably kept over him, he was permitted to wander in the grounds or in the forest—in fact to lead a life as much as possible like his old one but without its attendant worries.

Allen seems to have thought that those worries were the cause of Clare's breakdown, for in 1840 he wrote of the poet's entry to the asylum:

> He was then exceedingly miserable, every instant bemoaning his poverty, and his mind did not appear so much lost and deranged as suspended in its movements by the oppressive and permanent state of anxiety, and fear, and vexation, produced by the excitement of excessive flattery at one time, and neglect at another, his extreme poverty and over-exertion of body and mind, and no wonder that his feeble bodily frame, with his wonderful active powers of mind, was overcome.
>
> I had not then the slightest hesitation in saying that if a small pension could be obtained for him, he would have recovered instantly and most probably remained well for life.

There were, in fact, one or two appeals published in the autumn of 1837 for help which would relieve Clare's distress, but the writers did not know that he was already in an asylum. Allan Cunningham spoke of his unhappy situation in *The Anniversary*, and S. C. Hall inserted in *The Book of Gems* an article which drew forth a letter from the Marquis of Northampton; the latter, though he was not disposed to place Clare in the same rank as Hogg, Bloomfield, or Crockford, thought that his poverty was a disgrace to the county, and suggested that a collection of his poems should be published by subscription. He thought that some of the big landowners of the county would contribute, but his scheme never came to anything.

It was not until November, 1837, that Mrs. Emmerson heard of Clare's removal from home, and then her information was inaccurate, for she believed that he had gone to York Asylum. She wrote to Patty begging that one of the children would send her news of him.

In April, 1838, she wrote again:

> It is a great comfort to hear, that your dear Husband enjoys a more tranquil state of mind—and, that his general health is so much improved by the change of air, and kind treatment of Dr. Allen—I am glad to find my poor friend! has pleasure in his rambles, among the beautiful scenery where he now abideth. . . . I have recently . . . paid "five pounds" into the care of Mr. Taylor, as my portion of the "subscription" which is to pay Doctor Allen's charge for the medical and kind care of our dear Clare.

Of Mrs. Emmerson we hear no more; she had been in very bad health for several years, and it is probable that she did not live long after 1838. She had been a good friend to Clare, in adversity and in prosperity, and he understood and appreciated the friendship that she and her husband gave to him; he said of them that "two of kinder intentions and warmer feelings never existed, for time hath made no change in them".

Taylor continued to handle Clare's affairs, and it was to him or his new partner, Walton, that Dr. Allen made his reports. Both partners contributed towards the expenses of keeping Clare at High Beech, and Allen himself helped in this matter; so, too, did Lord Fitzwilliam, Dr. Darling, De Wint and various others.

There is little to tell of Clare in the next three years. In December, 1839, Allen wrote to Walton that Clare was "improved and improving—in appearance wonderfully—stout and rosy". He was now working and was in good spirits—"all life and fun".

On 19th June, 1840, a report of Clare's death, previously printed in *The Halifax Express*, appeared in *The Times*, and Dr. Allen wrote to contradict the statement and to appeal for subscriptions to help Clare. His letter, which was published on 23rd June, subsequently appeared in the *London Saturday Journal*, and *The Athenaeum* devoted a paragraph to the subscription scheme. Allen reported that Clare was in excellent health and looked very well, while his mind, though full of strange delusions, was "in a much more comfortable and happy state" than when he came. He commented on the strange fact that Clare was able to write beautiful poetry that showed no indication of insanity, yet when he talked or wrote prose his derangement was at once evident.

On 8th July, 1840, Allen again wrote to Walton, enclosing a certificate which stated that Clare was still insane and under his care. "He is looking very well," Allen wrote, "and his mind is not worse." The doctor was hopeful of the results of his letter to *The Times*, and believed that some money had already been offered.

Allen's aim was to raise £500, which would purchase an annuity for Clare, and the following year a number of leaflets were printed giving details of Clare's financial position and stating that Allen thought his recovery would be complete if his anxiety for the welfare of his family could be relieved; but in spite of the doctor's zeal the subscriptions did not reach that sum. The Queen Dowager gave £50, and Lord Fitzwilliam contributed generously, but these with a few smaller amounts were not enough for the annuity and went, presumably, towards the payment of Clare's expenses at High Beech.

On 17th March, 1841, Clare wrote to Patty. His letter is rational except for one or two rambling and incoherent sentences, but it is unutterably tragic, full of homesickness and longing for his children and his own fireside.

My dear Wife Patty

It makes me more than happy to hear that you and my dear family are all well—and you will all be as well pleased to hear that I have been so long in good health and spirits as to have forgotten that I ever was any otherways—My situation here has been even from the beginning more than irksome but I shake hands with misfortunes and wear through the storm—The spring smiles and so shall I—but not while I am here—I am very happy to hear my dear boy mention his "brother's and sister's" so kindly as I feel assured that they love one another as they ever have done—It was my lot to seem as living without friends until I met with you and though we are now parted my affection is unaltered—and we shall meet again. I would sooner wear the trouble's of life away single-handed than share them with others—As soon as I get relieved on duty here I shall be in Northamptonshire—though Essex is a very pleasant county—yet to me "there is no place like home". . . . For what reason they keep me here I cannot tell for I have been no otherways than well a couple of year's at the least and never was very ill only harrassed by perpetual bother —and it would seem by keeping me here one year after another that I was destined for the same fate again and I would sooner be packed in a slave ship for Affrica than belong to the destiny of mock friends and real enemies—Honest men and modest women are my friends.

Give my love to my dear children and kiss the little ones for me goodbye and God be with all for ever. I had three separate dream's about three of my boys, or your boys—Frederick John and William— not any ways remarkable only I was in a wreck with the latter— Such things never trouble me now in fact nothing troubles me and thank God it is so—I hope the time is not long ere I shall see you all by your own fireside though every day in absence seems to me longer than year's.

At about the same time, he wrote in his notebook a letter which was addressed to his "other wife", but apparently meant for both of them:

My dear Wife Mary,

I might have said my first wife and first love and first everything but I shall never forget my second wife and second love for I loved her once as dearly as yourself—and almost do so now so I determined to keep you both forever—and when I write to you I am writing to her at the same time and in the same letter God bless you both forever —and both your families also—I still keep writing though you do not write to me. . . . No one knows how sick I am of this confinement possessing two wives that ought to be my own and cannot see either one or the other; if I was in prison for felony I could not be served worse than I am—wives used to be allowed to see their husbands anywhere—religion forbids their being parted but I have not even religion on my side and more's the pity. . . . I wrote a new canto of *Don Juan* to pass the time away, but nothing seemed to shorten it in the least, and I fear I shall not be able to wear it away. Nature to me seems dead and her very pulse seems frozen to an icicle in the summer sun—what is the use of shutting me up from women in a petty paltry place as this merely because I am a married man and I dare say though I have two wives if I got away I should soon have a third and I think I should serve you both right in the bargain by doing so for I don't care a damn about coming home now—so you need not flatter yourselves with many expectations of seeing me nor do I expect you want to see me or you would have contrived to have done it before now—My dear Mary take all the good wishes from me as your heart can feel for your own husband and kiss all your dear family for their abscent father and Patty's children also and tell Patty that her husband is the same man as he was when she married him 20 years ago in heart and good intentions—God bless you both and your familys also I wish you both to keep in good health and be happy as I shall soon be when I have the good luck to be with you all at home once again—the love I have for you my dear Mary was never altered by time but always increased by absence.

I am my dear Mary
Your affectionate husband John Clare.

The allusion to the canto of *Don Juan* is the earliest hint of a delusion which was later to appear frequently in Clare's conversation and in his notebooks—an identification of himself with Byron. It would be idle to attempt to explain the deep and hidden workings of Clare's disordered brain, but it is reasonable to suppose that the connection can be traced back at least to the day when he saw Byron's funeral cortège, and was so impressed by the sight and by the grief of the crowd who watched it.

He did, in fact, during this period at High Beech, write a long poem called "Don Juan", in the style of that by Byron, and in it he sometimes compared himself with the other poet and sometimes assumed his identity.

> Lord Byron, poh!—the man wot rites the verses,
> And is just what he is and nothing more,
> Who with his pen lies like the mist disperses,
> And makes all nothing as it was before;
> Who wed two wives and oft the truth rehearses,
> And might have had some twenty thousand more,
> Who has been dead, so fools their lies are giving,
> And still in Allen's madhouse caged and living.

There is a sort of savage despair about it, a bitterness and cynicism unparalleled in any of his other work. It was as though, in these verses, he poured out all his accumulated anger against the pattern of life in general and his own life in particular, and afterwards came by way of weariness and terrible anguish to resignation and even to joy.

Something of that anguish and of the calm beyond it, we learn from the other long poem which Clare wrote at this time and called "Child Harold", still thinking of Byron but not imitating him as he did in *Don Juan*. There are lines in *Child Harold* that come near perfection, and, although there are others where the melody is not sustained, it contains some of Clare's most beautiful poetry.

> Life is to me a dream that never wakes;
> Night finds me on this lengthening road alone;
> Love is to me a thought that ever aches,
> A frost-bound thought that freezes life to stone.
> Mary, in truth and nature still my own,
> That warms the winter of my aching breast,
> Thy name is joy, nor will I life bemoan;
> Midnight, when sleep takes charge of nature's rest,
> Finds me awake and friendless—not distrest.
>
> Tie all my cares up in thy arms, O Sleep,
> And give my weary spirits peace and rest.
> I'm not an outlaw in this midnight deep
> If prayers are offered from sweet woman's breast.

. . . . .

Clare mentioned Byron to Cyrus Redding, who visited him at High Beech in May, 1841, but only to request his works when asked what books he wanted. His mind, on that occasion, was apparently occupied with another delusion.

Redding, in his account of the visit, says that he was accompanied by a friend who had known Clare previously. They found the poet hoeing in a field near the house, and called him away from his work to talk to him; Redding's companion was surprised to see how much his appearance had changed, for he had put on weight, and was no longer pale and haggard as he had once been.

> We found a little man, of muscular frame and firmly set, his complexion clear and forehead high, a nose somewhat aquiline, and long full chin. The expression of his countenance was more pleasing but somewhat less intellectual than that in the engraved portrait prefixed to his works in the edition of *The Village Minstrel*, published in 1821. . . . He spoke of the quality of the ground which he was amusing himself by hoeing, and the probability of its giving an increased crop the present year, a continued smile playing upon his lips.

Clare told them of his homesickness and of how lonely he was away from his wife. In the middle of the conversation, during which he spoke freely and without embarrassment, Clare suddenly began to talk about prize-fighting, in which he seemed to think he was to engage. He broke off another subject to introduce this one and then as suddenly abandoned it, with no apparent line of thought connecting one subject with another. Redding said that it was "as if the machinery of thought were dislocated, so that one part of it got off its pivot, and protruded into the regular workings; or as if a note had got into a piece of music which had no business there."

The prize-fighter idea occurred repeatedly in Clare's conversation, and in his notebook at about that time he wrote:

> Jack Randall's Challenge to All the World.
> Jack Randall the champion of the prize ring begs leave to inform the sporting world that he is ready to meet any customer in the ring or on the stage to fight for the sum of £500.
> He is not particular to weight, colour or country; he wishes to meet with a customer who has pluck enough to come to the scratch.
> So let thine enemies perish, Oh Lord.

Clare had written of his enthusiasm for the ring in an account of the visit that he made to the Fives Court with Rippingille in 1824, and presumably he had seen a certain amount of boxing at country fairs, but there is no record that he had ever tried it himself. It is strange that something that had entered so little into his life should play such an important part in his aberrations, but it is possible to suppose that this 'and the Byron delusion were more closely linked than would at first appear, and that both had a symbolical significance. In his notebook he made an entry which connected the two ideas:

> "Boxer Byron
> made of Iron, alias
> Boxiron
> at Springfield."

Springfield was the name of one of the High Beech houses, and it seems that Clare was referring to himself in the person of Byron and the boxer both at once. It has already been suggested that Clare's preoccupation with the author of *Childe Harold* was due to the fact that Byron had achieved the immortality which Clare so much desired and despaired of attaining, and that he therefore saw him as a personification of the success that had eluded his own grasp. All of Clare's life had been a struggle, and he had often felt that he fought alone against the world; thus it is not unlikely that the thought of this long and weary fight became identified in his mind with the prize fight that he had seen in London, and he himself became Jack Randall issuing his challenge to the world. But he felt himself an *invincible* fighter, and the idea of success could not be separated from the idea of Byron—therefore he was Boxer Byron.

Such theories are only shadowy speculations, and it is not particularly useful to speculate about anything of which we know so little. It is, however, interesting to note in this connection that— though it may be a coincidence and not of special significance —three of the subjects which now and in later years formed delusions in Clare's mind had all been occupying his thoughts in the year 1824. It was then that, during his visit to London, he saw Byron's funeral cortège, and also attended the fight at the Fives Court; and in the same year he wrote several sea-fighting songs, including one about Nelson.

An aspect of Clare's aberrations of which it is possible to speak with more certainty, is the way in which he kept his thoughts of Mary entirely to himself. The people who visited him at High Beech or, in later years, at Northampton, all describe how he told them he was Shakespeare or Byron, a prize-fighter or one of Nelson's seamen, but to none of them, apparently, did he ever mention Mary. Perhaps to those who were constantly with him he sometimes spoke of her, for he told Dr. Allen in the letter he wrote after leaving High Beech that he did not know what had become of her, but his mention of her name was certainly rare. Yet, in his notebook, he was constantly writing letters and poems to her, and we find such entries as:

God Almighty bless Mary Joyce Clare and her family now and forever—Amen.

God Almighty bless Martha Turner Clare and her family now and forever—Amen.

In his aberrations he continued the habit of silence that had been his in sanity, for he had loved Mary through a separation of nearly thirty years and had not spoken of her except in his poems which were the expression of his inmost thoughts:

Love is a secret
Like a bird in a shell
Like a rose ere it blossom
All unseen will it dwell.[1]

Clare's children were often in his thoughts. On Easter Sunday, 1841, he wrote in his notebook:

Went in the morning to Buckhurst Hill Church and stood in the Churchyard, when a very interesting boy came out while the organ was playing, dressed in a slop-frock like a plough boy and seemingly about nine years of age. He was just like my son Bill when he was about the same age and as stout made. He had a serious, interesting face and looked as weary with the working days as a hard-working man. I was sorry I did not give him the last halfpenny I had and ask him a few questions as to his age and name and parents, but perhaps I may see him again.

Of all the strange and puzzling aspects of Clare's insanity, the strangest and most wonderful is that he was able not only

[1] "Love."

to go on writing poetry, but to write poems that could take their place with the best things he had ever written. The best of the asylum poems were written later on at Northampton, but to the High Beech period belong some lovely verses which already show that quality of youthful, joyous and spontaneous melody which Clare, so strangely, brought to perfection in the years of his confinement.

> By a cottage near a wood
> Where the small birds build and sing,
> In my dreaming hours she stood,
> To review the lovely spring:
> There once dwelt a lovely maiden
> Whose name I sought in vain—
> Some called her lovely Lucy,
> And others honest Jane.
>
> By that cottage near a wood
> I have often stood alone
> In sad and happy mood
> And wished she was my own.
> The small birds flitted round me,
> But nature pleased in vain;
> For the dark and lovely maiden
> I never saw again. . . .

And there is one to Patty, in which he was thinking, evidently, of the days when he left the lime-kiln on summer evenings, and went to find her at Walkherd Lodge:

> Maid of Walkherd meet agen,
> By the wilding in the glen:
> By the oak against the door,
> Where we often met before.
> By thy bosom's heaving snow,
> By thy fondness none shall know;
> Maid of Walkherd meet agen,
> By the wilding in the glen.
>
> By thy hand of slender make,
> By thy love I'll ne'er forsake,
> By thy heart I'll ne'er betray,
> Let me kiss thy fears away!

I will live and love thee ever,
Leave thee and forsake thee never!
Though far in other lands to be,
Yet never far from love and thee.[1]

The flame of Clare's genius, which not poverty nor sickness nor discouragement could extinguish, burned still as brightly and as purely in the darkness of his clouded mind.

[1] "Maid of Walkherd."

25

HOMELESS AT HOME

O_N 20TH JULY, 1841, CLARE escaped from High Beech and in three days walked back to Northamptonshire. He made this journey of eighty miles practically without food, for he had nothing on the first two days but a half-pint of beer, and on the third day a little bread and cheese, some grass and some tobacco which he swallowed after chewing it. The day after his arrival at Northborough he wrote in his note-book:

> Returned home out of Essex and found no Mary—her and her family are nothing to me now though she herself was once the dearest of all—and how can I forget.

For the next three days he was occupied in writing a detailed account of his journey, from the time he planned his escape from High Beech to the time he reached Northborough. It is surely one of the most remarkable and most tragic stories in all the history of literature.

> July 18, 1841. Sunday. Felt very melancholly—went a walk on the forest in the afternoon—fell in with some gipseys one of whom offered to assist in my escape from the mad house by hiding me in his camp to which I almost agreed but told him I had no money to start with but if he would do so I would promise him fifty pounds and he agreed to do so before Saturday. On Friday I went again but he did not seem so willing so I said little about it—On Sunday I went and they were all gone—I found an old wide-awake hat, and an old straw bonnet of the plumb pudding sort was left behind—and I put the hat in my pocket thinking it might be useful for another opportunity and as good luck would have it, it turned out to be so.
>
> July 19. Monday. Did nothing.
>
> July 20. Reconnoitred the rout the Gipsey pointed out and found it a legible one to make a movement and having only honest courage and myself in my army I led the way and my troops soon followed; but being careless in mapping down the rout as the Gipsey told me I

John Clare in 1844
From the portrait by Thomas Grimshaw

missed the lane to Enfield town and was going down Enfield highway till I passed "The Labour in vain" Public house where a person I knew coming out of the door told me the way.

I walked down the lane gently and was soon in Enfield Town and bye and bye on the great York Road where it was all plain sailing and steering ahead; meeting no enemy and fearing none I reached Stevenage where being Night I got over a gate crossed over the corner of a green paddock where seeing a pond or hollow in the corner I [was] forced to stay off a respectable distance to keep from falling into it for my legs were nearly knocked up and began to stagger. I scaled some old rotten paleings into the yard and then had higher pailings to clamber over to get into the shed or hovel which I did with difficulty being rather weak. To my good luck I found some trusses of clover piled up about six or more feet square which I gladly mounted and slept on—there was some rags in the hovel on which I could have reposed had I not found a better bed. I slept soundly but had a very uneasy dream. I thought my first wife lay on my left arm and somebody took her away from my side which made me wake up rather unhappy. I thought as I woke somebody said "Mary" but nobody was near—I lay down with my head towards the north to show myself the steering point in the morning.

July 21. Daylight was looking in on every side and fearing my garrison might be taken by storm and myself be made prisoner I left my lodging by the way I got in and thanked God for his kindness in procureing it (for anything in a famine is better than nothing and any place that giveth the weary rest is a blessing). I gained the north road again and steered due north—on the left hand side the road under the bank like a cave I saw a Man and boy coiled up asleep which I hailed and they woke up to tell me the name of the next village. Somewhere on the London side the "Plough" Public house a Man passed me on horseback in a slop frock and said "here's another of the broken down haymakers" and threw me a penny to get a half pint of beer which I picked up and thanked him for and when I got to the "Plough" I called for a half pint and drank it and got a rest and escaped a very heavy shower in the bargain by having a shelter till it was over—afterwards I would have begged a penny of two drovers who were very saucy so I begged no more of anybody, meet who I would.

Having passed a lodge on the left hand within a mile and half or less of a town—I think it might be St. Ives but I forget the name[1]—I sat down to rest on a flint heap where I might rest half an hour or more and while sitting here I saw a tall Gipsey come out of the lodge gate and make down the road towards where I was sitting. When she got

---

[1] Clare noted at the foot of the page "It was St. Neots".

up to me on seeing she was a young woman with an honest looking countenance rather handsome I spoke to her and asked her a few questions which she answered readily and with evident good humour so I got up and went on to the next town with her—She cautioned me on the way to put something in my hat to keep the crown up, and said in a lower tone "You'll be noticed" but not knowing what she hinted—I took no notice and made no reply. At length she pointed to a small tower church which she called Shefford Church and advised me to go on a footway which would take me direct to it and I should shorten my journey fifteen miles by doing so. I would gladly have taken the young woman's advice feeling that it was honest and a nigh guess towards the truth but fearing I might lose my way and not be able to find the north road again I thanked her and told her I should keep to the road when she bade me "good day" and went into a house or shop on the left hand side the road. I passed three or four good built houses on a hill and a public house on the roadside in the hollow below them. I seemed to pass the Milestones very quick in the morning but towards night they seemed to be stretched further asunder. I got to a village further on and forget the name; the road on the left hand was quite overshaded by some trees and quite dry so I sat down half an hour and made a good many wishes for breakfast but wishes was no hearty meal so I got up as hungry as I sat down— I forget here the names of the villages I passed through but reccolect at late evening going through Potton in Bedfordshire where I called in a house to light my pipe in which was a civil old woman and a young country wench making lace on a cushion as round as a globe, and a young fellow, all civil people—I asked them a few questions as to the way and where the clergyman and overseer lived but they scarcely heard me or gave me no answer. I then went through Potton and happened with a kind talking country man who told me the Parson lived a good way from where I was—or overseer I don't know which—so I went on hopping with a crippled foot for the gravel had got into my old shoes one of which had now nearly lost the sole. Had I found the overseer's house at hand or the Parson's I should have gave my name and begged for a shilling to carry me home but I was forced to brush on pennyless and be thankful I had a leg to move on—I then asked him wether he could tell me of a farm yard anywhere on the road where I could find a shed and some dry straw and he said "Yes and if you will go with me I will show you the place—it's a public house on the left hand side the road at the sign of the 'Ram'"; but seeing a stone or flint heap I longed to rest as one of my feet was very painfull, so I thanked him for his kindness and bid him go on—but the good-natured fellow lingered awhile as if wishing to conduct me and then suddenly reccolecting that he had a hamper on his shoulder and a lock-up bag in his hand cram full to meet the coach which he feared missing he started hastily and was soon out of sight—I followed, looking in vain for the country man's straw bed and not being able to meet it I lay down by a shed side under some Elm trees, between the wall and the trees. Being a thick row planted some five or six feet from the buildings I lay there and tried to sleep but the wind came in between them so cold that I lay till I quaked like the ague and quitted the lodging for a better at the "Ram" which I could hardly hope to find —It began to grow dark apace and the odd houses on the road began to light up and show the inside tenants' lot very comfortable and my outside lot very uncomfortable and wretched—still I hobbled forward as well as I could and at last came to the "Ram". The shutters were not closed and the lighted window looked very cheering but I had no money and did not like to go in; there was a sort of shed or gig-house at the end but I did not like to lie there as the people were up so I still travelled on. The road was very lonely and dark in places being overshaded with trees; at length I came to a place where the road branched off into two turnpikes, one to the right about and the other straight forward, and on going bye my eye glanced on a milestone standing under the hedge so I heedlessly turned back to read it to see where the other road led too and on doing so I found it led to London. I then suddenly forgot which was north or south and though I narrowly examined both ways I could see no tree or bush or stone heap that I could reccolect I had passed; so I went on mile after mile almost convinced I was going the same way I came and these thoughts were so strong upon me that doubt and hopelessness made me turn so feeble that I was scarcely able to walk; yet I could not sit down or give up but shuffled along till I saw a lamp shining as bright as the moon which on nearing I found was suspended over a Tollgate. Before I got through the man came out with a candle and eyed me narrowly but having no fear I stopt to ask him wether I was going northward and he said "When you get through the gate you are", so I thanked him kindly and went through on the other side and gathered my old strength as my doubts vanished; I soon cheered up and hummed the air of "Highland Mary" as I went on. I at length fell in with an odd house all alone near a wood but I could not see what the sign was though the sign seemed to stand oddly enough in a sort of trough or spout. There was a large porch over the door and being weary I crept in and glad enough I was to find I could lye with my legs straight. The inmates were all gone to roost for I could hear them turn over in bed as I lay at full length on the stones in the porch—I slept here till daylight and felt very much refreshed as I got up—I blest my two wives and both their familys when I lay down and when I got up, and when I thought of some former difficultys on a like occasion I could not help blessing the Queen—I have but a slight reccolection of my journey between here and Stilton for I was knocked up and noticed little or nothing—one night I lay in a dyke bottom from the wind and went to sleep for half an hour when I suddenly awoke and found one side wet through from the sock[1] in the dyke bottom so I got out and went on—I remember going down a very dark road hung over with trees on both sides very thick which seemed to extend a mile or two. I then entered a town and some of the chamber windows had candle lights shining in them—I felt so weary here that I [was] forced to sit down on the ground to rest myself and while I sat here a coach[2] that seemed to be heavy laden came rattling up and stopt in the hollow below me and I cannot reccolect its ever passing by me. I then got up and pushed onward seeing little to notice for the road very often looked as stupid as myself and I was very often half asleep as I went on. The third day I satisfied my hunger by eating the grass by the roadside which seemed to taste something like bread. I was hungry and eat heartily till I was satisfied and in fact the meal seemed to do me good. The next and last day I reccolected that I had some tobacco and, my box of lucifers being exhausted, I could not light my pipe so I took to chewing tobacco all day and eat the quids when I had done and I was never hungry afterwards—I remember passing through Buckden and going a length of road afterwards but I don't reccolect the name of any place untill I came to Stilton where I was compleatly foot foundered and broken down. When I had got about half way through the town a gravel causeway invited me to rest myself so I lay down and nearly went [to] sleep. A young woman (as I guessed by the voice) came out of a house and said "Poor creature" and another more elderly said "Oh he shams" but when I got up the latter said "O no he don't" as I hobbled along very lame, I heard the voices but never looked back to see where they came from—When I got near the Inn at the end of the gravel walk I met two young women and I asked one of them wether the road branching to the right by the end of the Inn did not lead to Peterborough and she said "Yes" it did, so as soon as ever I was on it I felt myself in home's way and went on rather more cheerfull though I [was] forced to rest oftener than usual. Before I got to Peterborough a man and woman passed in a cart and on hailing me as they passed I found they were neighbours from Helpstone where I used to live—I told them I was knocked up which they could easily see and that I had neither eat or drank anything since I left Essex.

[1] Flood water.
[2] Clare put a * here and noted at the foot of the page: "The Coach did pass me as I sat under some trees by a high wall and the mud splashed in my face and wakened me up from a doze—when I knocked the gravel out of my shoes and started."

When I told my story they clubbed together and threw me fivepence out of the cart; I picked it up and called at a small public house near the bridge were I had two half pints of ale and two penn'o'th of bread and cheese. When I had done I started quite refreshed, only my feet was more crippled than ever and I could scarcely make a walk of it over the stones and being half ashamed to sit down in the street I forced myself to keep on the move and got through Peterborough better than I expected. When I got on the high road I rested on the stone heaps as I passed till I was able to go on afresh and bye and bye I passed Walton and soon reached Werrington and was making for the "Beehive" as fast as I could when a cart met me with a man and woman and a boy in it. When nearing me the woman jumped out and caught fast hold of my hands and wished me to get into the cart, but I refused and thought her either drunk or mad; but when I was told it was my second wife, Patty, I got in and was soon at North-borough. But Mary was not there, neither could I get any information about her further than the old story of her being dead six years ago which might be taken from a bran new old Newspaper printed a dozen years ago; but I took no notice of the blarney having seen her myself about a twelvemonth ago alive and well and as young as ever —So here I am homeless at home, and half gratified to feel that I can be happy anywhere.

When Clare had completed his story, he wrote a letter which he addressed to "Mary Clare—Glinton":

Northborough.
July 27, 1841.

My dear Wife,

I have written an account of my journey or rather escape from Essex for your amusement and hope it may divert your leisure hours —I would have told you before now that I got here to Northborough last friday night but not being able to see you or to hear where you was I soon began to feel homeless at home and shall bye and bye feel nearly hopeless but not so lonely as I did in Essex—for here I can see Glinton Church, and feeling that Mary is safe if not happy and I am gratified, though my home is no home to me, my hopes are not entirely hopeless while even the memory of Mary lives so near me. God bless you My dear Mary. Give my love to your dear beautiful family and to your Mother—and believe me as I ever have been and ever shall be,

My dearest Mary
Your affectionate husband.
John Clare.

About a month later Clare wrote to Dr. Allen, having first composed a draft of the letter round the edges of a local newspaper.

Dear Sir,

Having left the Forest in a hurry I had not time to take leave of you and your family but I intended to write and that before now. But dullness and disappointment prevented me for I found your words true on my return home here having neither friends nor home left. But as it is called the "Poet's Cottage" I claimed a lodging in it where I now am. One of my fancies I found here with her family and all well. They met me on this side Werrington with a horse and cart and found me all but knocked up for I had travelled from Essex to North-amptonshire without ever eating or drinking all the way—save one pennyworth of beer which was given me by a farm servant near an old house called "The Plough". One day I eat grass to keep on my [feet] but on the last day I chewed tobacco and never felt hungry afterwards.

Where my poetical fancy is I cannot say for the people in the neighbourhood tell me that the one called "Mary" has been dead these eight years; but I can be miserably happy in any situation and any place and could have staid in yours on the Forest if any of my old friends had noticed me or come to see me. But the greatest annoy-ance in such places as yours are those servants styled keepers who often assumed as much authority over me as if I had been their prisoner, and not liking to quarrel I put up with it till I was weary of the place altogether so heard the voice of freedom and started and could have travelled to York with a penny loaf and a pint of beer; for I should not have been fagged in body, only one of my old shoes had nearly lost the sole before I started and let in water and silt the first day and made me crippled and lame to the end of my journey.

I had eleven books sent me from How and Parsons, Booksellers— some lent and some given me; out of the eleven I only brought 5 vols here, and as I don't want any part of Essex in Northamptonshire agen I wish you would have the kindness to send a servant to get them for me. I should be very thankful—not that I care about the books altogether only it may be an excuse to see me and get me into company that I do not want to be acquainted with—one of your labourer's—Pratt's—wife borrowed [. . . . . . .] of Lord Byron's— and Mrs. Fish's daughter has two or three more, all Lord Byron's poems; and Mrs. King late of The Owl Public House Leppit Hill and now of Endfield Highway has two or three—all Lord Byron's and one is the *Hours of Idleness*.

You told me something before haytime about the Queen allowing

me a yearly salary of £100 and that the first quarter had then commenced—or else I dreamed so. If I have, the mistake is not of much
consequence to any one save myself, and if true I wish you would get
the quarter for me (if due) as I want to be independent and pay for
board and lodging while I remain here. I look upon myself as a
widow or bachelor—I don't know which. I care nothing about the
women now for they are faithless and deceitful; and the first woman
when there was no man but her husband found out means to cuckold
him by the aid and assistance of the devil—but women being more
righteous now, and men more plentiful they have found out a more
godly way to do it without the devil's assistance. And the man who
possesses a woman possesses losses without gain. The worst is the
road to ruin and the best is nothing like a good cow. Man I never did
like—and woman has long sickened me. I should like to be to myself
a few years and lead the life of a hermit, but even there I should wish
for her whom I am always thinking of—and almost every song I
write has some sighs and wishes in ink about Mary. If I have not
made your head weary by reading this I have tired my own by
writing it so I will wish you good-bye. . . .

In his reply, dated 18th November, 1841, Dr. Allen said that he
was glad to find that Clare realised how much he had wished to
make him happy and that if he had not always been so it was
through no fault of the doctor's. As to the income, he was sorry
to tell him that it was a single donation, not a yearly sum, and it
was only £50 instead of £100.

Your account of your weary Journey is painfully interesting, and
though hope and some delusive feelings about freedom made you
start and led you on I am sorry to find all these dreams are not realised, but that you find something wrong where you are as well as
here. I hope however you will find yourself more comfortable and
whenever you like a little change you are welcome to come here and
get Bed and Board for nothing, and be at liberty to go and come as
you choose, provided you do nothing to make you unpleasant as a
Visitor—You might lead the life of a Hermit as much as you choose
and I would contrive to give you some place for the purpose.

To Taylor, Allen had written sending a statement of expenses
for Clare's time at High Beech.

I sent for Clare [he said] but his wife thought him so much better
that she wished to try him for a while. Should he not remain well I
hope his friends will send him here rather than elsewhere, as I should
feel hurt after the interest I have felt and do feel for him.

But Clare never returned to High Beech, and Allen saw him no more.

Throughout the autumn Clare evidently led much the same sort of life as he had done in times past when mind and body were both healthy. He wrote a good many poems and fragmentary verses, and most of them contained thoughts of

> Mary, the muse of every song I write.

Sometimes he expressed his loneliness and the hopelessness of searching for her whom he could not find, and he repeatedly used the phrase "homeless at home" to describe what he felt.

> I've wandered many a weary mile
> —Love in my heart was burning—
> To seek a home in Mary's smile,
> But cold is life's sojourning.
> The cold ground was a feather-bed,
> —Truth never acts contrary—
> I had no home above my head,
> My home was love and Mary.

There was an echo of overburdening sadness when he felt himself, as it were, on the fringe of the world, struggling to keep himself from drifting away into the darkness of a lost mind. But there were happy verses, too, and the tides of joy ebbed and flowed as well as those of grief.

As in the earlier days, he wandered in the fields and noted lovingly every detail of the blooming of flowers and the life of birds and animals.

> . . . Here are heather bells[1] of a bright blue living for shelter close by the cart ruts where the wind can scarcely come at them, sheltered as if they had a house of their own.
> Oct. 19, 1841. William found a cowslip in flower.
> The mornings now are often frosty and the grass and wild herbs are often covered with rime as white as a shower of snow.
> 4th Nov. An immense flock of starnels settled in an ash tree in the orchard and when they took wing it was like a large roll of thunder.

During this brief interlude between one weary exile and another, Clare, though his mind was darkened now and then by that black and terrible despair, found a great tranquillity in the golden days

[1] Harebells.

of autumn when the larks rose singing from the stubbles, and the jewelled cobwebs lay each misty morning upon leaf and stone. There is a strangely prophetic mention of this time, and, indeed, of his whole latter life, in a poem called "The Fate of Genius" which he wrote sometime between 1821 and 1824. It could not have told the story more accurately if it had been written twenty years after, instead of twenty years before, Clare's illness.

> He dwindled down from too severe a blast,
> And hopes might wish to live that died as fast.
> Still he did live till real life seemed as gone,
> And his soul linger'd in a shadow'd one.
> And yet he mingled in his favour'd ways
> And bared his forehead to the sunny days,
> Listening the lark or fountain's moaning wave,
> As like a ghost as ever left its grave,
> And fled the world at last without a sigh,
> And died as gentle as a lamb would die.

But although Clare's mind was tolerably calm, his delusions remained as obstinate as ever. Mr. Mossop had already suggested that he should go to the new asylum at Northampton, and now, on the advice of Lord Fitzwilliam, Dr. Skrimshire came to see him again and certified him insane. On 29th December, 1841, he was taken from home and entered as a patient at the Northampton General Lunatic Asylum.

26

NORTHAMPTON—THE LAST YEARS

T̲h̲e̲ NORTHAMPTON ASYLUM, which had been opened in 1838, stood then about a mile outside the town, on high ground which overlooked the valley of the River Nen. Clare was entered there as a farmer, and Lord Fitzwilliam undertook to pay the eleven shillings a week which was charged for pauper patients, but in spite of this he was treated as a private patient throughout his long confinement in the asylum. On the form which was filled in by the asylum authorities when Clare was admitted there, his insanity was described as hereditary, and the question "Was it preceded by any severe or long continued mental emotion or exertion?" was answered: "After years addicted to poetical prosing."

The superintendent at the time of Clare's admission was Dr. Thomas S. Prichard, a man of strong character who believed, like Allen, that better results could be obtained by treating the patients with kindness than with harshness. He therefore allowed all those who were well enough to go out unattended and to visit the town if they wished, and he relied on their respect for his authority to prevent them from attempting to escape. His methods appear to have been very effective, and Clare was so convinced of the enormous and almost supernatural power of the doctor that when some fellow patients invited him to escape with them he refused, saying that they did not know the length of that man's arm nor his far-seeing as to their whereabouts.

It is difficult to reconstruct in any detail the fluctuations in Clare's state of mind during the years at Northampton, but certain broad outlines emerge clearly. That there *were* fluctuations, as indeed there had always been, is evident; there were days when he talked quite rationally, and others when he spoke rambling incoherent sentences, and at times he broke his usual habit of frequent writing and could not be induced to take any interest in poetry. But it seems that his mind was calmer than it had been at High Beech, and although he was often homesick and mourned his captivity, the darkest and most terrible depths were left behind him and he attained a measure of tranquillity. He wrote an enormous number of poems during these years, some of them fragmentary and tailing off into nonsense, but others which were among the most beautiful things he ever wrote. His physical health was excellent until almost the end of his life.

In May, 1843, Spencer T. Hall visited him and described him as "rather burly, florid, with light hair and somewhat shaggy eyebrows, and dressed as a plain but respectable farmer, in drab or stone-coloured coat and smalls, with gaiters, and altogether as clean and neat as if he had just been fresh brushed up for market or fair."

Hall recounts his conversation with Clare, in which the old delusion of being a prize fighter immediately appeared.

> On my asking him how he was, he said, "Why, I'm very well, and stout, but I'm getting tired of waiting here so long, and want to be off home. They won't let me go, however: for, you see, they're feeding me up for a fight; but they can get nobody able to strip to me; so they might as well have done with it and let me go." "But, Mr. Clare," said I, "are you not more proud of your fame as a poet than of your prowess as a prize-fighter?" When, rather abstractedly, as if considering or trying to recollect something, he answered, "Oh, poetry, ah, I know, I once had something to do with poetry, a long while ago: but it was no good."

Hall then mentioned having sent him a copy of the *Sheffield Iris* when he was at High Beech, and Clare replied that he had edited the paper and went to York Castle where he wrote an "Address to Robin". On that occasion he evidently identified himself with James Montgomery.

In November, 1843, Prichard reported on Clare's condition:

> Poor Clare is in good health but the state of his mind has not improved it rather appears to become more and more impaired; he used at one time to write many and very good pieces tho' he scarcely ever finished them, he now writes but little and in a coarse style very unlike his former compositions.

But in the following year Clare was writing, among other things, the beautiful "Graves of Infants":

> Infants' graves are steps of angels, where
> Earth's brightest gems of innocence repose.

God is their parent, and they need no tear:
He takes them to His bosom from earth's woes,
A bud their lifetime and a flower their close.
Their spirits are an Iris of the skies,
Needing no prayers; a sunset's happy close.
Gone are the bright rays of their soft blue eyes;
Flowers weep in dew-drops o'er them, and the gale
    gently sighs.

There is no hint of the "coarse style" there! Clare, the loving father, had perhaps a thought of his own children in past years when he wrote so tenderly of the "soft blue eyes". In this year, 1844, Anna died, and Frederick, his eldest son, had died in the previous May, but if he was ever told of their deaths he forgot and believed them still living at home.

De Wilde, editor of the *Northampton Mercury*, who often saw Clare in the town, described him as "a short, heavy man with the peculiar tread of one accustomed to follow the plough". There was, he said, still a striking likeness to Hilton's portrait, "though he had even then that peculiar heaviness of brow which increased with his years and seemed to overweight his brain and prevent its free action. . . . As he advanced in years the eye was almost lost beneath a heavy pent-house of brow." One day, in course of conversation, Clare quoted to him some lines of Shakespeare and some from *Childe Harold* and said they were his own. De Wilde, who did not know to whom he was talking, exclaimed in astonishment that they were Byron's and Shakespeare's. "It's all the same," Clare answered. "I'm John Clare now. I was Byron and Shakespeare formerly."

This delusion, which persisted so strongly, appears again and again in the notebooks.

> Lord Byron was 16 years when he began to write *Childe Harold* and finished it in 1818 when he was 25; when he wrote the 4th Canto he was courting one Martha Turner, the daughter of Mr. Wm. Turner, Walk Lodge. He began it one Sunday afternoon and finished it in three or four hours under an Ash Tree in her father's home close.

The question of identity troubled Clare deeply, not so much because he confused himself with other people, but because he had some idea that the whole world was concerned in a vast conspiracy to make him forget himself. Perhaps it was an echo from the years when he had been deeply wounded to find himself cast aside by a public who had been entertained for a brief season by the novelty of a peasant poet.

During the period before his removal from Northborough to Northampton, he had written in his notebook:

A very good commonplace counsel is *Self-Identity* to bid our own hearts not to forget our own selves and always to keep self in the first place lest all the world who always keeps us behind it should forget us all together—forget not thyself and the world will not forget thee—forget thyself and the world will willingly forget thee till thou art nothing but a living-dead man dwelling among shadows and false-hood. . . . But I cannot forget that I'm a man and it would be dishonest and unmanly in me to do so. . . . I am often troubled at times to know that should the world have the impudence not to know me but willingly forgetting me wether any single individual would be honest enough to know me—such people would be useful as the knocker to a door or the bell of a cryer to own the dead alive or the lost found. . . .

Mary Russell Mitford described the visit which a friend of hers paid to Clare at about this time, when the poet gave an account of the execution of Charles I as though he had been an eyewitness, "with an accuracy as to costume and manners far exceeding what would probably have been at his command if sane". He also "would relate the battle of the Nile, and the death of Lord Nelson with the same perfect keeping, especially as to seamanship, fancying himself one of the sailors who had been in the action, and dealing out nautical phrases with admirable exactness."

Clare used to visit the town frequently, as well as wandering about the fields and wooded grounds near the asylum; he had a favourite seat under the portico of All Saints' Church, and would sit there for hours, chewing tobacco and watching the passers-by. He was taciturn, apparently, and answered very briefly when spoken to, but the people of Northampton were invariably kind to him and it was not unusual for him to receive some little gift, such as a screw of tobacco.

There is an account of Clare written shortly after his death by a man called Jerom, a fellow patient at Northampton. In speaking of Clare's appearance, he mentioned how thickset and muscular

he was, and how easily he might have been taken for the prize-
fighter of his delusions. His hair turned from light flaxen colour
to a silvery white, and although he was bald on top it grew, in
the latter years of his life, very long—almost to his shoulders.
". . . He was like the King of the Forest, there was a prowess in his
limbs and a majesty in his fiery eye that showed the vigour and
energy of a mind whose greatness even in ruins reminded one
forcibly of what is said in Scripture of the Leviathan: 'None dare
stir him up, nor make him afraid.'"

He took a keen interest in great trials and was able to discuss
many of them in detail; naval battles formed another favourite
subject of conversation, and there was a verse that he used to
recite in which he was believed to be referring to Nelson.

> Fight on my boys, he said,
> Till I die, till I die,
> Fight on my boys, he said,
> Till I die.

In November, 1844, when Queen Victoria and Prince Albert
passed through the town on their way to visit the Marquis of
Exeter at Burghley House, Clare was given a good place from
which to watch the procession.

In April, 1845, W. F. Knight was appointed as steward to the
asylum and became a good friend to Clare. Not only did he show
him much kindness in many ways, but he transcribed an immense
number of poems, written in the asylum years, which would otherwise probably have been lost or destroyed. Many of them were
written in pencil on scraps of paper, and Clare gave them to
Knight to keep safely for him; others were presented to people who
visited the asylum and were afterwards given to the steward for
transcription. In some cases, the originals were so much obliter-
ated that Knight was unable to decipher them without reference
to Clare, and he explained why some pieces were left unfinished:
". . . for Clare will seldom turn his attention to pieces he has
been interrupted in while writing: and in no instance has he ever
rewritten a single line. Whenever I have wished him to correct a
single stanza, he has ever shown the greatest disinclination to take
in hand what seems to him a great task."

In July of that year, Prichard wrote to the Revd. Mr.
Chalklen of Northborough, through whom, probably, he

communicated with Patty: "John Clare is in excellent health, but his mind is becoming more and more obscured by his distressing malady—He enjoys perfect liberty here, and passes all his time out of doors in the fields or the Town, returning home only for his meals and bed."

There is no record that Patty ever went to see Clare, and she and his children have been blamed for neglecting him; later biographers have exonerated them, but in passing it is only fair to state again what appears to be the truth of the matter. Clare's second son, John, went several times to visit him, and likewise William. Charles, the youngest, who wrote most often to his father, was articled to a solicitor and probably found it difficult to make the long journey from Northborough to Northampton in his few leisure hours. He died in 1852. Patty herself may well have had good reason for not going—it is quite likely that she was asked not to do so lest her presence should distress Clare, and anyway, she was often sick herself in those latter years of her life, and her circumstances were too straitened to allow her to make the expensive journey to Northampton more than very occasionally. The details of her appearance, her character and opinions are unfortunately so few as to make her but a shadowy figure, and in this, as in other things, we can only guess at the part that she played; but as we know that she tried to save Clare from the asylum and nursed him at home with care and tenderness, it can safely be assumed that she was not guilty of neglecting him afterwards.

In 1846, Parker Clare died at the age of eighty-one. Clare was told of his father's death, but he had forgotten it soon afterwards. The routine of his life at Northampton continued unbroken; his moods veered between melancholy and a tranquil resignation, and the health of his short, muscular body remained better than it had ever been in the days of sanity. He wrote steadily and gave manuscript poems to a number of visitors who came to the asylum.

In June, 1847, he wrote to Charles:

I insist that Frederick and John had better not come unless they wish to do so for it is a *bad Place* and I have fears that they may get trapped as prisoners as I hear some have been and I may not see them nor even hear they have been here.

Clare did not know that Frederick had been dead four years.

In the draft of a letter to Patty we find him remembering the childhood of this eldest son, whose entry into Christ's Hospital he had
once so much desired yet so much dreaded because it would mean
a parting. He told her that he often thought of the family at
Northborough, and particularly the children:

> Freddy when I led him by the hand in his childhood I see him
> now in his little pink frock, sealskin cap and gold band—with his
> little face as round as a apple and as red as a rose—and now a stout
> Man both strangers to each other, the father a prisoner under a bad
> government so bad in fact that its no government at all but prison
> discipline where everybody is forced to act contrary to their own
> wishes.

Clare's feeling for children was not merely an objective affection; he did not look upon them from afar with the superior
kindliness that so often characterises the adult attitude to childhood, but rather seemed to feel himself one with them. He was
one of the blessed few who never lose the simplicity of heart with
which all men set out upon their pilgrimage, and to the end of his
life he looked on the things of the earth with the wonder of a child,
who sees them for the first time and feels each weed and leaf and
snail's shell to be a miracle of beauty.

Some years before, Clare had written of the "Fairy Things"
that had delighted his childhood and lost nothing of their
enchantment when he saw them as a man.

> . . . And fairy money-pots are often found
> That spring like little mushrooms out of ground,
> Some shaped like cups and some in slender trim
> Wineglasses like, that to the very rim
> Are filled with little mystic shining seed;
>
> .   .   .   .   .
>
> Acres of little yellow weeds,
> The wheat-fields constant blooms,
> That ripen into prickly seed
> For fairy curry-combs,
> To comb and clean the little things
> That draw their nightly wain;
> And so they scrub the beetle's wings
> Till he can fly again.

And flannel felt for the beds of the queen
From the soft inside of the shell of the bean,
Where the gipsies down in the lonely dells
Had littered and left the plundered shells.

Nothing that belonged to the earth was commonplace to Clare; everything had its part in the order of creation, and man was not so much above the animals and birds and plants that he could treat them with disdain. It was a mixture of protective tenderness and awe that he felt for them, rather as one might feel for a younger brother possessed of surpassing beauty and grace. It was a feeling born of that sense of kinship with all living creatures which is a part of childhood, and in Clare, instead of fading away as he came to manhood it grew stronger and more tender until it shone through all his work with a radiance that is almost blinding. He had called the snail "frail brother of the morn" and had watched the bees "stroke their little legs across their wings"; now, in the asylum years, when he was exiled both in space and time from the well-loved meadows round Helpston, he remembered how he had lain in the grass and watched the ladybird—or, as he called her, the clock-a-clay—in her home in the cowslip blossom:

While grassy forests quake surprise,
And the wild wind sobs and sighs,
My gold home rocks as like to fall,
On its pillar green and tall;
When the parting rain drives by
Clock-a-clay keeps warm and dry.

If a child could write beautiful poetry and achieve mastery of words and rhythms, he would write of the ladybird just as Clare did—without condescension or sentimentality, only smiling a little because she was so much smaller in stature than himself. In the same vein he addressed "Little Trotty Wagtail" who

. . . waddled in the mud
And left his little footmarks, trample where he would.

And like a child who has not yet accepted the suffering of the lesser creatures but feels it like the suffering of humanity, Clare grieved for the cruelty of the world.

17

> The tears of dew night leaves
> Upon the grass at morn
> Show nature inly grieves
> For deeds that day has done,
> For beetles trod upon,
> Moths and butterflies destroyed,
> Nests with the young ones gone,
> Left desolate and void. . . .

The sorrows of his own imprisonment were, for the moment, forgotten while he mourned for these tragedies that are to most men no more than the normal course of the world.

In February, 1848, Clare was writing to Charles with advice for all his children as to how they must meet life. They were to "love truth, be honest and fear nobody" and to study mathematics, astronomy, languages and botany. Once he had expressed the hope that his infant daughter would never "itch at rhymes", but now it seems that he wanted his children to follow in his footsteps.

> I loved nature [he wrote] and painted her both in words and colours better than many Poets and Painters and by Perseverance and attention you may all do the same—in my boyhood solitude was the most talkative vision I met with. Birds bees trees flowers all talked to me incessantly, louder than the busy hum of men, and who so wise as nature out of doors on the green grass by woods and streams under the beautiful sunny sky—daily communings with God and not a word spoken.

On 19th July, he wrote to Patty:

> My dear Wife,
> I have not written to you a long while, but here I am in the land of Sodom where all the people's brains are turned the wrong way. I was glad to see John yesterday, and should like to have gone back with him, for I am very weary of being here. You might come and fetch me away, for I think I have been here long enough.
> I write this in a green meadow by the side of the river agen Stokes Mill, and I see three of your daughters and a son now and then. The confusion and roar of mill dams and locks is sounding very pleasant while I write it, and its a very beautiful evening; the meadows are greener than usual after the shower and the rivers are brimful. I think it is about two years since I was first sent up in this Hell and not allowed to go out of the gates. . . . Keep yourselves

happy and comfortable and love one another. Bye and bye I shall be
with you, perhaps before you expect me. There has been a great
storm here with thunder and hail that did much damage to the glass
in the neighbourhood. Hailstones the size of hen's eggs fell in some
places. Did your brother John come to Northborough or go to
Barnack? His uncle John Riddle came the next morning but did not
stay. I thought I was coming home but I got cheated. I see many of
your little brothers and sisters at Northampton, weary and dirty with
hard work; some of them with red hands, but all in ruddy good
health: some of them are along with your sister Ruth Dakken who
went from Helpston a little girl. Give my love to your Mother,
Grandfather and sisters, and believe me, my dear children, hers and
yours.   Very affectionately
                                                 John Clare.

By the end of the letter he seems to have thought that he was
writing to the children.

In April, 1849, he wrote again to Charles, begging him for news
from home: ". . . tell me how the flowers go on and don't forget
your Latin and Greek and Hebrew. . . ."

In all his letters Clare spoke of his longing for home and asked
when he was to be fetched away from his "captivity". His son,
Charles, wrote back with assurances that the family were all well,
and generally said that there was no news to tell him. But things
were not easy at Northborough; Patty's health was no longer
good, and the two elder boys were often out of work, so that it was
difficult to make ends meet.

In 1851 we find Charles writing to Taylor to ask for help.
They were in arrears with the rent, and he was afraid that Patty
might lose her home. John was now in work, but William was not
and had for some time been obliged to live at his mother's expense,
while Charles' salary for his work in the attorney's office amounted
to £4 a year "which will not find me clothes". In the following
year Charles died. William lived on at Northborough with his
mother, working as a farm labourer; John eventually got a good
job on the railway and went away to live in Wales. Eliza married
a man called Sefton and moved to Spalding, while Sophia
remained at home and died in 1863.

Meanwhile Clare's life followed a steady routine, with little
variety. The poems which he was writing through these years are
startling indeed. The majority of them were love poems, and they
spoke of youth and happiness; their melody is as joyous and

spontaneous as the whistle of a blackbird in April, and there is a
sense of liberation in them, as though Clare had come through
the horrors of the darkness out into the dew-laden freshness of a
spring morning. With the inevitable ebb and flow of mood there
were poems that were pensive, too, and some that mourned his lost
liberty, but they only make the others the more remarkable.

> 'Tis Spring, my love, 'tis spring,
> And the birds begin to sing:
> If 'twas Winter, left alone with you,
> Your bonny form and face
> Would make a Summer place
> And be the finest flower that ever grew.
>
> 'Tis Spring, my love, 'tis Spring,
> And the hazel catkins hing,
> While the snowdrop has its little blebs of dew;
> But that's not so white within
> As your bosom's hidden skin—
> That sweetest of all flowers that ever grew.[1]

Who, reading such verses, could ever guess the circumstances in
which they were written. And, again:

> There's something i' the time so sweet, when lovers i' the evening
> meet,
> The air so still, the sky so mild, like slumbers o' the cradled child,
> The moon looks over fields of love, among the ivy sleeps the dove;
> To see thee is to love thee.
>
> So come, my Mary, now's the hour to feel the evening's soothing
> power,
> The ladybird has sought repose on golden pillows in the rose,
> The white moth's round the whitethorn bush, on its blue eggs sits
> the thrush,
> And I'll ever after love thee.[2]

The predominant impression in these and many more of the
poems of this period is one of carefree youth, a happiness so great
that the poet cannot help singing. We cannot—indeed, dare not—
attempt explanations or hazard guesses as to what moved Clare
to write thus. The biographer must accept limitations and it is
enough to know that they *were* written and to listen to their
melody.

[1] " 'Tis Spring, my love, 'tis Spring."   [2] "There's Something in the Time."

The poems that Clare's moods of sorrow produced were beautiful, too. In "I am", perhaps the best known of them, he wrestled again with the problem of self-identity, and contemplated "the vast ship-wreck of my life's esteems". In terrible weariness, he looked for rest:

> I long for scenes where man hath never trod;
> A place where woman never smiled or wept;
> There to abide with my Creator, God,
> And sleep as I in childhood sweetly slept:
> Untroubling and untroubled where I lie;
> The grass below—above the vaulted sky.

In 1854, Dr. Prichard left Northampton to establish an asylum of his own, and he was succeeded by Dr. Nesbitt and Dr. Wing. The change resulted in Clare's freedom being restricted, and he was no longer allowed to wander alone outside the asylum grounds. It is said that various people in the town had shown mistaken kindness in giving Clare ale, which was injurious in its effects, and that this was the reason for curtailing his privileges.

Knight, the steward, had gone from Northampton, too; he had proposed in 1850 that some of Clare's later poems should be published by subscription, as he had preserved with great care the transcripts that he had made from verses which Clare had written and given to him, but nothing more was heard of his scheme. Nesbitt, too, had a great admiration for Clare's poems and took a keen interest in him. He described how Clare had once said, on being asked how he wrote his poetry, that he "kicked it out of the clods".

During the next few years the state of Clare's mind became gradually more impaired, and his physical strength declined. He ceased to write at all, and when it was suggested to him, he would say that he had forgotten how to do it. In the spring of 1850, he was persuaded to take up his pen again and he wrote a few sonnets, including an "Address to John Clare".

In August of that year, Agnes Strickland visited the asylum with Lord Spencer, and Clare wrote down for her the little poem beginning "The daisy is a happy flower". She told him that she was pleased with the lines, and Clare, without appearing gratified by her praise, said that it was "a tidy little thing".

"I am glad you can amuse yourself by writing," Miss Strickland said.

"I can't do it," Clare answered gloomily: "they pick my brains out."

When she asked his meaning, he said, "They have cut off my head and picked out all the letters in the alphabet—all the vowels and consonants—and brought them out through my ears; and then they want me to write poetry! I can't do it!"

This last period of work lasted only until 1861, and then Clare wrote no more; his mind seems to have been, for the most part, calm and untroubled during 1860 and 1861, but thereafter the darkness deepened, he became apathetic, and at the last could rarely even delight in flowers and sunshine. He grew steadily weaker, and had to be put in a wheel-chair when he went out in the asylum grounds. Several times he said, "I want to go home" and "I have lived too long".

On Good Friday, 1864, he went out for the last time, and on 10th May he had a paralytic seizure. He lived on for ten days, and then died quietly on the afternoon of 20th May, 1864, within two months of his seventy-first birthday.

His body was taken to Helpston, and he was buried there, as was his wish, on 25th May. Patty, Eliza, and William were present, and so were Mr. Mossop and a few other old friends.

Forty years before, Clare had written the epitaph of genius:

> Here sleep the hopes of one whose glowing birth
> Was found too warm for this unfeeling earth.

But neither this nor the inscription which he had desired was put on his tombstone. It bore, instead, the words, "Sacred to the Memory of John Clare, the Northamptonshire Peasant Poet. Born July 13 1793. Died May 20 1864. Poeta nascitur, non fit."

A few words suffice to tell of the others who had played an important part in Clare's life. John Taylor died two months after him, aged eighty-three, after ten years of an illness which forced him to lead an invalid life. Patty lived on at Northborough for another seven years and died in 1871.

So the last of the characters in the story of John Clare finished their pilgrimage as he had done, and it is left to us to wonder at the life which contained so much of glory, so much of tragedy. The beautiful poem which Clare wrote in the latter years sums up the whole story more perfectly than any other words could do.

I lost the love of Heaven above
I spurned the lust of Earth below,
I felt the sweets of fancied love
And Hell itself my only foe.

I lost Earth's joys, but felt the glow
Of Heaven's fame abound in me
Till loveliness and I did grow
The bard of Immortality.

I loved, but woman fell away;
I hid me from her faded fame.
I snatched the sun's eternal ray
And wrote till Earth was but a name.

In every language upon earth,
On every shore, o'er every sea
I gave my name immortal birth
And kept my spirit with the free.

A BIBLIOGRAPHICAL OUTLINE

THE WORKS OF JOHN CLARE

Poems Descriptive of Rural Life and Scenery. London: Printed for Taylor and Hessey. 1820. Second and third editions, 1820. Fourth edition, 1821.
The Village Minstrel, and Other Poems. Taylor and Hessey. 1821. Two volumes. Second edition, 1823.
The Shepherd's Calendar; with Village Stories, and Other Poems. Taylor. 1827.
The Rural Muse. London: Whittaker and Co. 1835.

BIOGRAPHIES AND SELECTIONS

The Life of John Clare. By Frederick Martin. London and Cambridge: Macmillan & Co. 1865.
Life and Remains of John Clare. By J. L. Cherry. London: Frederick Warne & Co. Northampton: J. Taylor & Son. 1873.
Poems by John Clare. Selected and introduced by Norman Gale. With a Bibliography by C. Ernest Smith. George E. Over. Rugby, 1901.
Poems by John Clare, edited with an Introduction by Arthur Symons. London: Frowde. 1908.
Northamptonshire Botanologia: John Clare. By G. Claridge Druce. 1912. (Includes a memoir, and a classification of the flowers described in Clare's poems.)
John Clare: Poems Chiefly from Manuscript. Edited by Edmund Blunden and Alan Porter. With an Introduction by Edmund Blunden. London: Richard Cobden-Sanderson. 1920.
Madrigals and Chronicles. Being newly found poems written by John Clare. Edited, with a Preface and Commentary, by Edmund Blunden. London: The Beaumont Press. 1924.
Sketches in the Life of John Clare. By Himself. With an Introduction, Notes, and Additions by Edmund Blunden. London: R. Cobden-Sanderson Ltd. 1931.
John Clare. A Life. By J. W. and Anne Tibble. London: R. Cobden-Sanderson Ltd. 1932.
The Poems of John Clare. Edited, with an Introduction, by J. W. Tibble. London: J. M. Dent & Sons Ltd. New York: E. P. Dutton & Co. Inc. 1935.

MISCELLANEOUS CLARE VOLUMES

Four Letters from the Rev. W. Allen to the Right Honourable Lord Radstock, G.C.B., on the Poems of John Clare, the Northamptonshire Peasant. Hatchards. 1823.

Three Very Interesting Letters (two in curious rhyme) by the celebrated poets Clare, Cowper and Bird. With an Appendix (Clare's *Familiar Epistle to a Friend*) Charles Clarke's private press, Great Totham, 1837. Only 25 copies printed.
The John Clare Centenary Exhibition Catalogue. Introduction by C. Dack. Peterborough Natural History Society, 1893. Pamphlet.

A List of all the known volumes which contain references to Clare would be very long, and the following list, therefore, includes only those books that I have found to contain new or specially interesting material.

Baker, Miss A. E. *Glossary of Northamptonshire Words and Phrases,* 1854.
Blunden, Edmund. *Nature in English Literature,* 1929;
          Keats's Publisher: A Memoir of John Taylor, 1936.
Cary, H. F., Memoir of, 1947.
De Quincey, T. *London Reminiscences,* 1897.
De Wilde, G. J. *Rambles Round About,* 1872.
Dobell, B. *Sidelights on Charles Lamb,* 1903.
Hall, S. C. *Book of Gems,* 1838;
          A Book of Memories, 1871.
Hammond, J. L., and Barbara. *The Village Labourer, 1760–1832,* 1927.
Hood, Thomas. *Works,* ii, 1882.
Lamb, Charles. *Letters* (Everyman), 1909.
Lucas, E. V. *Life of Charles Lamb,* 1905.
Lombroso, Cesare. *The Man of Genius,* 1891.
Mitford, M. R. *Recollections of a Literary Life,* 1857.
Redding, Cyrus. *Fifty Years' Recollections,* 1859;
          Past Celebrities Whom I Have Known, ii, 1866.
Strickland, Agnes, Life of.
Symons, Arthur. *The Romantic Movement in English Poetry,* 1908.
Taylor, John. *Bibliotheca Northantonensis,* 1869.

After this book had gone to the printer, *Poems of John Clare's Madness,* edited by Geoffrey Grigson, was published (Routledge and Kegan Paul Ltd.), and I have altered one or two quotations to accord with the reading given there when it has differed from that of previous published selections.

                                        J. W.

INDEX

Ackermann, R., 193
Albert, Prince, 254
Alfred, The, 214, 218
Allen, Dr. Matthew, 228, 229, 230, 231, 248; and subscription for Clare, 231–2; letter from Clare, 246–7; letter to Clare, 247; on Clare's future, 247
Allen, Revd. W., 130, 132
Analectic Magazine, The, 72
Anniversary, The, 194, 222, 230
Annuals, Clare writes for, 165–6, 178, 188, 192, 193, 197
Antijacobin Review, The, 72
Arnold, Dr., 41, 136, 138
Artis, E. T., 116, 129, 154, 164, 165, 181, 182
Athenaeum, The, 206, 214, 225, 231
Autobiography, Clare's, 147, 148, 151

Bacon's Essays, 151
Bains, Granny, 22, 23
Baker, George, 194
Beattie's Minstrel, 83, 112
Bedford, Duke of, 89
Bee, The, 202, 214, 218
Behnes Burlowe, Henry, 180–1, 185–6, 189, 192, 199
Bell, Dr., 89
Bellamy, Counsellor, 28–9, 119
Bellars, Mrs., 28
Bennion, Thomas, 119, 126, 128, 134, 138, 139, 140
Billings, James, 47, 48, 116, 156
Billings, John, 47, 48, 116, 156
Birch-Reynardson, General, 74, 82
Blackwood's Magazine, 225
Bloomfield, Robert, 72, 112, 118, 135, 146, 152, 155, 230
Bone and Cleaver Club, The, 205
Boston, Mayor of, 190
Bowles, Revd. W. Lisle, 119, 144
Brooke, Henry, 190
Brown, Charles, 100
Bullimore, Mrs., 22
Burghley House, 33, 41, 74, 254
Burkhardt, 77
Burns, Robert, 62, 72, 112, 114
Byron, Lord, 88, 117, 119, 149; funeral of, 143–4; and Clare's delusions, 233–5, 252

Campbell, Thomas, 119, 228
Cary, Revd. H. F., 67, 80, 121, 127, 130–1, 147, 148, 192, 215, 228; on

Clare, 78; Clare on, 124; Clare visits, 124, 185
Chalklen, Revd. Mr., 255
Champion, The, 203
Chatterton, Thomas, 59, 88, 149
Chaucer, Geoffrey, 202
Child Harold (Clare), 234
Childe Harold (Byron), 144, 236, 252
Christie, J., 102
Clare, Ann, 18–20, 23, 26, 27, 28, 29, 34, 62, 69, 73, 81, 93, 185, 198, 226
Clare, Anna Maria, 91, 114, 132–3, 140, 157, 160, 163, 169, 204, 252
Clare, Charles, 218, 255, 258, 259
Clare, Eliza Louisa, 126, 160, 163, 174, 204, 259, 262
Clare, Frederick, 136, 201, 204, 220, 232, 252, 255, 256
Clare, John, birth, 19; infancy, 20–1; school, 22, 23, 25, 26; Mary Joyce, 25, 36–9; threshing, 22; night-school, 26; plough-boy, 28; goes to Wisbech, 28–9; at Blue Bell, 29–30; first poems, 32–3; leaves Blue Bell, 40; Burghley House, 41–2; runs away, 42; works at Newark, 42–3; home, 43; day labourer, 44–5, 47–9; militia, 45–7; lime-burning, 50–1, 55–6, 57; meets Patty Turner, 52–3, and courts her, 54, 64–6; gardening, 51, 64, 65; endeavours to publish poems, 54–9; meets Drury, 61; meets Taylor, 66–8; publication of *Poems Descriptive*, 71; visits Milton, 74; visits Burghley, 74–5; in London, 77–80; marriage, 81; visits Holywell Hall, 82–3; daughter born, 91; importunate visitors, 75, 93–4, 113; publication of *Village Minstrel*, 109; second visit to London, 119–25; second daughter born, 126; love affairs, 131–2, 169–71; first son born, 136; third visit to London, 138–45; visits Fives Court, 140–1; French Playhouse, 142–3; sees Byron's funeral cortège, 143–4; visits Artis and Henderson, 163–4; second son born, 174; publication of *Shepherd's Calendar*, 177; fourth visit to London, 185–7; travelling bookseller, 186, 188, 189, 194; third son born, 189; at Boston, 190–1; mental breakdown, 198–9; third daughter born, 200; moves to Northborough, 209; mis-statements in newspapers, 214–15; fourth son born, 218; grant from Literary Fund, 220; publication of

Clare, John,—*contd.*
Rural Muse, 221; visited by Taylor, 226–7; sent to High Beech, 229; escapes, 240; journey home, 240–5; sent to Northampton, 249; last illness and death, 262; appearance, 78, 123, 186, 235, 251, 252, 253–4; health (fits), 40–1, 84, (depression) 96, 101, 118, 127–8, 135–6, 137–8, 146–7, 149, 150, 185, 202, 204, 218, 219, 220, 221, 225–6, (physical symptoms) 118, 127–8, 136, 138, 146–7, 165, 183, 191, 204, (treated by Dr. Darling) 139–40, 145, 147, 152, 153, 169, 185, 200, 219, (mental symptoms) 198–200, 226–8, 230, 231, 250–1; drinking, 83–4, 104–5, 106–7, 114, 115, 126–7, 131, 133, 134, 145, 156, 165, 192; financial affairs, 94, 115, 128, 147–8, 171, 174–5, 181, 188, 194, 195–7, 202, 204, 207, 208, 211–12, 213, 214, 219, 220; on his work, 85, 116–17, 209, 215, 258; his methods of work, 115, 172; on his parents, 20; on Lord Radstock, 78–9, 99, 164; on Mrs. Emmerson, 79, 231; on Keats, 86; on grammar, 102; on Crabbe, 112, 146; and childhood, 111–12, 256–8; and children's books, 218; his faith, 113, 136–7, 201, 221–2, 223–4; on "The Londoners", 121–4, 141; and fame, 143–4; on Taylor, 159; on politics, 203–4; relations with Patty, 91–2, 106, 131, 132, 201; dreams, 157–8, 179, 216–17, 232; delusions, 227, 233–7, 252–3
Clare, John (Clare's son), 174, 232, 255, 258, 259
Clare, Martha (Patty), 93, 113, 120, 125, 145, 174, 180, 182, 183, 184, 185, 189, 192, 198, 202, 206, 218, 226, 228, 255, 259, 262; meets Clare, 52–3; Clare's courtship of, 53, 54, 64–6; marriage, 81; relations with Clare, 91–2, 106, 131, 132, 201; health, 126, 163, 201; from Mrs. Emmerson, 140, 199, 230; Clare's letters to, 186, 232, 233, 256, 258–9; Clare's "second wife", 227, 237, 245; Clare's poem to, 238; death, 262
Clare, Sir Michael, 135
Clare, Parker, 18–20, 22, 23, 26, 27, 28, 29, 34, 40, 50, 54, 69, 73, 81, 114, 120, 185, 198, 220, 226, 255
Clare, Sophia, 200, 259
Clare, Sophy, 19, 81, 93, 120
Clare, William Parker, 189, 232, 237, 248, 255, 259, 262
Cobbett's *Rural Rides*, 203
Coleridge, Samuel Taylor, 114, 117, 151, 194; Clare on, 141
Compleat Angler, 148, 167
Corrie, Haydn, 74, 77

Cousins, George, 42, 43
Cowper, William, 114
Crabbe, George, 112, 114, 146
Crockford, 230
Cunningham, Allan, 114, 146, 185, 186, 187, 193–4, 213, 214, 226, 230; Clare on, 124
Currie's *Life of Burns*, 88

Darley, George, 141, 176, 182, 185, 193
Darling, Dr., 136, 138, 139, 140, 145, 147, 152, 153, 157, 160, 165, 169, 183, 185, 200, 204, 219, 221, 225, 228, 231
Davenant, William, 168
Davies, Tom, 168
De Quincey, Thomas, 100, 139, 185, 191; Clare on, 141
Deville, 142, 147
Devonshire, Duke of, 89
De Wilde, G. J., 252
De Wint, Peter, 176, 177, 231
Diary, Clare's, (1824–1825) 148–55, 157–8, 162, 163, 166, 173; (of journey from Essex) 240–5
Dolben, Sir John E., 63
Don Juan (Byron), 149
Don Juan (Clare), 233–4
Drakard and Wilson, 202
Drury, Edward, 60–1, 64, 66, 67, 68, 74, 84, 89, 93, 95, 104, 106, 195, 196–7; meets Clare, 61–2; sends Clare's poems to Taylor, 63; plans to send Clare to National School, 69–70; anxieties for Clare, 71; quarrels with Taylor, 86–8, 93; claim on Clare, 174–5, 181
Dryden, John, 88

Eclectic Review, The, 72, 112
Elizabethan poets, Clare and, 150, 166–7, 192
Elm trees, 103, 109
Elton, C. A., 125, 141, 142, 151
Emery (actor), 77
Emmerson, Mrs. E. L., 79, 88, 89, 94, 98, 99, 102, 107, 113, 114–15, 118, 127, 128, 130, 131, 132, 135–6, 138, 139, 140, 141, 143, 147, 150, 154, 156, 158, 160, 161, 164, 169–71, 173, 174, 180, 181, 186, 188, 189, 195, 199, 202, 212, 214, 216, 219, 228, 230; first letter to Clare, 76; meets Clare, 79; on Lord Radstock, 90; relations with Clare, 91–2, 228, 230; her portrait, 92, 140; and Taylor, 93, 96, 98, 106–7, 176, 196, 207, 208; Clare stays with, 119, 185; godmother to Eliza Clare, 126; gifts to Clare, 132, 169, 180, 183, 206, 207, 210–11, 212, 226; visits Market Deeping, 169; pays Eliza's schooling, 174, 183; illness, 183, 220, 226; invites Clare to London, 184; and Clare's cottage, 190; Clare's poem

Emmerson, Mrs. E. L.,—*contd.*
to, 194; and Frederick's school, 201; and *Rural Muse*, 213, 218–19; new house, 226; subscribes to Clare's expenses at High Beech, 230

Emmerson, Thomas, 107, 139, 150, 154, 169, 210–11, 213, 219, 231

Enclosure, 19, 39–40, 45

Etty, William, 140

European Magazine, The, 194

Exeter, Marquis of, 41, 75, 89, 95, 102, 107, 147, 175, 204, 254

Fate of Genius, The, 249

Fitzwilliam, Earl, 73, 74, 89, 198

Fitzwilliam, Earl (formerly Lord Milton —see also under that title), 221, 228, 231, 232

Foxe's *Book of Martyrs*, 148

Fricker, the Misses, 194

Fund money, Clare's, 79–80, 89, 116, 128, 137, 147, 202, 204, 207, 208, 211, 212, 213

Gentleman's Magazine, The, 72, 112

Gifford, William, 72–3, 119

Gilchrist, Octavius, 63, 71, 80, 81, 84, 93, 104, 159, 207; meets Clare, 67–8; reviews Clare's poems in *Quarterly Review*, 72; takes Clare to London, 77; literary battle, 119, 144; joins Clare in London, 119; death, 133

Gilchrist, Mrs., 174

Gordon, Stephen, 50, 51, 56

Gray, Thomas, 150

Gregory, Francis, 29–30, 33, 36, 40

Gypsies, 48–9, 149

Halifax Express, The, 231

Hall, S. C., 185–6, 193, 197, 230

Hall, S. T., 251

Harrington, Sir John, 168

Hatchard & Son, 130

Hazlitt, William, 67, 100, 106, 121, 151, 191; Clare on, 123

Helpston, 18

Henderson, T., 116, 129, 136, 153, 154, 164, 181, 182, 206, 209, 213

Henson, J. B., 54, 55, 56, 57, 58, 59, 61

Hessey, J. A., 66, 84, 91, 95, 96, 107, 118, 130, 134, 137, 138, 141, 145, 152, 153, 157, 160–1, 164, 166, 171, 172, 175, 201; meets Clare, 78; sends Clare his fiddle, 88; on Taylor, 93; on *Shepherd's Calendar*, 135, 152, 157, 176; dissolution of partnership with Taylor, 163; on Lord Radstock, 164; on Clare's troubled conscience, 183; goes bankrupt, 194; book and print auctioneer, 196

High Beech, 228; Clare admitted to, 229; Clare escapes from, 240

Hilton, William, R.A., 78, 109, 114, 195, 228, 252

Hogg, James, 230

Holland, Revd. Isaac Knowles, 62, 69, 73

Hood, Thomas, 66, 100, 121, 193; on Clare, 123–4

How, J., 213, 214, 218–19, 220

Inskip, Thomas, 146, 152

Iris, The, 166, 251

Jacob (printer), 212, 214

Jerom, William, 253–4

Jones, the Sailor Boy, 142

Joyce, Mary, 108, 131, 132, 240, 246; childhood friendship with Clare, 25–6; Clare in love with, 36–9, 65; Clare's poems to, 36–7, 108, 111, 132, 155, 216, 217, 223, 248; becomes spiritualised in Clare's mind, 216–18; Clare's "first wife", 227, 233, 237, 241, 245; Clare's letters to, 233, 245

Kean, Edmund, 77

Keats, John, 67, 78, 85, 86, 95–6, 100, 101, 102, 104, 109, 111, 114, 136, 191, 202, 211, 220; Clare on, 86

Kent, Elizabeth, 173

Knight (actor), 77

Knight, W. F., 254, 261

Knox's *Essays*, 151

Lamb, Charles, 100, 106, 124, 127, 141, 151, 164, 191, 220; Clare on, 121–2

Landon, Miss, 194

Landor, W. S., 100

Lawrence, Sir Thomas, 142

Leopold, Prince, 89, 142

Literary Fund, grant to Clare, 220

Literary Gazette, The, 112, 206, 225

Lloyd, Charles, 151

Lockhart, J. G., 102

Lolham Brigs, 114, 151

London Magazine, The, 68, 106, 107, 113, 115, 119, 128, 129–30, 141, 159, 164, 195; contributors' dinners, 120–4, 134, 138

London Saturday Journal, 231

Macready, W. C., 77

Marsh, Herbert (Bishop of Peterborough), 88, 181–2, 198

Marsh, Mrs. Marianne, 181–2, 184, 198, 199, 200, 208, 213

Marshall, publisher, 193

Martin, Frederick, *Life of John Clare*, 22, 66, 73, 79, 137, 142, 165, 186, 188, 191, 198, 227

Marvell, Andrew, 167
Meeting, The, 74, 77
Midsummer Cushion, The, 212–13, 215, 218–19, 221, 223
Militia, Clare and, 42–3, 45–7
Milton, Viscount, 69, 73, 74, 81, 101, 116, 154, 206, 214. (See also Earl Fitzwilliam)
Milton, Viscountess, 74, 136, 157, 165
Mitford, Mary Russell, 253
Montgomery, James, 166–7, 168, 251
Monthly Magazine, The, 72
Mossop, Revd. Charles, 74, 198, 201, 206, 207, 208, 212, 228, 249, 262
Mounsey, Revd. T., 59
Munden, J. S., 77
Murray, John, 119, 130
Murry, J. M., 86

Natural History notes, Clare's, 115, 148, 149, 156, 161, 173, 198, 248
Nell (music publisher), 202
Nelson, Horatio, Lord, 236, 253, 254
Nesbitt, Dr., 261
Newbon, Elizabeth, 49
Newcomb, Robert, 61, 62
New Monthly Magazine, The, 72, 112, 164, 225
Northampton General Lunatic Asylum, 249, 250
Northampton, Marquis of, 230
Northborough, 206, 207, 208, 214; Clare moves to, 209–10

Oliver, T., 141

Parish, The, 128–9, 205
Parker, John Donald, 18
Peterborough, Bishop of. (See Marsh, Herbert)
Phillips, Charles, 138
Pickworth, 55–6
Pierrepoint, Hon. H. M., 74
Pleasures of Spring, The, 193
Poems Descriptive of Rural Life and Scenery, 148, 171, 195; Taylor's Introduction to, 32, 71–2; publication of, 71; reviews of, 72; third edition, 72, 89–90; fourth edition, 72, 92–3
Pope, Alexander, 62, 88, 119, 151
Porter, Tom, 30, 34, 60, 61
Price, Revd. Thomas, 78
Prichard, Dr. T. S., 250, 251, 254, 261
Pringle, Thomas, 193, 208

Quarterly Review, The, 72, 119
Queen Dowager, 232
Queen Victoria, 254

Radstock, Admiral the Lord, 76–7, 81, 88, 92, 102, 111, 114, 115, 126, 158, 160, 182; Clare on, 78–9, 99, 151, 164; introduces Clare to Mrs. Emmerson, 79; starts fund for Clare, 79–80, 89, 195; quarrels with Taylor, 87, 89–90 92–3, 96–9, 106–7, 130; death, 164
Ramsay, Allan, 193
Randall, Jack, 235–6
Ranters, 137
Recruiting Party, The, 128–9
Redding, Cyrus, 235
Reynolds, J. H., 67, 78, 121, 129, 138, 185; Clare on, 122; on Clare, 123
Riots, (1795) 19; (1816) 51; (1830–1831) 203
Rippingille, Edward, 29, 119–20, 127, 141–3, 185, 226, 236
Rural Muse, The, 135, 209, 212–13, 226, 228; preparation of, 218–19, 220; publication of, 221; contents, 221–3; reviews, 225; sales, 225
Russell, Lord John, 89
Ryde, H., 190

Savage, Richard, 150
Scott, John, 102
Scott, Sir Walter, 84, 88, 102, 142
Seasons, The, 32–3, 47
Seaton, 23
Sell, Betty, 65
Severn, Joseph, 102
Shakespeare, William, 252; sonnets of, 149; plays of, 151
Sharpe, W., 197
Shelley, Percy Bysshe, 117
Shenstone, W., 62
Shepherd's Calendar, The, 141, 157, 165, 189, 221; preparation of, 134, 135, 136, 152, 153, 157, 158, 160–1, 162–3, 171–2, 176; publication of, 177; sales, 178, 195; contents, 178–80; reviews, 180
Sherwill, Captain, 84, 88
Simpson, Frank, 199, 202, 213, 219
Simpson, Mrs., 199–200, 213
Sketches in the Life of John Clare, 32, 81, 105, 106
Skrimshire, Dr., 101, 153, 157, 163, 198, 218 249
Smith, Elder & Co., 209
Southern, Henry, 164
Southey, Robert, 88, 97, 117, 194
Spencer, Earl, 89, 115, 128, 147, 175, 190, 204, 261
Stimson, Ann. (See Clare, Ann)
Stimson, Morris, 28, 29
Strickland, Agnes, 261–2

Tannahill, Robert, 31, 151
Taylor, John, 60, 63, 70, 71, 84, 85, 86, 91, 93, 95, 101, 103, 104, 105, 106, 113, 116, 117, 129, 130, 133, 134, 135, 136,

Taylor, John,—*contd.*
137, 138, 141, 143, 169, 174, 176, 188, 192, 202, 204, 205, 206, 212, 216, 219, 220, 221, 225, 226, 259; early life, 66; meets Clare, 67–8; his literary dinners, 77–8, 120–4, 134, 138; on Clare, 78, 114, 126; relations with Drury, 86–8, 174–5; quarrels with Lord Radstock, 89–90, 92–3, 96–9; Clare's trustee, 89, 207–8, 211, 214; on Keats, 95–6, 102, 104; edits *Village Minstrel*, 98, 101–2, 106–8, 109–10; relations with Clare, 99–100, 138, 158–9, 176, 182, 218; edits *London Magazine*, 106, 107; visits Clare, (at Helpston) 113–14, (at Northborough) 226–7; Clare visits in London, 119; edits *Shepherd's Calendar*, 136, 152, 153, 157, 158, 161, 162–3, 171–2, 176, 177; Clare on, 164, 200; publisher to London University, 182–3, 191–2; plan for sale of Clare's book, 186, 189, 206; on Clare's accounts, 196; and Mrs. Emmerson, 207; and subscription for Clare (1832), 210–11, 212; and *Rural Muse*, 213, 219, 220; and newspaper falsehoods, 214–15, 218; arranges for Clare at High Beech, 228–9, 231, 247; death, 262
Taylor & Hessey, firm of, 67, 78, 87, 95, 106, 154, 202; financial dealings with Clare, 94, 100, 115, 128, 147–8, 171, 181, 194, 195–7; dissolution of partnership, 163; and *London Magazine*, 106, 164
Thompson, 60, 61
Thomson, James, 32, 33, 124, 193
Times, The, 231

Townsend, Chauncy Hare, 83, 112
Turner, John, 81
Turner, Martha. (See Clare, Martha)
Turner, William, 52, 64
Turnill, John, 30
Turnill, Richard, 25, 111
Twopenny, Revd. Mr., 62

Van Dyk, H., 141, 152, 154, 157, 159, 160, 161, 185
Vestris, Madame, 74, 77
Village Minstrel, The, 52, 91, 114, 117, 148, 154, 174, 235; preparation of, 85, 101, 106–8; Taylor's Introduction to, 87, 107, 109–10, 195, 211; publication of, 109; contents, 110–11; reviews, 112; sales, 113, 117, 171, 195

Wainewright, T. G., 106, 123, 125; on Clare and Lamb, 121; Clare on, 124
Walker (apothecary), 136, 157
Walton, 231
Watts, Alaric, 193
What is Life?, 56–7
Whittakers, 213, 219, 220
Wilders, 51
Will, Clare's, 137–8
Williamson, Samuel, 204
Wilson, Professor, 225
Wing, Dr., 261
Withers, 42, 43
Woodhouse, Richard, 89, 101, 137, 208, 211, 212, 220
Wootton, Sir Henry, 168
Wordsworth, William, 31, 88, 114, 117, 151, 209